Foundations of Tensor Analysis for Students of Physics and Engineering With an Introduction to the Theory of Relativity

NASA Technical Reports Server (NTRS), Joseph C. Kolecki

The BiblioGov Project is an effort to expand awareness of the public documents and records of the U.S. Government via print publications. In broadening the public understanding of government and its work, an enlightened democracy can grow and prosper. Ranging from historic Congressional Bills to the most recent Budget of the United States Government, the BiblioGov Project spans a wealth of government information. These works are now made available through an environmentally friendly, print-on-demand basis, using only what is necessary to meet the required demands of an interested public. We invite you to learn of the records of the U.S. Government, heightening the knowledge and debate that can lead from such publications.

Included are the following Collections:

Budget of The United States Government
Presidential Documents
United States Code
Education Reports from ERIC
GAO Reports
History of Bills
House Rules and Manual
Public and Private Laws
Code of Federal Regulations
Congressional Documents
Economic Indicators
Federal Register
Government Manuals
House Journal
Privacy act Issuances
Statutes at Large

NASA/TP—2005-213115

Foundations of Tensor Analysis for Students of Physics and Engineering With an Introduction to the Theory of Relativity

Joseph C. Kolecki
Glenn Research Center, Cleveland, Ohio

April 2005

The NASA STI Program Office . . . in Profile

Since its founding, NASA has been dedicated to the advancement of aeronautics and space science. The NASA Scientific and Technical Information (STI) Program Office plays a key part in helping NASA maintain this important role.

The NASA STI Program Office is operated by Langley Research Center, the Lead Center for NASA's scientific and technical information. The NASA STI Program Office provides access to the NASA STI Database, the largest collection of aeronautical and space science STI in the world. The Program Office is also NASA's institutional mechanism for disseminating the results of its research and development activities. These results are published by NASA in the NASA STI Report Series, which includes the following report types:

- TECHNICAL PUBLICATION. Reports of completed research or a major significant phase of research that present the results of NASA programs and include extensive data or theoretical analysis. Includes compilations of significant scientific and technical data and information deemed to be of continuing reference value. NASA's counterpart of peer-reviewed formal professional papers but has less stringent limitations on manuscript length and extent of graphic presentations.

- TECHNICAL MEMORANDUM. Scientific and technical findings that are preliminary or of specialized interest, e.g., quick release reports, working papers, and bibliographies that contain minimal annotation. Does not contain extensive analysis.

- CONTRACTOR REPORT. Scientific and technical findings by NASA-sponsored contractors and grantees.

- CONFERENCE PUBLICATION. Collected papers from scientific and technical conferences, symposia, seminars, or other meetings sponsored or cosponsored by NASA.

- SPECIAL PUBLICATION. Scientific, technical, or historical information from NASA programs, projects, and missions, often concerned with subjects having substantial public interest.

- TECHNICAL TRANSLATION. English-language translations of foreign scientific and technical material pertinent to NASA's mission.

Specialized services that complement the STI Program Office's diverse offerings include creating custom thesauri, building customized databases, organizing and publishing research results . . . even providing videos.

For more information about the NASA STI Program Office, see the following:

- Access the NASA STI Program Home Page at ***http://www.sti.nasa.gov***

- E-mail your question via the Internet to help@sti.nasa.gov

- Fax your question to the NASA Access Help Desk at 301–621–0134

- Telephone the NASA Access Help Desk at 301–621–0390

- Write to:
  NASA Access Help Desk
  NASA Center for AeroSpace Information
  7121 Standard Drive
  Hanover, MD 21076

NASA/TP—2005-213115

Foundations of Tensor Analysis for Students of Physics and Engineering With an Introduction to the Theory of Relativity

Joseph C. Kolecki
Glenn Research Center, Cleveland, Ohio

National Aeronautics and
Space Administration

Glenn Research Center

April 2005

Acknowledgments

To Dr. Ken DeWitt of Toledo University, I extend a special thanks for being a guiding light to me in much of my advanced mathematics, especially in tensor analysis. Years ago, he made the statement that in working with tensors, one must learn to find—and feel—the rhythm inherent in the indices. He certainly felt that rhythm, and his ability to do so made a major difference in his approach to teaching the material and enabling his students to comprehend it. He read this work and made many valuable suggestions and alterations that greatly strengthened it.

I wish to also recognize Dr. Harold Kautz's contribution to the section Magnetic Permeability and Material Stress, which was derived from a conversation with him. Dr. Kautz has been my colleague and part-time mentor since 1973.

Available from

NASA Center for Aerospace Information
7121 Standard Drive
Hanover, MD 21076

National Technical Information Service
5285 Port Royal Road
Springfield, VA 22100

Available electronically at http://gltrs.grc.nasa.gov

Contents

Foundations of Tensor Analysis for Students of Physics and Engineering With an Introduction to the Theory of Relativity

Joseph C. Kolecki
National Aeronautics and Space Administration
Glenn Research Center
Cleveland, Ohio 44135

Summary

Although one of the more useful subjects in higher mathematics, tensor analysis has the tendency to be one of the more abstruse seeming to students of physics and engineering who venture deeper into mathematics than the standard college curriculum of calculus through differential equations with some linear algebra and complex variable theory. Tensor analysis is useful because of its great generality, computational power, and compact, easy-to-use notation. It seems abstruse because of the intellectual gap that exists between where most physics and engineering mathematics end and where tensor analysis traditionally begins. The author's purpose is to bridge that gap by discussing familiar concepts, such as denominate numbers, scalars, and vectors, by introducing dyads, triads, and other higher order products, coordinate invariant quantities, and finally by showing how all this material leads to the standard definition of tensor quantities as quantities that transform according to certain strict rules.

Introduction

This monograph is intended to provide a conceptual foundation for students of physics and engineering who wish to pursue tensor analysis as part of their advanced studies in applied mathematics. Because an intellectual gap often exists between a student's studies in undergraduate mathematics and advanced mathematics, the author's intention is to enable the student to benefit from advanced studies by making languagelike associations between mathematics and the real world. Symbol manipulation is not sufficient in physics and engineering. One must express oneself in mathematics just as in language.

I studied tensor analysis on my own over a period of 13 years. I was in my twenties and early thirties at that time and was interested in learning about tensors because Einstein had used them and I was reading Einstein. Family and work responsibilities prevented me from daily study, so I pursued the subject at my leisure, progressing through my numerous collected texts as time permitted. I found that tensor manipulation was quite simple, but the "language aspects" of tensor analysis—what the subject actually was trying to tell me about the world at large—were extremely difficult. I spent a great deal of time disentangling concepts such as the difference between a curved coordinate system and a curved space, the physical-geometrical interpretation of covariant versus contravariant, and so forth. I also followed up a number of very necessary side branches, such as the calculus of variations (required in deriving the general form of the geodesic) and the application of tensors in the general theory of mechanics.

My studies culminated in my taking a 12-week course from the University of Toledo in Toledo, Ohio. I was pleased that I could keep pace with the subject throughout the 12. My instructor seemed interested in my approach to solving problems and actually kept copies of my written homework for reference in future courses. Afterwards, I decided to write a monograph about my 13 years of mathematical studies so that other students could benefit. The present work is the result.

Algebra

Statement of Core Idea

Physical quantities are coordinate independent. So should be the mathematical quantities that model them. In tensor analysis, we seek coordinate-independent quantities for applications in physics and engineering; that is, we seek those quantities that have component transformation properties that render the quantities independent of the observer's coordinate system. By doing so, the quantities have a type of objective existence. That is why tensors are ultimately defined strictly in terms of their transformation properties.

Number Systems

At the heart of all mathematics are numbers. Numbers are pure abstractions that can be approximately represented by words such as "one" and "two" or by numerals such as "1" and "2." Numbers are the only entities that truly exist in Plato's world of ideals and they cast their verbal or numerical shadows upon the face of human thought and endeavor.

The abstract quality of the concept of "number"[1] is illustrated in the following example: Consider three cups of different sizes all containing water. Imagine that one is full to the brim, one is two-thirds full and the last is one-third. Although we can say that there are three cups of water, where exactly does the quality of "threeness" reside?

The number systems we use today are divided into these categories:

- Natural or counting numbers: 1, 2, 3, 4, 5
- Whole numbers: 0, 1, 2, 3, 4, 5
- Integers: …, –3, –2, –1, 0, 1, 2, 3, 4, 5
- Rational numbers: numbers that are irreducible ratios of pairs of integers
- Irrational numbers: numbers such as $\sqrt{2}$ that are not irreducible ratios of pairs of integers
- Real numbers: all the rational and irrational numbers taken together
- Complex numbers: all the real numbers in addition to all those that have $\sqrt{-1}$ as a factor

Irrational numbers.— These are numbers that can be shown to be not irreducible ratios of pairs of integers. That $\sqrt{2}$ is such a number is easily demonstrated by using proof by reductio ad absurdum:

> Let a and b be two integers such that $\sqrt{2} = a/b$ where the ratio a/b is assumed irreducible. Then, $2 = a^2/b^2$ and $2b^2 = a^2$. Thus a^2 and therefore a are even integers, and there exists a number k such that $a = 2k$ and $a^2 = 4k^2$. Thus, $b^2 = 2k^2$, and b^2 and therefore b are also even integers. But when a and b are both even, the ratio a/b is reducible since a factor of 2 may be taken from both the numerator and the denominator. This last statement violates the assumption that the ratio a/b must be irreducible and therefore we conclude by reductio that no two such integers as a and b can exist. Q.E.D.

Real numbers.—These numbers may also be divided into two different groups, other than rational and irrational.

Algebraic numbers: Algebraic numbers are all numbers that are solutions of the general, finite equation

$$a_n x^n + a_{n-1} x^{n-1} + \ldots + a_1 x + a_0 = 0 \tag{1}$$

where all the a_i are rational numbers and all the superscripts and subscripts are integers. Note that $\sqrt{2}$ is such a number since it is a solution to the equation

$$x^2 - 2 = 0 \tag{2}$$

So is the complex number $\sqrt{-1}$ since it is a solution to the equation

$$x^2 + 1 = 0 \tag{3}$$

Transcendental numbers: All numbers that are not solutions to the same general, finite equation (1) are called transcendental numbers. The numbers π and e (base of the natural logarithms) are two such numbers. The transcendental numbers are a subset of the irrational numbers.

Difference between transcendental and non-transcendental irrational numbers.—The difference between transcendental irrational numbers and non-transcendental irrational numbers can be understood by considering classical Greek constructions. In a finite number of steps, using a pencil, a straightedge, and a compass, it is possible to construct a line segment with length equal to the non-transcendental irrational number $\sqrt{2}$. First, draw an (arbitrary) unit line. Second, draw another unit line at right angles to the first unit line at one of its endpoints. Third, connect the free endpoints of the two lines. The result is the required line segment of length $\sqrt{2}$. A similar construction is possible for $\sqrt{3}$ and other such irrational numbers.

However, for the transcendental irrational number π, no such construction is possible in a finite number of steps. Recall that π is the ratio of the circumference of a circle to its diameter. Equivalently, it is the length of the circumference of a circle of unit diameter. We now

[1]Number is an abstract concept; numeral is a concrete representation of number. We write numerals such as 1, 2, 3…to represent the abstract concepts one, two, three… .

ask, is it possible, using only the classical Greek methods, to construct a line segment of length π? Suppose that we begin with an n-gon of an arbitrary finite number of sides to approximate the circle. We then use the length of one of the sides and repeat it, end to end along a reference line n times. This result represents our first approximation of the required line segment.

We then double the number of sides in the n-gon, making it a $2n$-gon, and repeat the procedure. The new result is our second approximation, and so on as the procedure is repeated. It turns out that to reproduce the actual circumference length precisely, an infinite number of approximations is necessary. Thus, we are forced to conclude that using only the Greek classical methods, it is impossible to achieve the goal of constructing a line segment of length π because it exceeds our abilities by requiring an infinite number of steps. All finite approximations are close but not exact.

A similar argument may be made for the number e. The value of the natural logarithm $\ln(\mu)$ is obtained from the integral with respect to x of the function $1/x$ from 1 to μ. For $\mu = e$, the integral becomes $\ln(e) = 1$, since e is the base of the natural logarithm. We start by not knowing exactly where e lies on the x-axis. We may use successive trapezoidal approximations to find where it lies by finding to what position $x > 1$ on the x-axis we must integrate to obtain an area of unity, but the process is extremely complicated and involves convergence from below and above. As was the case with π, the process exceeds our abilities by requiring an infinite number of steps.

Numbers, Denominate Numbers, and Vectors

Numbers can function in an infinite variety of ways. For example, they can be used to count items. If I were to ask how many marbles you had in a bag, you might answer, "Three," a satisfactory answer. The bare number three, a magnitude, is sufficient to provide the information I seek. If you wanted to be more complete, you could answer, "Three marbles." But inclusion of the word "marbles" is not required for your answer to make sense. However, not all number designations are as simple as naming the number of marbles in the bag. Suppose that I were to ask, "How far is it to your house?" and you answered, "Three." My response would be "Three what?" Evidently, for this question, more information is required, another word or quantity or something has to be attached to the word "three" for your answer to make sense. This time I require a "denominate" number, a number with a name (Latin de meaning "with" and nomos meaning "name"). An answer of "3 km" names the number three so that it no longer strands alone as a bare magnitude. These numbers are sometimes referred to as "scalars." Temperature is represented by a scalar. The total energy of a thermodynamic system is also represented by a scalar.

Let us pause here to define some basic terminology. Consider any fraction, which is a ratio of two integers such as two-thirds. You know from school that two is called the numerator and three, the denominator. The quantity two-thirds is a kind of denominate number. It tells how many (enumerates) of a particular fraction of something (denominated or named a third) I have. If the distance to your house is 2/3 km, then there are formally two denominations to contend with: a third and a kilometer.

Proceeding on, if I were then to ask, "Then how do I get to your house from here?" and you said, "Just walk 3 km," again I would look at you quizzically. For this question, not even a denominate number is sufficient; it is not only necessary to specify a distance but also a direction. "Just walk 3 km due north," you say. Now your answer makes sense. The denominate number 3 km now includes the additional information of direction. Such a quantity is called a vector. The study of vectors is a very broad study in mathematics.

Finally, suppose that we were at your house and I stopped to examine a support beam in the middle of the main room. I might ask, "What is the net load on this beam?" and you would answer, "(So many) pounds downward." You answered appropriately using a vector. But now I ask, "What is the stress in the beam?" You answer, "Which stress? There are three tensile and six shear stresses. Which do you want to know? And in what part of the beam are you interested?" Thus, the subject of tensors is introduced because not even a vector is sufficient to answer the question about stresses.

You might have noticed that as we took our first step from bare number to scalar to vector, we added new terminology to deal with the concepts of denominability and directionality. We will begin our approach to tensors specifically by examining vectors and then by extending our concept of them.

Formal Presentation of Vectors

Vectors give us information such as how far and in what direction. The "how far" part of a vector is formally called the magnitude, roughly its size. The "what direction" part of a vector is formally called the direction. Thus, a vector is a quantity that possesses magnitude and direction.

Now that we have acquired an intuitive sense of what vectors are, let us consider their more formal characteristics. To do so, take a commonly used vector from the toolkit of physics, velocity. Velocity is a vector because it has magnitude and direction. Its magnitude, usually called speed, is a denominate number such as 50 mph or 28 000 km/s. Its direction is chosen to be the same as that in which the object is moving in space. Note the use of the word "chosen." Mathematicians and physicists are free, within certain limits, to choose and define the terms and even the systems they are talking about; that is, they can choose and define how they will construct their model or theory. This point might seem subtle but in the long run, it is important.

In the angular quantities, such as angular velocity or angular momentum, the magnitude of the vector is obviously the number of revolutions per minute or the number of radians turned per second. But what direction should the vector have? The axis of rotation is the only direction that is unique in a rotating system, so we choose to place the vector along this axis. But should it point up or down? Tradition in physics has resolved that the direction be assigned via the right-hand rule: the fingers of the right hand curl in the direction of the motion and the thumb of the right hand then points in the assigned direction of the vector. Such a vector is called a right-handed vector. Had the left hand been used, the result would have been the reverse.

Electrical current density is also a vector. It is usually designated by the letter **j** and has units of amperes per square meter. Current density is a measure of how much charge passes through a unit area perpendicular to the current flow in a unit time. The direction assigned to **j** is somewhat peculiar in that physicists and engineers use opposite conventions. For the engineer, **j** points in the direction that conventional current would flow. Conventional current is the flow of positive charge, and the use of this convention goes back to the times and practices of investigators such as Benjamin Franklin. It is now known that electrical current is a flow of electrons and that electrons (by convention) carry a negative charge. (The positive charge carriers barely move if at all.) Physicists have adopted the convention that **j** point in the direction of electron current, not conventional current. Hence, the student should be aware of this difference.

Resuming the discussion of velocity as a vector, suppose that I were driving northeast on a level road at 34 mph. How would I specify my velocity? Well, the speed is known, but what about the direction? I could say "34 mph northeast on a level road." "On a level road" specifies that I am going neither up nor down but horizontally. However, I am still unable to do many calculations because my direction combines two compass headings, north and east. If I am going exactly northeast, then I could say that I am traveling x mph east and x mph north. The following triangle represents my situation:

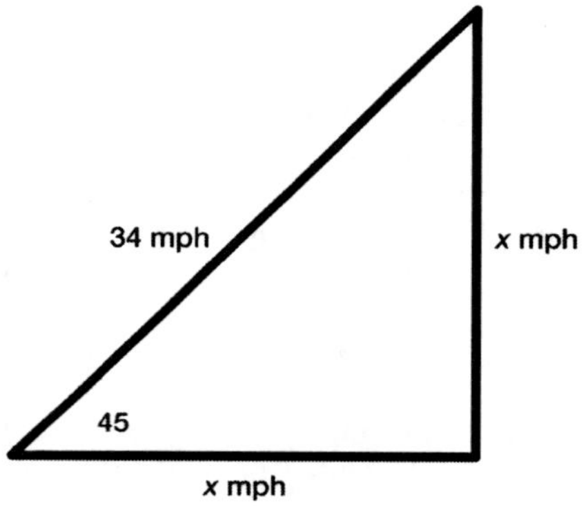

I can solve for x using Pythagoras's theorem: $x = 24$ mph approximately. Thus, I write the velocity vector as 34 mph NE = 24 mph E + 24 mph N, understanding that the equation represents the situation shown in the triangle. I drop the caveat "on a level road" because the directions east and north are implicitly measured in the local horizontal plane.

To simplify, I use a unit vector **u** to represent the directions. A unit vector has a magnitude equal to one and any direction I choose. When I multiply the denominate number by the unit vector, the magnitudes combine as 1 × 24 mph and the direction attaches automatically.

Let $\mathbf{u}_E$ and $\mathbf{u}_N$ be unit vectors pointing east and north, respectively, and let $\mathbf{u}_{NE}$ be a unit vector pointing northeast so that the velocity vector becomes

$$(34 \text{ mph})\mathbf{u}_{NE} = (24 \text{ mph})\mathbf{u}_E + (24 \text{ mph})\mathbf{u}_N \quad (4)$$

The vector (34 mph) $\mathbf{u}_{NE}$ is said to have components 24 mph eastward and 24 mph northward. This method of representing vectors will be used throughout the remainder of this text.

If I divide through by the denominate number 34 mph, I obtain the expression

$$\mathbf{u}_{NE} = (0.71)\mathbf{u}_E + (0.71)\mathbf{u}_N \tag{5}$$

Note that cos 45° = sin 45° = 0.71 to two decimal places. I use trigonometry to write

$$(34 \text{ mph})\mathbf{u}_{NE} = (34 \text{ mph} \times \cos 45°)\mathbf{u}_E + (34 \text{ mph} \times \sin 45°)\mathbf{u}_N \tag{6}$$

The components of the velocity can be obtained solely from the velocity itself and the directional convention adopted. This method of writing vectors should already be familiar to students of this text.

Let us now refine the method just introduced. We know that we live in a world of three spatial dimensions, forward, across, and up. Let us choose a standard notation for writing vectors as follows:

i represents a unit vector forward
j represents a unit vector across
k represents a unit vector up

Let us also agree to represent vectors in bolded type. Now, let **V** be a vector with components[2] *a*, *b*, and *c* in the forward, across, and up directions, respectively. Then the vector **V** is formally written as

$$\mathbf{V} = a\mathbf{i} + b\mathbf{j} + c\mathbf{k} \tag{7}$$

With this notation, we can now define arithmetic rules for combining vectors.

By the conventions of modern physics, we live in a world, not of three, but of four dimensions—three spatial and one temporal. We therefore introduce a fourth unit vector **l** to represent the forward direction of time from past to future. The resulting four-vector[3] **V** is formally written as

$$\mathbf{V} = a\mathbf{i} + b\mathbf{j} + c\mathbf{k} + d\mathbf{l} \tag{8}$$

In the case of the spacetime continuum of special relativity, the component *d* is usually an imaginary number. For example, if *a*, *b*, and *c* are the usual spatial locations *x*, *y*, and *z*, then *d* is the temporal location *ict* where $i = \sqrt{-1}$. This situation leads to the result that

$$V^2 = \mathbf{V} \cdot \mathbf{V} = x^2 + y^2 + z^2 - c^2 t^2 \tag{9}$$

In relativistic spacetime, the theorem of Pythagoras does not strictly apply. The properties of four-vectors were extensively explored by Albert Einstein.

Vector Arithmetic

Equality.—A basic rule in vector arithmetic is one that tells us when two vectors are equal. Suppose there are two vectors

$$\mathbf{U} = \alpha\mathbf{i} + \beta\mathbf{j} + \chi\mathbf{k} \tag{10a}$$

$$\mathbf{V} = a\mathbf{i} + b\mathbf{j} + c\mathbf{k} \tag{10b}$$

Whenever **U** = **V** is written, it will always mean that the individual components associated with each of the unit vectors **i**, **j**, and **k** are equal. Thus, the single vector equation **U** = **V** gives three independent scalar equations:

$$\alpha = a \tag{11a}$$

$$\beta = b \tag{11b}$$

$$\chi = c \tag{11c}$$

Consider now the single statement **U** = **V** on the one hand and the triad $\{\alpha = a, \beta = b, \chi = c\}$ on the other as completely synonymous.

Next consider cases where there are different sets of unit vectors in the same space. Let us say that **i**, **j**, and **k** comprise one set (the set *K*) and **u**, **v**, and **w** comprise a second set (the set *K**). Now consider a vector **V**. Let us write

$$\mathbf{V} = a\mathbf{i} + b\mathbf{j} + c\mathbf{k} \tag{12a}$$

$$\mathbf{V} = \alpha\mathbf{u} + \beta\mathbf{v} + \chi\mathbf{w} \tag{12b}$$

---

[2]We might also say "scalar" components since the individual components of a quantity such as velocity are all scalars. However, there are also cases in which the components are differential operators such as in the gradient operator $\nabla = (\partial/\partial x)\mathbf{i} + (\partial/\partial y)\mathbf{j} + (\partial/\partial z)\mathbf{k}$. Herein, therefore, we will use the more generic term "components" as being inclusive of all possible cases.

[3]A four-vector is a four-dimensional vector in the spacetime of special relativity. The components of a four-vector transform according to the familiar Lorentz-Einstein transformation for unaccelerated motion.

Now, we cannot equate components because the unit vectors are not the same. However, we can invoke the trivial identity and say that for all vectors **V**, it is true that **V** = **V**. From this trivial identity, we acquire the nontrivial result that

$$a\mathbf{i} + b\mathbf{j} + c\mathbf{k} = \alpha\mathbf{u} + \beta\mathbf{v} + \chi\mathbf{w} \tag{13}$$

If the vectors **u**, **v**, and **w** can be expressed as functions of **i**, **j**, and **k**, then the components α, β, and χ can also be expressed as functions of *a*, *b*, and *c*. In other words, if

$$\mathbf{u} = u_1\mathbf{i} + u_2\mathbf{j} + u_3\mathbf{k} \tag{14a}$$

$$\mathbf{v} = v_1\mathbf{i} + v_2\mathbf{j} + v_3\mathbf{k} \tag{14b}$$

$$\mathbf{w} = w_1\mathbf{i} + w_2\mathbf{j} + w_3\mathbf{k} \tag{14c}$$

we can write

$$\begin{aligned} a\mathbf{i} + b\mathbf{j} + c\mathbf{k} &= \alpha\mathbf{u} + \beta\mathbf{v} + \chi\mathbf{w} \\ &= \alpha\left(u_1\mathbf{i} + u_2\mathbf{j} + u_3\mathbf{k}\right) + \beta\left(v_1\mathbf{i} + v_2\mathbf{j} + v_3\mathbf{k}\right) \\ &\quad + \chi\left(w_1\mathbf{i} + w_2\mathbf{j} + w_3\mathbf{k}\right) \\ &= \left(\alpha u_1 + \beta v_1 + \chi w_1\right)\mathbf{i} + \left(\alpha u_2 + \beta v_2 + \chi w_2\right)\mathbf{j} \\ &\quad + \left(\alpha u_3 + \beta v_3 + \chi w_3\right)\mathbf{k} \end{aligned} \tag{15}$$

so that

$$a = \alpha u_1 + \beta v_1 + \chi w_1 \tag{16a}$$

$$b = \alpha u_2 + \beta v_2 + \chi w_2 \tag{16b}$$

$$c = \alpha u_3 + \beta v_3 + \chi w_3 \tag{16c}$$

This last set of equations represents a set of component transformations for the vector **V** between the two sets of unit vectors *K* and *K**. Coordinate transformations will be used later to formally define tensors. In the meantime, we will use what we have learned about vector equalities to develop many important ideas about tensors.

Addition.—Suppose that I traveled 6 km north and 3 km more north. How far north would I have gone? A total of 9 km north. Now, suppose that I went 3 km east, 6 km north, and 5 more km east. How far north and how far east would I have gone? I would have gone 6 km north, but I would also have gone 3 km + 5 km = 8 km east. Evidently, when vectors are added, they are added component by component. To formalize this as a rule, let us say that two vectors **U** and **V** can be added to produce a new vector **W** as

$$\mathbf{W} = \mathbf{U} + \mathbf{V} \tag{17}$$

provided that the vectors **U** and **V** are added component by component. If

$$\mathbf{U} = \alpha\mathbf{i} + \beta\mathbf{j} + \chi\mathbf{k} \tag{18a}$$

$$\mathbf{V} = a\mathbf{i} + b\mathbf{j} + c\mathbf{k} \tag{18b}$$

then

$$\mathbf{U} + \mathbf{V} = (\alpha + a)\mathbf{i} + (\beta + b)\mathbf{j} + (\chi + c)\mathbf{k} \tag{19}$$

and

$$\mathbf{U} - \mathbf{V} = (\alpha - a)\mathbf{i} + (\beta - b)\mathbf{j} + (\chi - c)\mathbf{k} \tag{20}$$

Multiplication.—Vector addition provides a good beginning for defining vector arithmetic. However, vector arithmetic also consists of multiplication. We will next formally define several different types of products[4] that all involve pairs of vectors.

Scalar or inner product: The first type of vector product to be defined is the scalar or inner product, so called because when two vectors are thus combined, the result is not a vector but a scalar. In physics, scalar products are useful in determining quantities such as power in a mechanical system (the scalar product of force and velocity). For the vectors

$$\mathbf{U} = \alpha\mathbf{i} + \beta\mathbf{j} + \chi\mathbf{k} \tag{21a}$$

$$\mathbf{V} = a\mathbf{i} + b\mathbf{j} + c\mathbf{k} \tag{21b}$$

the scalar product will be denoted by the symbol **U** · **V** where the vector symbols **U** and **V** are written side by side with a dot in between (hence, the scalar product is sometimes referred to as the "dot product"). The vectors **U** and **V** are combined via the scalar product to produce a scalar η:

[4]We will not formally define division of vectors. We will encounter reciprocal vector sets, but strict division is not formally defined because there are so many different types of vector products.

$$\mathbf{U}\cdot\mathbf{V}=\eta \tag{22}$$

The scalar may be obtained in one of two ways. The first way is component-by-component multiplication and summing (analytical interpretation):

$$\mathbf{U}\cdot\mathbf{V}=\alpha a+\beta b+\chi c \tag{23}$$

The second way is the product of vector magnitudes and enclosed angle (geometrical interpretation):

$$\mathbf{U}\cdot\mathbf{V}=|\mathbf{U}||\mathbf{V}|\cos\theta \tag{24}$$

where |**U**| and |**V**| are the lengths of **U** and **V**, respectively, and θ is the angle enclosed between them.

Note that in developing these formal definitions, we have stated the "new" (i.e., the "unknown") in terms of the "known." This point might seem trivial, but it is often important to bring it to mind, especially when you are involved in a complicated proof or other type of argument. Arguments usually run aground because terms are not sufficiently defined.

Let us look at the two definitions of inner product more closely and ask whether they are consistent, one with the other. Take the vectors **U** and **V** and form the term-by-term inner product according to basic algebra:

$$\begin{aligned}\mathbf{U}\cdot\mathbf{V}&=(\alpha\mathbf{i}+\beta\mathbf{j}+\chi\mathbf{k})\cdot(a\mathbf{i}+b\mathbf{j}+c\mathbf{k})\\ &=\alpha\mathbf{i}\cdot(a\mathbf{i}+b\mathbf{j}+c\mathbf{k})+\beta\mathbf{j}\cdot(a\mathbf{i}+b\mathbf{j}+c\mathbf{k})\\ &\quad+\chi\mathbf{k}\cdot(a\mathbf{i}+b\mathbf{j}+c\mathbf{k})\\ &=\alpha\mathbf{i}\cdot a\mathbf{i}+\alpha\mathbf{i}\cdot b\mathbf{j}+\alpha\mathbf{i}\cdot c\mathbf{k}+\beta\mathbf{j}\cdot a\mathbf{i}+\beta\mathbf{j}\cdot b\mathbf{j}\\ &\quad+\beta\mathbf{j}\cdot c\mathbf{k}+\chi\mathbf{k}\cdot a\mathbf{i}+\chi\mathbf{k}\cdot b\mathbf{j}+\chi\mathbf{k}\cdot c\mathbf{k}\\ &=\alpha\mathrm{a}(\mathbf{i}\cdot\mathbf{i})+\alpha\mathrm{b}(\mathbf{i}\cdot\mathbf{j})+\alpha\mathrm{c}(\mathbf{i}\cdot\mathbf{k})+\beta\mathrm{a}(\mathbf{j}\cdot\mathbf{i})\\ &\quad+\beta\mathrm{b}(\mathbf{j}\cdot\mathbf{j})+\beta c(\mathbf{j}\cdot\mathbf{k})+\chi a(\mathbf{k}\cdot\mathbf{i})+\chi b(\mathbf{k}\cdot\mathbf{j})\\ &\quad+\chi c(\mathbf{k}\cdot\mathbf{k})\end{aligned} \tag{25}$$

At this point, what are we to do with the inner products (**i** · **i**), (**i** · **k**), (**j** · **k**), and so on. We know that these vectors are unit vectors and that they are (by definition) mutually perpendicular. A little thought (and a lot of comparison with historical results in field theory) leads us to choose the definition

$$\mathbf{i}\cdot\mathbf{i}=\mathbf{j}\cdot\mathbf{j}=\mathbf{k}\cdot\mathbf{k}=1 \tag{26}$$

All other combinations = 0.

Remember, everything that is done in mathematics must be defined at some point in time by a human agency. Historically, applications in areas of physics such as field theory have produced certain recurrent forms of equations that eventually lead to the writing of definitions such as the foregoing. Study these definitions carefully. You will notice that the information about the inner products of unit vectors is neatly summarized in the geometric interpretation of inner product:

$$\mathbf{U}\cdot\mathbf{V}=|\mathbf{U}||\mathbf{V}|\cos\theta \tag{27}$$

where in the case of the unit vectors |**U**| = |**V**| = 1 and cos θ = 1 or 0, depending on whether θ = 0° or 90°. The student may now proceed to complete the argument.

We have already said that the scalar product is also called the inner product. The terminology "inner product" is actually the preferred term in books on tensor analysis and will be adopted throughout the remainder of this text.

One special case of the inner product is of particular interest; that is, the inner product of a vector with itself is the square of the magnitude (length) of the vector:

$$\mathbf{U}\cdot\mathbf{U}=U^2 \tag{28}$$

Cross or vector product: Another type of product is the cross or vector product. The terminology "cross" is derived from the symbol used for this operation, **U** × **V**. The terminology "vector" is derived from the result of the cross product of two vectors, which is another vector. The direction of the new vector is perpendicular to the plane of the two vectors being combined and is specified as being "up" or "down" by the right-hand rule: rotate the first vector in the product **U** × **V** towards the second. The resultant will point in the direction in which a right-handed thread (of a screw) would advance.

This rule may seem somewhat arbitrary—and indeed it is—but it is useful in physics nonetheless, particularly when dealing with rotational quantities such as angular velocity. If an object is spinning at a rate of ω radians per second, we define a vector **ω** whose direction is along the spin axis by the right-hand rule. Now, select a point away from the axis in the rotating system and ask, "What is the velocity of the point?" Remember that velocity has both magnitude (speed) and direction. Let **r** be a vector from an arbitrary point (reference or datum) on the spin axis to the point whose velocity we wish to determine. The desired velocity is given by the cross product $\boldsymbol{\omega} \times \mathbf{r}$. The vector resulting from a cross product is sometimes also called a pseudovector (or false vector), perhaps because of the arbitrary and somewhat ambiguous way in which its direction is defined.

Two vectors **U** and **V** in three-dimensional space may be combined via a cross product to produce a new vector **S**:

$$\mathbf{U} \times \mathbf{V} = \mathbf{S} \tag{29}$$

where **S** is perpendicular to the plane containing **U** and **V** and has a sense (direction) given by the right-hand rule. The vector **S** is obtained via the rule (geometrical interpretation):

$$\mathbf{S} = |\mathbf{U}||\mathbf{V}|(\sin\theta)\mathbf{u} \tag{30}$$

where $|\mathbf{U}|$ and $|\mathbf{V}|$ are the lengths of **U** and **V**, respectively, θ is the angle enclosed between them, and **u** is a unit vector in the appropriate direction.

An equivalent formulation of the cross product is as a determinant (analytical interpretation):

$$\mathbf{U} \times \mathbf{V} = \det \begin{vmatrix} \mathbf{i} & \mathbf{j} & \mathbf{k} \\ u_x & u_y & u_z \\ v_x & v_y & v_z \end{vmatrix} \tag{31}$$

Because of the use of the right-hand rule, note that $\mathbf{U} \times \mathbf{V}$ does not equal $\mathbf{V} \times \mathbf{U}$, but rather

$$\mathbf{U} \times \mathbf{V} = -(\mathbf{V} \times \mathbf{U}) \tag{32}$$

Thus, the cross product is not commutative.

It is interesting to look at the cross products of the unit vectors **i**, **j**, and **k**. Since they are all mutually perpendicular, $\sin\theta = \sin(\pm 90°) = \pm 1$, and $|\mathbf{U}||\mathbf{V}| = 1 \times 1 = 1$. If we write the unit vectors in the order **i**, **j**, **k**, **i**, **j**, **k**, **i**, **j**, **k**, ..., we see that the cross product of any two consecutive unit vectors from left to right equals the next unit vector immediately to the right: $\mathbf{i} \times \mathbf{j} = \mathbf{k}$; $\mathbf{j} \times \mathbf{k} = \mathbf{i}$; $\mathbf{k} \times \mathbf{i} = \mathbf{j}$, and so on. On the other hand, the cross product of any two consecutive unit vectors from right to left equals negative one times the next vector immediately to the left: $\mathbf{j} \times \mathbf{i} = -\mathbf{k}$; $\mathbf{k} \times \mathbf{j} = -\mathbf{i}$; $\mathbf{i} \times \mathbf{k} = -\mathbf{j}$, and so on. These relations between unit vectors are often used to define or specify a right-handed coordinate system. (Note that for a left-handed coordinate system, the argument would run in reverse of the one presented here.)

Product of a vector and a scalar: It is not possible to form a scalar or a vector product using anything other than two vectors. Nonetheless, the operation of doubling the length of a vector cannot be represented by either of these two operations. So we introduce still another type of product: A given vector **V** may be multiplied by a scalar number α to produce a new vector $\alpha\mathbf{V}$ with a different magnitude but the same direction.

In the case of doubling the length of the given vector, $\alpha = 2$. In general, we let $\mathbf{V} = V\mathbf{u}$ where **u** is a unit vector; then

$$\alpha\mathbf{V} = \alpha V\mathbf{u} = (\alpha V)\mathbf{u} = \xi\mathbf{u} \tag{33}$$

where $\xi = \alpha V$ is the new magnitude.

Perhaps you are thinking that we are trying to make up the arithmetic of vectors as we go along. "You cannot really do this," you argue, "because it has all been put down already in the text books." True, it has. But where do you think that it all came from? It is important for students to approach their mathematics not from the perspective that "God said in the beginning..." but rather that somebody or many somebodies worked very hard to put it all together. Students must also realize, by extension, that they are perfectly capable of adding to what already is known or of inventing an entirely new system for inclusion in the ever growing body of mathematics.

Dyads and Other Higher Order Products

This section will define another more general type of vector multiplication. The first step is simply following instructions from high school algebra. To take this first step, we consider how we performed the multiplication of quantities in algebra. Multiply the two quantities $(a + b + c)$ and $(d + e + f)$:

$$\begin{aligned}(a+b+c)\times(d+e+f) &= ad + ae + af \\ &\quad + bd + be + bf + cd + ce + cf\end{aligned} \tag{34}$$

Recall that each term from the first parentheses is multiplied by each term in the second parentheses and the resultant partial products are summed together to form the product. The product actually results from an application of the associative and distributive laws of algebra. Each of the original quantities had three terms. Their product has $3^2 = 9$ terms.

Suppose that we multiplied two vectors the same way. What sort of entity would we produce? Remember that new entities must ultimately be defined in terms of those already known. Let us try. Multiply the vectors $\mathbf{A} = a\mathbf{i} + b\mathbf{j} + c\mathbf{k}$ and $\mathbf{D} = d\mathbf{i} + e\mathbf{j} + f\mathbf{k}$ using the same rules that were used to form the product of $(a + b + c)$ and $(d + e + f)$:

$$\begin{aligned}\mathbf{AD} &= \left(a\mathbf{i} + b\mathbf{j} + c\mathbf{k}\right)\left(d\mathbf{i} + e\mathbf{j} + f\mathbf{k}\right) = ad\mathbf{ii} + ae\mathbf{ij} \\ &\quad + af\mathbf{ik} + bd\mathbf{ji} + be\mathbf{jj} + bf\mathbf{jk} + cd\mathbf{ki} + ce\mathbf{kj} + cf\mathbf{kk}\end{aligned} \tag{35}$$

The right-hand side is a new entity, but does it make any sense or have any physical meaning? The answer is "Yes," but we must progressively develop and define just what that meaning is.

The second step is to name this new entity so that we can more easily refer to it. We call it a dyad or dyadic product from the Latin di or dy, meaning "two" or "double." Inserting a dot between the vectors **A** and **D** and between the corresponding unit vectors on the right-hand side would reduce the dyad to the ordinary inner product with the result being a scalar. Similarly, inserting the cross symbol would reduce the dyad to the ordinary cross product with the result being another vector. So the dyad appears to contain the inner and cross products[5] as special cases.

Before making any more formal definitions, we will review two pertinent concepts.

> First, in algebra when multiplying two terms, it makes little difference which term is taken first. If we multiply x and y, the result can be called xy or yx, since $xy = yx$ by the commutative law. However, we have already seen that the commutative law does not apply in all cases. For example, in the discussion of the vector cross product $\mathbf{U} \times \mathbf{V}$, we discovered that $\mathbf{U} \times \mathbf{V} = -(\mathbf{V} \times \mathbf{U})$ because of the unusual way we chose to assign direction to the result (i.e., the commutative law does not hold for cross-multiplication). Therefore, in a case such as this, we say that the cross product is anticommutative. In the cross product, one vector premultiplies and the other postmultiplies. The position of the two vectors makes a difference to the result. This concept of premultiplication and postmultiplication also plays a role in defining the properties of the dyad.
>
> Second, recall the multiplication of a vector by a scalar. A given vector **V** can be multiplied by a scalar number α to produce a new vector with a different magnitude, but the vector will have the same direction. Let $\mathbf{V} = V\mathbf{u}$ where **u** is a unit vector. Then
>
> $$\alpha\mathbf{V} = \alpha V\mathbf{u} = \left(\alpha V\right)\mathbf{u} = \xi\mathbf{u} \tag{36}$$
>
> where ξ is the new magnitude. Note that the result has a different magnitude but has the same direction as the original vector. In other words, this type of multiplication alters only the size of the vector but has no effect on the direction in which it points. Note also that $\alpha\mathbf{V} = \mathbf{V}\alpha$.

Having reviewed these concepts, we are prepared to consider the dyad **AD**, an unknown entity that has entered our mathematical world. Let us exercise it and see just what we can discover.

Suppose that we were to form the inner product of **AD** with another arbitrary vector **X**. Let us premultiply by **X** and see what happens. Formally, write

$$\mathbf{X} \cdot \mathbf{AD} \tag{37}$$

Now, we have another new entity to which we must give meaning. Let us agree that the vectors on each side of the dot will "attach" to one another just as in a normal inner product.

$$\mathbf{X} \cdot \mathbf{AD} = \left(\mathbf{X} \cdot \mathbf{A}\right)\mathbf{D} \tag{38}$$

Now we know exactly how to handle the quantity $(\mathbf{X} \cdot \mathbf{A})$, which is the usual inner product of two vectors and is equal to some scalar, say ξ. So, formally write

$$\mathbf{X} \cdot \mathbf{AD} = \left(\mathbf{X} \cdot \mathbf{A}\right)\mathbf{D} = \xi\mathbf{D} \tag{39}$$

where $\xi\mathbf{D}$ is the product of a vector and a scalar. This product has a magnitude different from the magnitude of **D** but has the same direction as **D**.

[5] The dyad has nine components whereas the cross product has three. Insertion of the cross symbol in **AD** works as follows using the usual rules for the cross products of the unit vectors: $\mathbf{A} \times \mathbf{D} = (a\mathbf{i} + b\mathbf{j} + c\mathbf{k}) \times (d\mathbf{i} + e\mathbf{j} + f\mathbf{k}) = ad\mathbf{i} \times \mathbf{i} + ae\mathbf{i} \times \mathbf{j} + af\mathbf{i} \times \mathbf{k} + bd\mathbf{j} \times \mathbf{i} + be\mathbf{j} \times \mathbf{j} + bf\mathbf{j} \times \mathbf{k} + cd\mathbf{k} \times \mathbf{i} + ce\mathbf{k} \times \mathbf{j} + cf\mathbf{k} \times \mathbf{k} = (bf - ce)\mathbf{i} + (cd - af)\mathbf{j} + (ae - bd)\mathbf{k}$.

It is significant that the product has its direction determined by the dyad and not by the premultiplying vector **X**. It appears that postoperating[6] on **X** with the dyad **AD** has given a vector with a new magnitude and a new direction as compared with **X**. This statement is so significant that we will consider it as part of the definition of a dyad.

Continuing on, suppose that we now postmultiply the dyad **AD** by the same vector **X**, again using the inner product. For consistency, use the same attachment rule as before. The result is

$$\mathbf{AD}\cdot\mathbf{X}=\mathbf{A}(\mathbf{D}\cdot\mathbf{X})=\mathbf{A}\psi=\psi\mathbf{A} \qquad (40)$$

where ψ is the scalar $(\mathbf{D}\cdot\mathbf{X})$

As before, we acquire a vector with a new magnitude and a new direction from **X**, but it is a different vector (both in magnitude and direction) from the one acquired when we premultiplied. Evidently, this type of operation with dyads is neither commutative (since $\mathbf{X}\cdot\mathbf{AD}\neq\mathbf{AD}\cdot\mathbf{X}$) nor anticommutative (since $\mathbf{X}\cdot\mathbf{AD}\neq-\mathbf{AD}\cdot\mathbf{X}$). This result should not be surprising. Commutativity in mathematics is never a given and when it does occur, it is somewhat a luxury because it simplifies our work.

The complete definition of a dyad can now be stated:

> A dyad is any quantity that operates on a vector through the inner product to produce a new vector with a different magnitude and direction from the original. The inner product of a vector and a dyad is noncommutative.

Dyad Arithmetic

Equality.—Suppose that we have two dyads:

$$\underline{\mathbf{A}}=a\mathbf{ii}+b\mathbf{ij}+c\mathbf{ik}+d\mathbf{ji}+\ldots \qquad (41a)$$

$$\underline{\mathbf{B}}=\alpha\mathbf{ii}+\beta\mathbf{ij}+\chi\mathbf{ik}+\delta\mathbf{ji}+\ldots \qquad (41b)$$

Whenever we say that $\underline{\mathbf{A}}=\underline{\mathbf{B}}$, we will always mean that the individual components associated with each of the unit dyads **ii**, **ij**, **jk**, … are equal. Thus, the single dyad equation $\underline{\mathbf{A}}=\underline{\mathbf{B}}$ will give us nine independent scalar equations:

$$\left.\begin{array}{l}\alpha=a\\ \beta=b\\ \chi=c\\ \delta=d\\ \text{etc.}\end{array}\right\}\ \text{Nine equalities altogether} \qquad (42)$$

We will thus consider the single statement $\underline{\mathbf{A}}=\underline{\mathbf{B}}$ on the one hand and the nine scalar equations $\{\alpha=a, \beta=b, \chi=c, \delta=d,\ldots\}$ on the other as being completely synonymous.

As in the discussion of vectors, with dyads we will also consider cases where there are different sets of unit vectors in the same space. Let us say that **i**, **j**, and **k** comprise one set (the set *K*) and that **u**, **v**, and **w** comprise a second set (the set *K**). Now consider a dyad $\underline{\mathbf{A}}$ and write

$$\underline{\mathbf{A}}=a\mathbf{ii}+b\mathbf{ij}+c\mathbf{ik}+\ldots \qquad (43a)$$

$$\underline{\mathbf{A}}=\alpha\mathbf{uu}+\beta\mathbf{uv}+\chi\mathbf{uw}+\ldots \qquad (43b)$$

Now, we cannot directly equate components because the unit dyads are no longer the same, but we can invoke the trivial identity and say that for all dyads $\underline{\mathbf{A}}$, it is true that $\underline{\mathbf{A}}=\underline{\mathbf{A}}$. From this trivial identity, we acquire the nontrivial result that

$$a\mathbf{ii}+b\mathbf{ij}+c\mathbf{ik}+\ldots=\alpha\mathbf{uu}+\beta\mathbf{uv}+\chi\mathbf{uw}+\ldots \qquad (44)$$

As before, if the vectors **u**, **v**, and **w** can be expressed as functions of **i**, **j**, and **k**, then the components α, β, and χ can also be expressed as functions of *a*, *b*, and *c*. The actual calculation will not be carried out here for the sake of space, but students are encouraged to attempt it on their own. The details are not complicated; just set up the linear transformation for the unit vectors

$$\mathbf{u}=u_1\mathbf{i}+u_2\mathbf{j}+u_3\mathbf{k} \qquad (45a)$$

$$\mathbf{v}=v_1\mathbf{i}+v_2\mathbf{j}+v_3\mathbf{k} \qquad (45b)$$

$$\mathbf{w}=w_1\mathbf{i}+w_2\mathbf{j}+w_3\mathbf{k} \qquad (45c)$$

and naively multiply everything together using algebra.

Sums and differences.—In defining the equality of two dyads, we followed a pattern already familiar to us from vector equality. Let us continue to reason along

[6]We preoperate on the dyad with **X** but postoperate on the vector **X** with the dyad. Note the terminology here.

these lines and next consider dyad addition. We will agree that dyad addition proceeds component by component as does vector addition. Also, we will always represent dyads (as we have already begun to do) by boldface type with an underscore, such as $\underline{\mathbf{A}}$ or $\underline{\mathbf{B}}$. Now, write the rule for dyad addition: Let $\underline{\mathbf{A}} = a\mathbf{ii} + b\mathbf{ij} + c\mathbf{ik} + d\mathbf{ji} + \ldots$ and $\underline{\mathbf{B}} = \alpha\mathbf{ii} + \beta\mathbf{ij} + \chi\mathbf{ik} + \delta\mathbf{ji} + \ldots$. Then

$$\underline{\mathbf{A}} + \underline{\mathbf{B}} = (a+\alpha)\mathbf{ii} + (b+\beta)\mathbf{ij} + (c+\chi)\mathbf{ik} + (d+\delta)\mathbf{ji} + \ldots \tag{46}$$

Dyad differences are handled the same as dyad sums:

$$\underline{\mathbf{A}} - \underline{\mathbf{B}} = (a-\alpha)\mathbf{ii} + (b-\beta)\mathbf{ij} + (c-\chi)\mathbf{ik} + (d-\delta)\mathbf{ji} + \ldots \tag{47}$$

Note from these definitions that

$$\underline{\mathbf{A}} + \underline{\mathbf{B}} = \underline{\mathbf{B}} + \underline{\mathbf{A}} \tag{48}$$

and

$$\underline{\mathbf{A}} - \underline{\mathbf{B}} = -(\underline{\mathbf{B}} - \underline{\mathbf{A}}) \tag{49}$$

Thus, dyad addition is commutative; dyad subtraction is anticommutative.

Multiplication.—As with vector multiplication, dyad multiplication may take one of several forms. The dyad products to be examined in the following sections are the inner product, the cross product, the product of a dyad and a scalar, and the direct product of two dyads.

Inner product: First, we must define the inner product of two dyads. Consider the dyads $\underline{\mathbf{A}}$ and $\underline{\mathbf{B}}$. Their inner product may be formally written as

$$\underline{\mathbf{A}} \cdot \underline{\mathbf{B}} \tag{50}$$

Now, as before, we must give meaning to the symbol. Let us begin by letting

$$\begin{aligned} \underline{\mathbf{A}} &= \mathbf{XY} \\ \underline{\mathbf{B}} &= \mathbf{ST} \end{aligned} \tag{51}$$

We now substitute for $\underline{\mathbf{A}}$ and $\underline{\mathbf{B}}$:

$$\underline{\mathbf{A}} \cdot \underline{\mathbf{B}} = \mathbf{XY} \cdot \mathbf{ST} \tag{52}$$

As before, it seems appropriate to allow the dot to attach to the vectors closest to itself. Therefore,

$$\underline{\mathbf{A}} \cdot \underline{\mathbf{B}} = \mathbf{XY} \cdot \mathbf{ST} = \mathbf{X}(\mathbf{Y} \cdot \mathbf{S})\mathbf{T} = \xi\mathbf{XT} \tag{53}$$

where ξ is the scalar $\mathbf{Y} \cdot \mathbf{S}$. The dot product of two dyads is thus another dyad. Is this result unexpected? Perhaps, but it is consistent with everything that we have done up to this point, so we will persist. Note that the inner product of two dyads is not commutative (i.e., $\underline{\mathbf{A}} \cdot \underline{\mathbf{B}} \neq \underline{\mathbf{B}} \cdot \underline{\mathbf{A}}$)

$$\underline{\mathbf{A}} \cdot \underline{\mathbf{B}} = \mathbf{XY} \cdot \mathbf{ST} = \mathbf{X}(\mathbf{Y} \cdot \mathbf{S})\mathbf{T} = \xi\mathbf{XT} \tag{54}$$

but

$$\underline{\mathbf{B}} \cdot \underline{\mathbf{A}} = \mathbf{ST} \cdot \mathbf{XY} = \mathbf{S}(\mathbf{T} \cdot \mathbf{X})\mathbf{Y} = \chi\mathbf{SY} \tag{55}$$

Since the inner product of two dyads is another dyad, it is just possible that one of the original dyads in the product is itself another inner product. Let $\underline{\mathbf{A}} = \underline{\mathbf{C}} \cdot \underline{\mathbf{D}}$ and see what we can discover. First, note that

$$\underline{\mathbf{A}} \cdot \underline{\mathbf{B}} = \underline{\mathbf{C}} \cdot \underline{\mathbf{D}} \cdot \underline{\mathbf{B}} \tag{56}$$

The question that now comes to mind is whether the order of performing the inner products makes any difference to the result; that is, whether

$$(\underline{\mathbf{C}} \cdot \underline{\mathbf{D}}) \cdot \underline{\mathbf{B}} = \underline{\mathbf{C}} \cdot (\underline{\mathbf{D}} \cdot \underline{\mathbf{B}}) \tag{57}$$

To answer this question, let $\underline{\mathbf{C}} = \mathbf{XM}$ and $\underline{\mathbf{D}} = \mathbf{NY}$. Then $\underline{\mathbf{A}} = \underline{\mathbf{C}} \cdot \underline{\mathbf{D}} = \mathbf{XM} \cdot \mathbf{NY} = \mathbf{X}(\mathbf{M} \cdot \mathbf{N})\mathbf{Y} = \psi\mathbf{XY}$. Recalling that $\mathbf{Y} \cdot \mathbf{S} = \xi$,

$$\begin{aligned} (\underline{\mathbf{C}} \cdot \underline{\mathbf{D}}) \cdot \underline{\mathbf{B}} &= \left[\mathbf{X}(\mathbf{M} \cdot \mathbf{N})\mathbf{Y}\right] \cdot \mathbf{ST} \\ &= \psi\mathbf{XY} \cdot \mathbf{ST} = \psi\xi\mathbf{XT} \end{aligned} \tag{58}$$

$$\begin{aligned} \underline{\mathbf{C}} \cdot (\underline{\mathbf{D}} \cdot \underline{\mathbf{B}}) &= \mathbf{XM} \cdot \left[\mathbf{N}(\mathbf{Y} \cdot \mathbf{S})\mathbf{T}\right] \\ &= \xi\mathbf{XM} \cdot \mathbf{NT} = \xi\psi\mathbf{XT} \end{aligned} \tag{59}$$

Thus, the result is independent of the order of performing the inner products, and so we conclude that the associative law holds for inner multiplication of dyads; that is, that

$$(\underline{\mathbf{C}} \cdot \underline{\mathbf{D}}) \cdot \underline{\mathbf{B}} = \underline{\mathbf{C}} \cdot (\underline{\mathbf{D}} \cdot \underline{\mathbf{B}}) \tag{60}$$

Cross product: We may also define the cross product of two dyads as

$$\underline{\mathbf{A}} \times \underline{\mathbf{B}} \tag{61}$$

With $\underline{\mathbf{A}} = \mathbf{XY}$ and $\underline{\mathbf{B}} = \mathbf{ST}$, we have

$$\underline{\mathbf{A}} \times \underline{\mathbf{B}} = \mathbf{XY} \times \mathbf{ST} = \mathbf{X}(\mathbf{Y} \times \mathbf{S})\mathbf{T} = \mathbf{XMT} \tag{62}$$

where $\mathbf{M} = \mathbf{Y} \times \mathbf{S}$. The result is another new entity, a triad. Its properties may be developed along lines analogous to those already laid out for dyads. Note how the attachment rule for the operator (in this case, the cross ×) has again been applied. In working with dyads and higher order products, this rule has become the norm, part of the internal "rhythm" of the mathematics.

Product of a dyad and a scalar: Given the dyad $\underline{\mathbf{A}} = \mathbf{XY}$ and the scalar α, form the product α $\underline{\mathbf{A}}$ and note the result:

$$\begin{aligned} \alpha\underline{\mathbf{A}} &= \alpha\mathbf{XY} = (\alpha\mathbf{X})\mathbf{Y} = (\mathbf{X}\alpha)\mathbf{Y} = \mathbf{X}\alpha\mathbf{Y} \\ &= \mathbf{X}(\alpha\mathbf{Y}) = \mathbf{X}(\mathbf{Y}\alpha) = \mathbf{XY}\alpha = \underline{\mathbf{A}}\alpha \end{aligned} \tag{63}$$

The product of a dyad and a scalar is thus commutative.

Direct (or dyad) products: We may do with dyads, triads, and other higher order products what we have already done with vectors; that is, we may multiply them directly without either the dot or the cross. Let $\underline{\mathbf{A}}$ be a dyad and $\underline{\mathbf{C}}$ be a triad. Then

$$\underline{\mathbf{AC}} = \underline{\mathbf{Q}} \tag{64}$$

is a pentad. If $\underline{\mathbf{A}}$ has 9 components and $\underline{\mathbf{C}}$ has 27 components, then $\underline{\mathbf{Q}}$ will have 9 × 27 = 243 components. Products of any order may thus be constructed and their properties defined in accordance with what we have already done with dyads. Such higher order products are called *n*-ads where *n* refers to the number of vectors involved in the product. Thus, a structure such as the one we have just worked with, $\underline{\mathbf{Q}}$ = **QRSTU** is a pentad because of the five component vectors **Q**, **R**, **S**, **T**, and **U**.

Contraction.—This section introduces contraction, one more new and as yet unfamiliar operation that will play a role in tensor analysis. Consider the dyad $\underline{\mathbf{R}} = \mathbf{MN}$. $\underline{\mathbf{R}}$ is contracted by placing a dot between the component vectors **M** and **N** and carrying out the inner product. The result will be a scalar *R*:

$$\underline{\mathbf{R}}(\text{contracted}) = \mathbf{M} \cdot \mathbf{N} = R \tag{65}$$

It is useful to introduce matrix notation at this point in our development. In linear algebra we deal with sets of linear equations such as

$$ax + by + cz = u \tag{66a}$$

$$dx + ey + fz = v \tag{66b}$$

$$gx + hy + mz = w \tag{66c}$$

Rewritten in matrix form, this set becomes

$$\begin{vmatrix} a & b & c \\ d & e & f \\ g & h & m \end{vmatrix} \begin{vmatrix} x \\ y \\ z \end{vmatrix} = \begin{vmatrix} u \\ v \\ w \end{vmatrix} \tag{67}$$

where the matrix premultiplies the column vector with components *x*, *y*, and *z* to obtain a new column vector with components *u*, *v*, and *w*. Recall that we wrote this expression in a shorthand notation similar to that which we have been using:

$$\underline{\mathbf{A}}\mathbf{x} = \mathbf{u} \tag{68}$$

The dot was probably not used in your linear algebra class because it was not required to complete the notation. In generalizing from the more specific forms of linear algebra and vector analysis to the more general forms of dyads and higher order products, however, the notation becomes incomplete without the dot.

In the notation that we have been using, the left-hand side is actually a triad:

$$\underline{\mathbf{A}}\mathbf{x} = \underline{\mathbf{T}} \tag{69}$$

To obtain the system of linear equations, we must contract the triad by inserting a dot between the dyad $\underline{\mathbf{A}}$ and the vector **x**. The result is

$$\underline{\mathbf{A}} \cdot \mathbf{x} = \mathbf{u} \tag{70}$$

As we generalize to include more information in less space, we must become more rigorous in bookkeeping our symbols.

In higher order *n*-ads, it is necessary to specify exactly where a contraction is to be made. Consider the pentad **ABDCE**. In any one of several ways, the dot can be introduced between the five component vectors to produce different results, all of which are legitimate contractions of the pentad:

$$\mathbf{AB} \cdot \mathbf{DCE} = \mu \mathbf{ACE} \tag{71a}$$

$$\mathbf{ABDC} \cdot \mathbf{E} = \lambda \mathbf{ABD} \tag{71b}$$

$$\mathbf{A} \cdot \mathbf{BDC} \cdot \mathbf{E} = \nu \mathbf{D} \tag{71c}$$

Note that each dot reduces the order of the result by two. Thus, the pentad with one dot produces a triad, with two dots, a monad (vector), and so on.

Components, Rank, and Dimensionality

The *n*-ads are mathematical entities that consist of components.

> Components are just the denominate (or nondenominate) numbers that premultiply the unit *n*-ads and are required to completely specify the entire *n*-ad.

As a general rule, when different observers are involved in a situation involving *n*-ads, the components (component values) they record will vary from observer to observer but only in a way that allows the *n*-ad as a whole to remain the same. The *n*-ad must be thought of as having an observer-independent reality of its own. We are already familiar with this concept from our knowledge of arithmetic. For example, the number eight may be written as the sum of different pairs of numbers:

$$8 = 5 + 3, 6 + 2, 3 + 3, +2, \ldots \tag{72}$$

The component numbers have been changed but their sum remains the same.

In physics and engineering, it is often the case that more than one observer is involved in a given situation, each simultaneously watching the same event from a different perspective. Although their individual descriptions may vary because of their perspectives, their overall accounts of the event must match because the event itself is one and the same for all. This situation should remind students of the trivial identities used in previous sections; namely, $\mathbf{V} = \mathbf{V}$ and $\underline{\mathbf{A}} = \underline{\mathbf{A}}$. In this case, the trivial identity is

$$\text{Event} = \text{Itself} \tag{73}$$

In other words, every event equals itself regardless of the perspective from which it is viewed. Herein lies the major reason why vectors and dyads and triads and so forth (more generally, tensors) are used in physics. The trivial identity parallels a sort of objective reality that mirrors what we believe of the universe at large. We used the trivial identity to obtain transformations between different sets of unit vectors. The transformations preserve the identities of the vector and/or the dyad so that it remains the same for both sets.

We can now replace the term "set of unit vectors" with "observer." Each observer sets up a set of unit vectors (measuring apparatus), but whatever phenomenon is being observed must be the same for all, despite possible different perspectives. Later, when we develop the component transformations that will formally define tensors, we will do so explicitly with this kind of mathematical objectivity in mind. Thus, tensors will be ideal mathematical objects for building models of the world at large.

Vectors and other higher order products are often "viewed" simultaneously from different coordinate systems. For any given vector (event), the components viewed within each individual coordinate system differ from those viewed in all other coordinate systems. However, the vector itself remains one and the same vector for all. Thus, the component values are coordinate dependent (they are the projections onto the particular coordinate axes chosen), whereas the vector itself is said to be coordinate independent (it represents an objective reality).

In a three-dimensional space, the actual number of individual components that comprise a vector or some higher order entity remains the same for everybody:

1. A scalar has one component; that is, the denominate number that represents it.
2. A vector has three components, one in each of the **i**, **j**, and **k** directions.
3. A dyad has nine components, one for each of the unit dyads **ii**, **ij**, **jk**, and so on.

The number of components provides a good index for making a distinction between one type of entity and another.

The entities[7] with which we are dealing are called tensors (a term to be defined) and their position in the component number hierarchy is designated by an index number called the rank. Table I presents this concept.

TABLE I.—TENSORS AND THEIR RANK

Type of tensor	Rank	Number of components
Scalar	0	1
Vector	1	3
Dyad	2	9

We have begun to build a sequence. Can you see the next term? It would be a tensor of rank 3 with 27 components followed by a tensor of rank 4 with 81 components. The terms that can be added to the list are unlimited. The relationship that exists between the rank and number of components is presented in table II.

TABLE II.—RELATIONSHIP BETWEEN RANK AND COMPONENTS

Type of tensor	Rank	Number of components
Scalar	0	1
Vector	1	3
Dyad	2	9
"Triad"	3	27
"Quartad"	4	81

Note that the rank, as we have defined it, is equal to the number of vectors directly multiplied to form the object. A scalar involves no vectors; a vector involves one vector; a dyad involves two vectors, and so on. In addition, another general relationship is apparent:

$$\text{Number of components} = 3^{(\text{Rank})} \tag{74}$$

To generalize further, the number three arises because we have been working in three-dimensional space, the space most familiar to all of us.

> A three-dimensional space is any space for which three independent numbers (coordinates) are required to specify a point.

However, the dimensionality of the space need not be restricted to three. A little reflection will show that we could repeat our development in any number of dimensions n.

> An n-dimensional space is any space for which n independent numbers (coordinates) are required to specify a point.

Therefore, for an n-dimensional space, it may be stated (herein without proof) that

$$\text{Number of components} = (\text{dimensionality of space})^{(\text{Rank})} \tag{75}$$

or

$$\text{Number of components} = n^{(\text{Rank})} \tag{76}$$

Dyads as Matrices

You should have noticed that the rules that we have been developing for dyads are extensions of the rules already developed for vectors and are the same as the rules developed for matrices and matrix algebra. This is not accidental. A knowledge of matrix algebra implies a rudimentary understanding of dyad algebra and vice versa. At this point, we will digress to explore this connection more thoroughly.

First, recall that in constructing a dyad from two vectors $\mathbf{A} = a\mathbf{i} + b\mathbf{j} + c\mathbf{k}$ and $\mathbf{D} = d\mathbf{i} + e\mathbf{j} + f\mathbf{k}$, we multiplied the vectors using the same rules as those for multiplying numbers in high school algebra:

$$\begin{aligned}\mathbf{AD} &= (a\mathbf{i} + b\mathbf{j} + c\mathbf{k}) \times (d\mathbf{i} + e\mathbf{j} + f\mathbf{k}) = ad\mathbf{ii} + ae\mathbf{ij} \\ &+ af\mathbf{ik} + bd\mathbf{ji} + be\mathbf{jj} + bf\mathbf{jk} + cd\mathbf{ki} + ce\mathbf{kj} + cf\mathbf{kk}\end{aligned} \tag{77}$$

Now, suppose that we wrote out the vectors **A** and **D** with a slightly different notation:

$$\mathbf{A} = a_1\mathbf{i} + a_2\mathbf{j} + a_3\mathbf{k} \tag{78}$$

and

$$\mathbf{D} = d_1\mathbf{i} + d_2\mathbf{j} + d_3\mathbf{k} \tag{79}$$

where $a_1 = a$, $a_2 = b, \ldots d_1 = d$, $d_2 = e$, … . Using this new notation, the dyad **AD** becomes

$$\mathbf{AD} = a_1d_1\mathbf{ii} + a_1d_2\mathbf{ij} + a_1d_3\mathbf{ik} + a_2d_1\mathbf{ji} \ldots \tag{80}$$

By setting $a_1d_1 = \mu_{11}$, $a_1d_2 = \mu_{12}, \ldots$, this dyad may be rewritten as

[7] In fact, tensors are proper subsets of scalars, vectors, dyads, triads, and so on. Thus, while all rank 2 tensors are dyads, for example, not all dyads are rank 2 tensors. The distinction will become more clear when we formally define tensors and tensor character.

$$\mathbf{AD} = \mu_{11}\mathbf{ii} + \mu_{12}\mathbf{ij} + \mu_{13}\mathbf{ik} + \mu_{21}\mathbf{ji}\ldots \qquad (81)$$

Students should see that the components μ_{ij} of the dyad **AD** can be arranged in the familiar configuration of a 3×3 square matrix (having the same number of rows as columns):

$$\begin{vmatrix} \mu_{11} & \mu_{12} & \mu_{13} \\ \mu_{21} & \mu_{22} & \mu_{23} \\ \mu_{31} & \mu_{32} & \mu_{33} \end{vmatrix} \qquad (82)$$

Hence, the components of all dyads of a given dimension can be represented as square matrices. (We shall not prove this statement herein.) In an n-dimensional space, the dyad will be represented by an $n \times n$ square matrix. Just as a given matrix is generally not equal to its transpose (the transpose of a matrix is another matrix with the rows and columns interchanged), so it is with dyads: it is generally the case that $\mathbf{UV} \neq \mathbf{VU}$; that is, the dyad product is not commutative.

We know that a matrix may be multiplied by another matrix or by a vector and also that given a matrix, the results of premultiplication and postmultiplication are usually different: matrix multiplication does not, in general, commute.

Using the known rules of matrix multiplication, we can write the rules associated with dyad multiplication. For example, to use matrices to show that the product of a dyad $\underline{\mathbf{M}}$ and a scalar α is commutative, let

$$\underline{\mathbf{M}} = \begin{vmatrix} \mu_{11} & \mu_{12} & \mu_{13} \\ \mu_{21} & \mu_{22} & \mu_{23} \\ \mu_{31} & \mu_{32} & \mu_{33} \end{vmatrix} \qquad (83)$$

Then for any scalar α,

$$\alpha\underline{\mathbf{M}} = \begin{vmatrix} \alpha\mu_{11} & \alpha\mu_{12} & \alpha\mu_{13} \\ \alpha\mu_{21} & \alpha\mu_{22} & \alpha\mu_{23} \\ \alpha\mu_{31} & \alpha\mu_{32} & \alpha\mu_{33} \end{vmatrix} = \begin{vmatrix} \mu_{11}\alpha & \mu_{12}\alpha & \mu_{13}\alpha \\ \mu_{21}\alpha & \mu_{22}\alpha & \mu_{23}\alpha \\ \mu_{31}\alpha & \mu_{32}\alpha & \mu_{33}\alpha \end{vmatrix} = \underline{\mathbf{M}}\alpha \qquad (84)$$

Fields

Tensor analysis is used extensively in field theory by physicists and engineers. Therefore, it is worthwhile to digress again and consider the concept of a field. Before doing so, we will digress even farther to consider mathematical models and their relationship to mathematical theories.

Physicists and engineers must often set up mathematical models of the systems they wish to study. The word "model" is very important here because it illustrates the relationship between physics and engineering on the one hand and the real world on the other. Models are not the same as the objects they represent in that they are never as complete. If the model were as complete as the object it represented, it would be a duplicate of the object and not a model. Sometimes a model is very simple, as was the model used earlier to represent the number of components in a tensor:

$$\text{Number of components} = n^{(\text{Rank})} \qquad (85)$$

Sometimes a model is elegant or very general, in which case it is a theory. Theories, even though logically consistent, can never be proven 100 percent correct. Wherever a given theory falls short of experimental reality, it must be modified, shored up, so to speak. Thus, in the 20th century, relativity and quantum mechanics were developed to shore up classical dynamics when its predictions diverged from experiment. Of course, relativity and quantum mechanics possess all the former predictive power of classical dynamics, but they are also accurate in those realms where classical dynamics failed.

Models in physics and engineering consist of mathematical ideas. When setting up a mathematical model, the physicist or engineer must first define a working region, a "space" in which the model will actually be built. This region is an abstraction, a substratum within which the equations will be written and the actual mathematical maneuvers will be made. Recall the closed systems that you have already studied in thermodynamics. These spaces have a definite boundary that partitions off a piece of the world that is just sufficient for dealing with the problem at hand.

Usually, the working region is considered to comprise an infinite number of geometrical points, with the proviso that for any point P in the region, there is at least one point also in the region that is infinitely close to P. Under the appropriate conditions, such a region is called a continuum (or geometric continuum), but a more rigorous statement declares the following:

For all points P in a given region, construct a sphere with P at the center. Then reduce the sphere to an arbitrarily small radius. If in the limit of smallness there is at least one other point P^* of the region inside the sphere with P, then the region is called a continuum. In topology, such an accumulation of points is also called a point set.

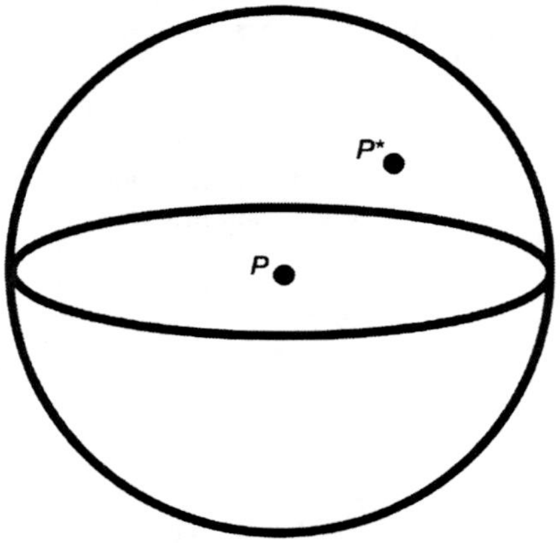

A field can be properly designated over this continuum. The field may be a scalar field, a vector field, or a higher-order-object field and is formed according to the following rule:

> At every point P of the continuum, we designate a scalar, a vector, or some higher order object called a field quantity. The same type of quantity must be specified for every point of the continuum.

Since we want the fields to be "well behaved," (i.e., we can use calculus and differential equations throughout the field), we impose another condition on the field quantities:

> Consider the specific field quantities that exist at two arbitrary points P and P^* in the continuum. Let A be the field quantity at P and A^* be the field quantity at P^*. Then as P approaches P^*, the field quantity A must approach the field quantity A^*; that is, the difference $A - A^*$ must tend to zero.

When this condition is satisfied, the field is said to be continuous. Wherever this condition is violated, a discontinuity exists. When discontinuities occur in a field, the usual equations of the field cannot be applied. Discontinuities are sometimes called shocks or singularities depending on their exact nature.

A punctured field is a field wherein the discontinuities are circumscribed and thereby eliminated. Punctured fields are dealt with in the calculus of residues in complex number theory.

Magnetic Permeability and Material Stress

This section provides two real-world examples of how second-rank tensors are used in physics and engineering: the first deals with the magnetic field and the second, with stresses in an object subjected to external forces.

Recall from basic electricity and magnetism that the magnetic flux density **B** in volt-seconds per square meter and the magnetization **H** in amperes per meter are related through the permeability of the field-bearing medium μ in henrys per meter by the expression

$$\mathbf{B} = \mu \mathbf{H} \tag{86}$$

If you are not familiar with these terms then, briefly, the magnetization **H** is a vector quantity associated with electrical current flowing, say, through a loop of wire. The magnetic flux density **B** is the amount per unit area of magnetic "field stuff" flowing through the loop in a unit of time, and the permeability is a property of the medium itself through which the magnetic field stuff is flowing (loosely analogous to the resistivity of a wire.)[8]

For free space, a space that contains no matter or stored energy, μ is a scalar with the particular value μ_0:

$$\mu_0 = 4\pi \times 10^{-7} \text{ H/m} \tag{87}$$

This denominate number is called the permeability of free space. Since μ is a scalar, the flux density and the magnetization in free space differ in magnitude only but not in direction. However, in some exotic materials (e.g., birefringent materials), the component atoms or molecules have peculiar electric or magnetic dipole properties that make these terms differ in both magnitude and direction. In these materials, a scalar permeability is insufficient to represent the relationship

[8] The resistivity of a wire or of any conducting medium enters the field equations as a proportionality between electric current density and electric field. Recall that Ohm's law for current and voltage states $V = IR$, where V is voltage (volts), I is current (amperes), and R is resistance (ohms). In field terms, this same law has the form $\mathbf{E} = \rho\mathbf{j}$, where **E** is electric field in volts per meter, ρ is resistivity in ohm-meters, and **j** is current density in amperes per square meter.

between **B** and **H**. The scalar permeability must be replaced by a tensor permeability, so that the relationship becomes

$$\mathbf{B} = \underline{\boldsymbol{\mu}} \cdot \mathbf{H} \tag{88}$$

The permeability $\underline{\boldsymbol{\mu}}$ is a tensor of rank 2. It is a physical quantity that is the same for all observers regardless of their frame of reference. Remember that **B** and **H** are still both vectors, but they now differ from one another in both magnitude and direction. This expression represents a generalization of the former expression **B** = μ**H** and, in fact, contains this expression as a special case.

To understand how the equation **B** = μ**H** is a special case of $\mathbf{B} = \underline{\boldsymbol{\mu}} \cdot \mathbf{H}$, select for the tensor $\underline{\boldsymbol{\mu}}$ the special form

$$\underline{\boldsymbol{\mu}} = \begin{vmatrix} \mu & 0 & 0 \\ 0 & \mu & 0 \\ 0 & 0 & \mu \end{vmatrix} \tag{89}$$

Then, $\underline{\boldsymbol{\mu}} \cdot \mathbf{H} = \mu H_x\mathbf{i} + \mu H_y\mathbf{j} + \mu H_z\mathbf{k} = \mu\mathbf{H}$.

The magnetic field represents a condition of energy storage in space. The field term for stored energy takes on the form of a fluid density and has the units energy-per-unit-volume or in meter-kilogram-second units,

$$\text{joules}/(\text{meter})^3 = \text{J}/\text{m}^3 \tag{90}$$

But joules = (force × distance) = newtons × meters = newton-meters so that energy density also appears as a fluid pressure:

$$\text{J}/\text{m}^3 = \text{N} \times \text{m}/\text{m}^3 = \text{N}/\text{m}^2 \tag{91}$$

that is, force per unit area. If you read older texts or the original works of James Clerk Maxwell, you will read of magnetic and electric pressure. The energy density of the field is what they are referring to.

The term with units of newtons per square meter is also called stress. Thus, some older texts also spoke of field stress. Doing so is not entirely inappropriate since many materials when placed in a field, experience forces that cause deformations (strains) with their associated stresses throughout the material.

The classical example of the use of tensors in physics deals with stress in a material object. Since stress has the units of force-per-unit-area (newtons per square meter), it is clear that

$$\text{Stress} \times \text{area} = \text{force} \tag{92}$$

that is, the stress-area product should be associated with the applied forces that are producing the stress. We know that force is a vector and that area is an oriented quantity that can be represented as a vector. The vector chosen to represent the differential area **dS** has magnitude dS and direction normal to the area element, pointing outward from the convex side.

Thus, the stress in equation (92) must be either a scalar or a tensor. If stress were a scalar, then a single denominate number should suffice to represent the stress at any point within a material. But an immediate problem arises in that there are two different types of stress: normal stress (normal force) and shear stress (tangential force). How can a single denominate number represent both? Furthermore, there are nine independent components of stress: three are normal stresses, one associated with each of the three spatial axes, and six others are shear stresses, one associated with each of the six faces of a differential cube.

Since force and area are both vectors, we must conclude that stress is a rank 2 tensor (3×3 matrix with nine components) and that the force must be the inner product of stress and area. The differential force **dF** is thus associated with the stress $\underline{\mathbf{T}}$ on a surface element **dS** in a material by

$$\mathbf{dF} = \underline{\mathbf{T}} \cdot \mathbf{dS} \tag{93}$$

The right-hand side can be integrated over any surface within the material under consideration as is actually done, say, in the analysis of bending moments in beams. The stress tensor $\underline{\mathbf{T}}$ was the first tensor to be described and used by scientists and engineers. The word tensor derives from the Latin tensus meaning "stress" or "tension."

Note that in the progression from single number to scalar to vector to tensor, and so on, information is being added at every step. The complexity of the physical situation being modeled determines the rank of the tensor representation we must choose. A tensor of rank 0 is sufficient to represent something like a single temperature or a temperature field across the surface of an aircraft compressor blade. A tensor of rank 1 is required to represent the electric field surrounding a point charge in space or the (classical)[9] gravitational field of a massive object. A tensor of rank 2 is necessary to represent a magnetic permeability in complex materials or the stresses in a material object or in a field, and so on.

Location and Measurement: Coordinate Systems

Once we have chosen a working space, we need to specify locations in that space. When we make a statement such as "Consider the point *P*," we must be able to say something about how to locate *P*.

We do so by setting up a reference or coordinate system with which to coordinate our observations. First, we choose a point P_0. Through P_0 draw three mutually perpendicular lines. Then select an interval on each of the lines (e.g., the width of a fist or the distance from the elbow to the tip of the longest finger) and repeatedly mark off the interval end to end along each line. We need not select equal intervals for all three lines, but the system is usually more tractable if we do.

Now, we place integer markers along each of the lines. At P_0, place the integer zero. At the first interval marker on each line, place a one; at the second marker, a two, and so on. We have now constructed a coordinate system. Each point *P* in the space may be assigned a location using the following rule:

> Through *P*, draw three lines perpendicular to and intersecting each of the coordinate lines. Note the number where the perpendiculars touch the coordinate lines. Agree on an order for the lines by labeling one *x*, one *y*, and one *z*. Write the numbers corresponding to *P* as a triad (*x*, *y*, *z*) and place the triad next to the point. If the perpendiculars do not fall directly on integers, interpolate to write the numbers as fractions or decimals.

The point P_0 will be named the "origin" of the coordinate system, since it is the point from which the three coordinate lines apparently originate. The three coordinate lines themselves will be named "coordinate axes" or just "axes." The numbers associated with any point *P* in the space will be given the name "coordinates." The axes will be ordered according to the following rule:

> Arbitrarily select one of the axes and call it *x*. Place integers along the axis and note the direction along which the integers increase. Call this direction positive. Now use the right-hand rule from the positive *x*-axis to the next axis. Call that axis *y*. The right-hand rule establishes the positive direction along *y*. Finally, use the right-hand rule again from the *y*-axis to determine the positive direction along the third axis and call it *z*.

This type of system is called a right-handed coordinate system for obvious reasons (see following sketch). We will continue to use right-handed systems unless otherwise specified.

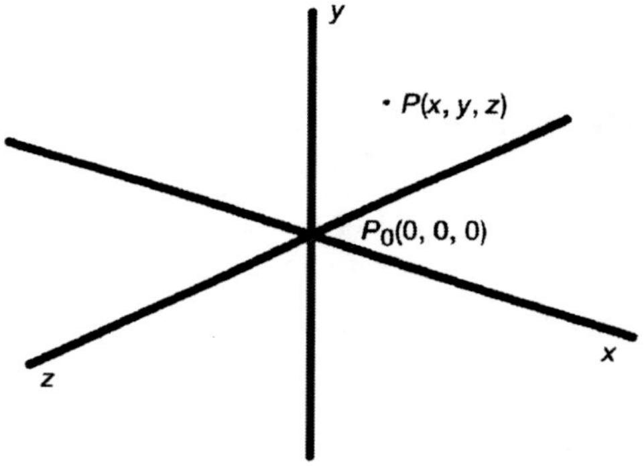

Now, put a vector into the space; represent the vector as a directed line segment (although this representation is artificial). The direction assigned to the vector is arbitrary. Place an arrow point on one end to show the direction and call this end the head. Call the other end the tail. The length of the line segment represents the magnitude of the vector. The arrow point represents its direction. The field point with which the vector is associated will be, by mutual agreement, the tail point (see sketch).

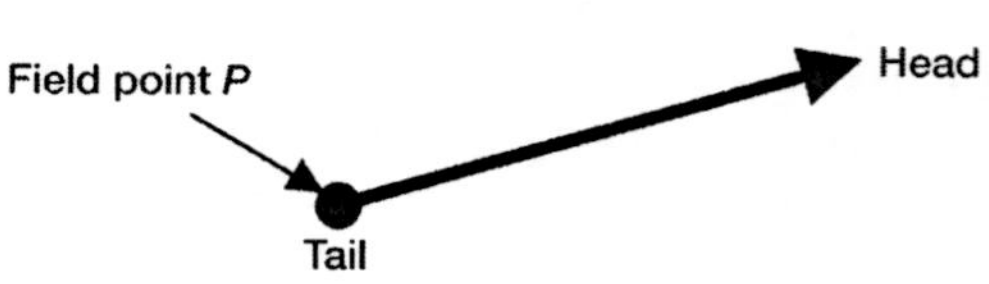

[9]In classical or Newtonian gravitation theory, the field term is the local acceleration **g** in meters per square second; the gravitational potential is a scalar energy-per-unit-mass term ϕ in square meters per square second; these terms are related by the Poisson equation $4\pi\mathbf{g} = \nabla\phi$. In general relativity, the components of the gravitational field (the field terms) are the Christoffel symbols Γ^{i}_{jk} in meters; the potentials are the components of the rank 2 metric tensor g_{jk} in square meters; and the equation relating these terms is a rank 2 tensor equation involving spacetime curvature and the local stress-energy tensor, the components of which are measured in joules per cubic meter.

When we speak of magnitude, we progress from the problem of location to that of measurement. Let us place the vector along the x-axis and imagine that its tail is located at $x = 1$ and its head, at $x = 2$. What is the magnitude of the vector? "Well," you say, "Its magnitude is 1, since $2 - 1 = 1$." But note that I am immediately forced to ask, "One what?" All that has been specified so far is a coordinate difference, not a length. We often set things up so that coordinate differences represent actual lengths in some system of units but to do so is purely a matter of choice.

Take a centimeter rule and measure the length of the x-axis between the markers 1 and 2. Suppose that we measure 2.345 cm. Then, the line segment with a coordinate "length" of one has a physical length of 2.345 cm. Call the physical length s and the coordinate length ξ. We now have the provisional relationship

$$s = 2.345\xi \text{ cm} \tag{94}$$

If we have been careful about constructing our coordinate system and have taken pains to keep all the coordinate intervals the same physical length, then this relationship holds throughout the space. Thus, for a coordinate difference of 5.20, we have

$$s = 2.345 \times 5.20 = 12.2 \text{ cm (approx.)} \tag{95}$$

The number 2.345 is a denominate number and has units of centimeter per unit-coordinate-difference, or just plain centimeters. It is called a metric. Remember it well, for in the general case, the metric associated with a coordinate system is a rank 2 tensor (see footnote 7 on the gravitational field) and plays a variety of important roles.

Multiple Coordinate Systems: Coordinate Transformations

Suppose that we were working together in a given space and that we each had attached to ourselves our own coordinate system. You make observations and measurements in your system and I make them in mine. Is it possible for us to communicate with one another and to make sense of what the other is doing? Well, we are observing and measuring the same physical phenomena in the same space. If these phenomena are "real" (as we must assume), then they must have an objective existence apart from what we see or think of them; they must exist independently of our respective coordinate systems. This concept is fundamental to all physics and engineering and is, in fact, an axiom so apparently self-evident as to remain implicit most of the time. To illustrate, suppose that we were each observing a new car at the dealer. I observe from the front and just a little to the right; you observe from the rear. I note a painted projection on one side of the car and ask you to tell me what the projection looks like to you. For you to know what I am referring to, you must first know where I am standing relative to you and the car. With this knowledge in hand, you observe that from your perspective, the projection is a driver-side rear-view mirror. I now know the function of the projection, and you know that it is housed in a painted metal housing.

The two different locations at which you and I were standing are taken as the origins of two different coordinate systems. Drawing the coordinate systems on a sheet of paper would enable us to note that the space represented by the sheet of paper (a plane) contains the two systems in such a way that each can be represented in terms of the other. This representation is called a coordinate transformation.

Let us give names to our two coordinate systems. I call my system K and we agree to call yours K^*. Instead of a car, let us now observe a single point P. The coordinates of P that I record will be labeled (x, y, z); those that you record will be labeled (x^*, y^*, z^*).

Next, we both observe a given vector **V** in our working space and we say that it is located at a definite field point P. We both record the coordinates of the points at the head and tail of the vector:

Head	You	(x_H^*, y_H^*, z_H^*)	Me	(x_H, y_H, z_H)
Tail	You	(x_T^*, y_T^*, z_T^*)	Me	(x_T, y_T, z_T)

We each use our respective results to determine the square of the coordinate magnitude of the vector:

Observer	Magnitude
You	$(x_H^* - x_T^*)^2 + (y_H^* - y_T^*)^2 + (z_H^* - z_T^*)^2$
Me	$(x_H - x_T)^2 + (y_H - y_T)^2 + (z_H - z_T)^2$

For simplicity, assume that for this particular experiment, coordinate magnitude equals physical magnitude in appropriate units (i.e., the metric is unity) in both coordinate systems. Does it make sense that we should determine different magnitudes for the same vector? Since the vector is an objective reality in space and is independent of our respective coordinate systems, the answer is a resounding "No." Therefore, we are able to write

$$\left(x_H^* - x_T^*\right)^2 + \left(y_H^* - y_T^*\right)^2 + \left(z_H^* - z_T^*\right)^2 = \left(x_H - x_T\right)^2 + \left(y_H - y_T\right)^2 + \left(z_H - z_T\right)^2 \tag{96}$$

At least we know that our respective measurements are related by some type of equation, in this case through the magnitude of the vector **V**, which magnitude must be the same for all observers. This assurance leads us to postulate that there must be mathematical functions that relate our respective coordinate observations to one another; perhaps functions that look like

$$x^* = x^*\left(x, y, z\right) \tag{97a}$$

$$y^* = y^*\left(x, y, z\right) \tag{97b}$$

$$z^* = z^*\left(x, y, z\right) \tag{97c}$$

Note that the last group of equations specifies a particular notation for the three functions. This notation is standard in books on tensor analysis and will be used throughout the remainder of this text. Also, because there is nothing particular about the order in which we choose between *K* and *K**, we might just as easily have written the variables in reverse:

$$x = x\left(x^*, y^*, z^*\right) \tag{98a}$$

$$y = y\left(x^*, y^*, z^*\right) \tag{98b}$$

$$z = z\left(x^*, y^*, z^*\right) \tag{98c}$$

That such functions as these do exist is easily argued by noting that the origin of my coordinate system is a point in your coordinate system (as is your origin a point in my system); my coordinate axes are straight lines in your system, and so on. From these considerations, the equations relating the two systems are obtained. The system of equations

$$x^* = x^*\left(x, y, z\right) \tag{99a}$$

$$y^* = y^*\left(x, y, z\right) \tag{99b}$$

$$z^* = z^*\left(x, y, z\right) \tag{99c}$$

or its reverse is called a coordinate transformation. The origin of my system, for example, is the point (x, y, z) = (0, 0, 0). In your system, this point is located at

$$x^* = x^*\left(0,0,0\right) \tag{100a}$$

$$y^* = y^*\left(0,0,0\right) \tag{100b}$$

$$z^* = z^*\left(0,0,0\right) \tag{100c}$$

The existence of such a family of coordinate transformations assures us that if I specify a point *P* at the coordinates (*x*, *y*, *z*) in my system, I can always calculate the coordinates (x^*, y^*, z^*) in your system and tell you exactly where to look to see the same point *P*. Objects like the vector **V** are formally said to be invariant under a coordinate transformation. This concept of invariance is of paramount importance in defining tensors.

Coordinate Independence

Think of a vector **V** at a point *P* in space. Imagine that you and I both observe it from our respective coordinate systems *K** and *K*. The symbol **V** represents something physical and has an existence independent of our choice of the locating and measuring apparatus; hence, **V** is a coordinate-independent entity. As such, it represents the first example of what we will eventually admit into that class of objects that will formally be called tensors.

Can we write a definition for coordinate independence in mathematical terms? Well, we can first say in *K* that I observe a vector **V**; in *K** you observe a vector **V***, the same vector that I observe (as **V**) in *K*. Coordinate independence is then specified by saying that **V** and **V*** are one and the same, identical, equal:

$$\mathbf{V} = \mathbf{V}^* \tag{101}$$

Although the vectors **V** and **V*** are identical, their components in *K* and *K**, respectively, generally are not. We have already touched upon this concept; now let us look at it a little more closely. Draw a representative picture in two-dimensions. In *K*, let $\mathbf{V} = \mathbf{v}_1 + \mathbf{v}_2$, and in *K**, let $\mathbf{V}^* = \mathbf{v}_1^* + \mathbf{v}_2^*$.

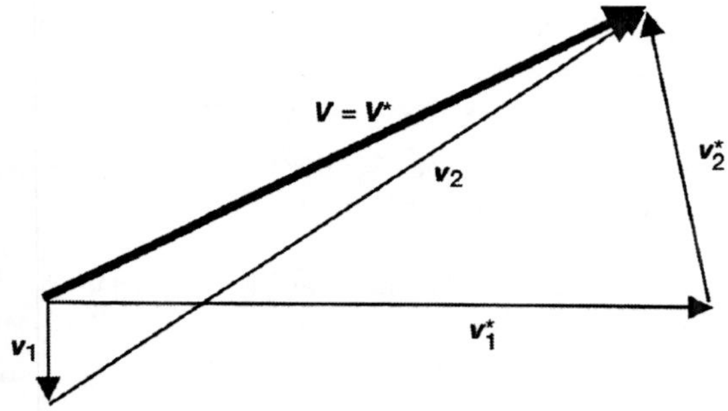

Obviously the coordinate systems K and K^* in the diagram are oblique since the component vectors, assumed parallel to the local coordinate axes, are not perpendicular. Here we have a situation wherein two different sets of components make up the same vector. One set belongs to K, the other to K^*. The vector **V** is itself a physical quantity, coordinate independent, the same for all observers. The components ($\mathbf{v}_1, \mathbf{v}_2, \mathbf{v}_1^*$, and $\mathbf{v}_2^*$) are coordinate dependent; they are determined by **V** and the particular observer's chosen coordinate system. In fact, the components are no more than the projections of the vector **V** onto the respective coordinate axes.

The physical reality of the vector **V** does not translate directly to the components $\mathbf{v}_1, \mathbf{v}_2, \mathbf{v}_1^*$, and $\mathbf{v}_2^*$. In the case of a car traveling at 50 mph due northeast, the velocity vector of the car is a measurable quantity. If I choose a coordinate system with axes oriented exactly due north and exactly due east, then the components along those axes (36 mph due north and 36 mph due east) are determined by the physical velocity vector and the angles made by that vector with the respective coordinate axes. A change in choice of axes will cause a change in the magnitudes and directions of the component vectors but not in **V** itself.

The two observers ought to be able to share their results and can do so through the coordinate transformations. It may be shown that each component vector in the K system is derivable from the component vectors in the K^* system and vice versa through the coordinate transformations. In other words, once we have established and agreed upon the coordinate transformations, we may write

$$\mathbf{v}_1 = \mathbf{v}_1\left(\mathbf{v}_1^*, \mathbf{v}_2^*\right) \tag{102a}$$

$$\mathbf{v}_2 = \mathbf{v}_2\left(\mathbf{v}_1^*, \mathbf{v}_2^*\right) \tag{102b}$$

$$\mathbf{v}_1^* = \mathbf{v}_1^*\left(\mathbf{v}_1, \mathbf{v}_2\right) \tag{102c}$$

$$\mathbf{v}_2^* = \mathbf{v}_2^*\left(\mathbf{v}_1, \mathbf{v}_2\right) \tag{102d}$$

The functions $\mathbf{v}_1, \mathbf{v}_2, \mathbf{v}_1^*$, and $\mathbf{v}_2^*$ must be specified to preserve the equality **V** = **V***, and in formal tensor analysis, this specification can always be accomplished.

Coordinate Independence: Another Point of View

When we spoke of the coordinate independence of the vector **V**, we argued that although the components were different for different coordinate systems, the magnitude of the vector must be the same for all observers. In other words,

$$\{\mathbf{V} = \mathbf{V}^*\} \Rightarrow \{\mathbf{V}\cdot\mathbf{V} = \mathbf{V}^*.\mathbf{V}^*\} \tag{103}$$

or

$$v^2 = v^{*2} \tag{104}$$

where v and v^* are the respective magnitudes.

Now with this idea in mind, consider a dyad. When viewed from K, call the dyad $\underline{\mathbf{S}}$ and when viewed from K^*, call the dyad $\underline{\mathbf{S}}^*$. We now assert that the dyad is coordinate independent so that $\underline{\mathbf{S}} = \underline{\mathbf{S}}^*$. Immediately, the question arises: Can we use the concept of magnitude, or more properly find an associated scalar, to gain understanding of the physical meaning of the relation $\underline{\mathbf{S}} = \underline{\mathbf{S}}^*$?

With the vector **V**, we found an associated scalar, the magnitude $\mathbf{V}\cdot\mathbf{V}$ of the vector. We agreed, on physical grounds, that this magnitude must be the same for all observers. Now, suppose that we contract the dyad to find its associated scalar. Let us write

$$\underline{\mathbf{S}}\left(\text{contracted}\right) = s \tag{105a}$$

$$\underline{\mathbf{S}}^*\left(\text{contracted}\right) = s^* \tag{105b}$$

What now can we say about s and s^*? That they are equal? First, observe that s and s^* are scalars; that is, they represent the inner product of the two component vectors comprising the dyad in each of the systems K and K^*, respectively. Set $\underline{\mathbf{S}}$ = **AB** and $\underline{\mathbf{S}}^*$ = **A*B***. Then

$$\underline{S} = \underline{S}^* \Rightarrow \mathbf{AB} = \mathbf{A^*B^*} \tag{106}$$

Now proceed formally as follows: Form the left inner product of both sides of the equation **AB** = **A*B*** with **A**:

$$\mathbf{A} \cdot \mathbf{AB} = \mathbf{A} \cdot \mathbf{A^*B^*} \tag{107}$$

$$(\mathbf{A} \cdot \mathbf{A})\mathbf{B} = (\mathbf{A} \cdot \mathbf{A^*})\mathbf{B^*} \tag{108}$$

$$a^2\mathbf{B} = (\mathbf{A} \cdot \mathbf{A^*})\mathbf{B^*} \tag{109}$$

$$\mathbf{B} = \left(\frac{\mathbf{A} \cdot \mathbf{A^*}}{a^2}\right)\mathbf{B^*} \tag{110}$$

We have now expressed the vector **B** as a function of **B***. In equation (110), call the term in parentheses β. We then have

$$\mathbf{B} = \beta\mathbf{B^*} \tag{111}$$

Now, return to equation (106) and form the right inner product of both sides with **B**:

$$\begin{aligned} \mathbf{AB} \cdot \mathbf{B} &= \mathbf{A^*B^*} \cdot \mathbf{B} \rightarrow \\ \mathbf{A}b^2 &= \mathbf{A^*B^*} \cdot \mathbf{B} = \mathbf{A^*}(\mathbf{B^*} \cdot \mathbf{B}) \rightarrow \\ \mathbf{A} &= \frac{\mathbf{A^*}(\mathbf{B^*} \cdot \mathbf{B})}{b^2} \\ &= \frac{\mathbf{A^*}(\mathbf{B} \cdot \mathbf{B})}{\beta b^2} = \frac{\mathbf{A^*}}{\beta} \end{aligned} \tag{112}$$

Using (111) and (112) in **A** · **B** finally gives

$$\mathbf{A} \cdot \mathbf{B} = \left(\frac{\mathbf{A^*}}{\beta}\right) \cdot (\beta\mathbf{B^*}) = \mathbf{A^*} \cdot \mathbf{B} \tag{113}$$

that is

$$s = s^* \tag{114}$$

The coordinate independence of the dyad $\underline{S}$ does indeed imply the coordinate independence of its associated scalar by contraction s. Thus

> A test for the coordinate independence of any dyad is to contract the dyad and check the coordinate independence of the resulting magnitude.[10]

However, the same must be true of a quartad or any other even-numbered product since

1. Contraction reduces rank by 2 (thus quartad → dyad → scalar, etc.).
2. Every even number is a multiple of 2.

Therefore, a more general rule states:

> A test for the coordinate independence of any even-numbered product is to repeatedly contract the product until a single magnitude is obtained and then check the coordinate independence of the result.

Then, what about odd-numbered products such as triads or pentads? It is stated without proof (the proof should be obvious) that their contractions will always result in a vector. Thus

> A test for the coordinate independence of any odd-numbered product is to repeatedly contract the product until a quantity with magnitude and direction is obtained and then check the coordinate independence of the result.

Coordinate Independence of Physical Quantities: Some Examples

Tensors are formally defined by the coordinate transformation properties of their components. The transformation properties of tensors are specified by remembering that the physical quantities they represent must appear the same to different observers with different points of view. This property ensures a type of objective reality in the mathematics that mirrors the objective reality of physical objects and events.

We assert that tensors must be quantities that are coordinate independent; conversely, only these coordinate independent quantities are admissible into that class of objects that we call tensors. Some quantities are coordinate dependent. If a quantity is coordinate dependent, then it cannot be admitted as a tensor. The individual components of a tensor may appear different to different observers, as the shadow of a stick may appear different when the light is held at

[10]We assert that $\underline{S} = \underline{S}^* \Rightarrow s = s^*$. By the theorem of the contrapositive, $s \neq s^* \Rightarrow \underline{S} \neq \underline{S}^*$; i.e., the quantity is not coordinate independent.

different angles; however, the overall tensor (like the actual stick) must remain the same for all.

So as not to get lost in the unfamiliar notational schemes that will be introduced later, consider some concrete examples from the real world.

Admissible scalars.—Suppose that I measure the temperature (°C) at a given point P at a given time. You also measure the temperature (°C) at P at the same time but from a different location. Say that P is a point in a beaker of fluid; I stand due north of the beaker whereas you stand due south. We both have identical thermometers, and so on. It would make no sense if you and I acquired different temperature readings; we both should expect to obtain, and both must obtain, the same numerical quantity from our respective measurements. If T is the temperature measured in K and T^* is the temperature measured in K^*, physics requires that

$$T = T^* \tag{115}$$

This simple expression is a scalar transformation law between K and K^* for the temperature T.

> We now specify that only scalars that transform according to this rule and are coordinate independent are considered admissible as tensors.

Inadmissible scalars.—Since we have also hinted that there are scalar quantities that are inadmissible as tensors, is a counterexample possible? Certainly. This time, let T represent the frequency of a light signal emanating from an ideal[11] monochromatic source at P. We both measure the frequency of the light at the same time using the same units of inverse seconds. This time, let us also assume that one of us is moving relative to the other and to the source.

If I am "stationary," the light will have a certain frequency, say $T = T_0$, where the subscript 0 implies a specific numerical value. If you are moving relative to me when you do your measurement, the light that you observe will be red or blue shifted and so will appear to you as having frequency $T^* = T_0 \pm \Delta T$, where ΔT is just the amount by which the light is frequency shifted. Obviously $T \neq T^*$ in this case, and although the frequency thus observed is a scalar quantity, it is evidently not admissible as a tensor.

This counterexample may seem odd at first glance, but it becomes important in special relativity. You might be inclined to argue that I (the stationary observer) have made the correct measurement simply because I was stationary. That being so, you (the moving observer) have only to correct for your motion and then $T = T^*$. Then you ask, "Isn't T admissible as a tensor after all?"

The answer is that in classical physics it is, but in relativity it is not. T would be a tensor only if the term "stationary" could be adequately defined. In classical physics, stationary means "not moving relative to absolute space." But in special relativity, the concept of absolute space is abandoned and replaced with the notion that the observation made in either coordinate system is equally valid. Since there is no absolute system available for comparison, both observations are correct. That they do not agree numerically is simply accounted for by the fact that the two systems are in relative motion.[12] But whether one or the other or both are "actually" moving is a meaningless question. The same argument holds for motion of the monochromatic source. The bottom line is that it makes no difference whether it is you or I or the source or all three that are moving. Only the relative motion counts. It is in this sense that the frequency of the monochromatic source is not a tensor.

Vectors.—As with scalars, neither are all quantities with magnitude and direction admissible as tensors. Let $\mathbf{V}$ represent a quantity with magnitude and direction observed in K and $\mathbf{V}^*$ represent the same quantity observed in K^*. If this quantity is to be admissible as a tensor, then it must be coordinate independent; that is, it must satisfy

$$\mathbf{V} = \mathbf{V}^* \tag{116}$$

This simple expression is a vector transformation law between K and K^*:

> We now specify that only quantities that transform according to this rule are considered admissible as tensors.

Is a counterexample possible here? Yes. The position vector whose components are the coordinate values themselves is obviously not coordinate independent. We will consider the position vector in greater detail

[11]We have evidently gotten our source from the same bin as we got the proverbial massless pulley and the nonstretch rope.

[12]In special relativity, time (and therefore frequency or inverse time) is a component of a four-dimensional vector in spacetime. This vector is called a four-vector and is a tensor. Recall that we have already said that although a tensor must be coordinate independent, its components usually are not. In this case, the distinguishing feature of the two coordinate systems is that they are in relative motion.

after we have formally defined tensors according to their component transformations.

Apply the test of finding associated scalars (magnitudes) for the position vector. First, let **R** be a position vector that locates a point in K and $\mathbf{R}^*$ be a position vector that locates the same point in K^*. Unless the origins of K and K^* coincide, we must have

$$\mathbf{R} = \mathbf{R}^* + \mathbf{C} \tag{117}$$

where **C** is the vector that locates the origin of K relative to K^*. Obviously, we cannot infer from this latter relationship that $\mathbf{R} = \mathbf{R}^*$ unless $\mathbf{C} = \mathbf{0}$ (the zero vector). Additionally, we must also have

$$\begin{aligned}\mathbf{R}\cdot\mathbf{R} &= (\mathbf{R}^*+\mathbf{C})\cdot(\mathbf{R}^*+\mathbf{C}) \\ &= (\mathbf{R}^*\cdot\mathbf{R}^*)+(2\mathbf{R}^*\cdot\mathbf{C})+(\mathbf{C}\cdot\mathbf{C})\end{aligned} \tag{118}$$

Apparently, the position vector does not pass this test either. The position vector is an example of a vector that is not admissible into the class of objects called tensors.

Admissible vectors.— Although the position vector **r** is not a tensor, its differential **dr** is. The differential position vector does not depend in any way on coordinate values, only on their differences; therefore, it is coordinate independent. Now, let us take a careful look at the differential position vector **dr**.

In college texts, **dr** is usually given as

$$\mathbf{dr} = (dx)\mathbf{i} + (dy)\mathbf{j} + (dz)\mathbf{k} \tag{119}$$

where **i**, **j**, and **k** are unit vectors. Again we assert that **dr** has as its components only the coordinate differentials, not the coordinate values themselves; **dr** is not specifically attached to any particular coordinate system.

Metric or Fundamental Tensor

The quantity $\mathbf{dr}\cdot\mathbf{dr} = (\mathrm{dr})^2$ represents the square of the magnitude of **dr** (a coordinate "distance"), but it may or may not represent a true length in meters or centimeters unless provision for doing so has been made in setting up the coordinate system.

Consider the case where such provision has not been made. In fact, look at the case where a different metric exists along each axis. We will associate the unit meters (m) with the metric quantities and not with the coordinate differentials or the unit vectors.

The vector **dr** still represents the vector resultant of the coordinate differentials dx, dy, and dz; but **dr** now has nothing to do with physical distance; it represents a coordinate distance. However, if α, β, and χ are the metric terms for x, y, and z, respectively, then the vector

$$\mathbf{du} = (\alpha\, dx)\mathbf{i} + (\beta\, dy)\mathbf{j} + (\chi\, dz)\mathbf{k} \tag{120}$$

does carry the necessary physical distance information. To find the physical length ds of **du**, we must form the inner product

$$(ds)^2 = \mathbf{du}\cdot\mathbf{du} = (\alpha\, dx)^2 + (\beta\, dy)^2 + (\chi\, dz)^2 \tag{121}$$

The square root of the right-hand side provides the required length in meters.

Can ds be directly related to the vector **dr**? Yes. Two approaches will now be presented to show how.

Approach 1: Take the expression $(ds)^2 = \mathbf{du}\cdot\mathbf{du} = (\alpha dx)^2 + (\beta dy)^2 + (\chi dz)^2$ and rewrite it as

$$(ds)^2 = \alpha^2\, dx\, dx + \beta^2\, dy\, dy + \chi^2\, dz\, dz \tag{122}$$

and note that this expression is the same as

$$\begin{aligned}(ds)^2 &= \left[(\alpha^2\, dx)\mathbf{i} + (\beta^2\, dy)\mathbf{j} + (\chi^2\, dz)\mathbf{k}\right]\cdot\mathbf{dr} \\ &= \left[(\alpha^2\mathbf{ii} + \beta^2\mathbf{jj} + \chi^2\mathbf{kk})\cdot\mathbf{dr}\right]\cdot\mathbf{dr} \\ &= \left[\underline{\mathbf{G}}\cdot\mathbf{dr}\right]\cdot\mathbf{dr}\end{aligned} \tag{123}$$

The components of the dyad $\underline{\mathbf{G}}$ are, in fact, components of a rank 2 tensor called the metric or fundamental tensor. As a matrix, $\underline{\mathbf{G}}$ has this appearance:

$$\underline{\mathbf{G}} \rightarrow \begin{vmatrix}\alpha^2 & 0 & 0 \\ 0 & \beta^2 & 0 \\ 0 & 0 & \chi^2\end{vmatrix} \tag{124}$$

The components of $\underline{\mathbf{G}}$ are arranged in a 3×3 square diagonal matrix whose terms each have the physical units square meters (m^2).

Approach 2: This approach is somewhat more elegant and introduces the style of argument that is often used when developing formal equations.

Since **dr** is a vector, assume the existence of a dyad $\underline{\mathbf{G}}$ whose properties are to be determined but for which

$\underline{\mathbf{G}} \cdot \mathbf{dr}$ is another vector. It should be obvious that we fully intend $\underline{\mathbf{G}}$ to carry the necessary metrical information. Specifically, we shall require $\underline{\mathbf{G}}$ to satisfy the condition that $(\mathrm{d}s)^2 = [\underline{\mathbf{G}} \cdot \mathbf{dr}] \cdot \mathbf{dr}$, where d$s$ is a distance in meters and $\underline{\mathbf{G}}$ will be called the metric dyad.

Note that in this approach, nothing restricts our choice of $\underline{\mathbf{G}}$ to be a diagonal matrix. Necessity forces $\underline{\mathbf{G}}$ to be a square matrix, but the possibility of $\underline{\mathbf{G}}$ possessing nonzero off-diagonal terms has not been eliminated.

In this second argument, you might wonder why we introduced the dyad $\underline{\mathbf{G}}$ only one time instead of introducing a dyad $\underline{\mathbf{g}}$ such that

$$(\mathrm{d}s)^2 = [\underline{\mathbf{g}} \cdot \mathbf{dr}] \cdot [\underline{\mathbf{g}} \cdot \mathbf{dr}] \tag{125}$$

The question is well taken. We could have done things this way, but the result would have turned out to be the same as the one we initiated above. Remember that the inner product is commutative. Therefore,

$$\begin{aligned}[\underline{\mathbf{g}} \cdot \mathbf{dr}] \cdot [\underline{\mathbf{g}} \cdot \mathbf{dr}] &= [\underline{\mathbf{g}} \cdot \underline{\mathbf{g}}] \cdot [\mathbf{dr} \cdot \mathbf{dr}] \\ &= \underline{\mathbf{G}} \cdot [\mathbf{dr} \cdot \mathbf{dr}] = [\underline{\mathbf{G}} \cdot \mathbf{dr}] \cdot \mathbf{dr}\end{aligned} \tag{126}$$

where $\underline{\mathbf{G}} = \underline{\mathbf{g}} \cdot \underline{\mathbf{g}}$ is the dyad introduced originally. The implicit lesson here is that there exists a sort of "economy of symbols" in dyad (and by extension, in tensor) notation. One learns this economy only with time and experience.

Let us now show that $\underline{\mathbf{G}}$ must be coordinate independent. Begin with the terms ds and $\mathbf{dr}$. We have already agreed that $\mathbf{dr}$ is a coordinate independent vector and can argue that since ds is the physical length of $\mathbf{dr}$, it must be a coordinate independent scalar. So, in the case of two coordinate systems K and K^*, we have

$$\mathrm{d}s^* = \mathrm{d}s \tag{127}$$

and by extension

$$(\mathrm{d}s^*)^2 = (\mathrm{d}s)^2 \tag{128}$$

Now, let $(\mathrm{d}s)^2 = (\underline{\mathbf{G}} \cdot \mathbf{dr}) \cdot \mathbf{dr}$ in K and $(\mathrm{d}s^*)^2 = (\underline{\mathbf{G}}^* \cdot \mathbf{dr}^*) \cdot \mathbf{dr}^*$ in K^*. We then have

$$(\underline{\mathbf{G}} \cdot \mathbf{dr}) \cdot \mathbf{dr} = (\underline{\mathbf{G}}^* \cdot \mathbf{dr}^*) \cdot \mathbf{dr}^* \tag{129}$$

But $\mathbf{dr}$ is coordinate independent, therefore $\mathbf{dr} = \mathbf{dr}^*$ and

$$(\underline{\mathbf{G}} \cdot \mathbf{dr}) \cdot \mathbf{dr} = (\underline{\mathbf{G}}^* \cdot \mathbf{dr}) \cdot \mathbf{dr} \tag{130}$$

or

$$(\underline{\mathbf{G}} \cdot \mathbf{dr}) \cdot \mathbf{dr} - (\underline{\mathbf{G}}^* \cdot \mathbf{dr}) \cdot \mathbf{dr} = 0 \tag{131}$$

Simplifying,

$$[(\underline{\mathbf{G}} - \underline{\mathbf{G}}^*) \cdot \mathbf{dr}] \cdot \mathbf{dr} = 0 \tag{132}$$

Consider what this last equation has to tell us. It states that

> There exists a quantity, namely $[(\underline{\mathbf{G}} - \underline{\mathbf{G}}^*) \cdot \mathbf{dr}] \cdot \mathbf{dr}$, which everywhere equals zero or, more precisely, which vanishes everywhere in the space under consideration. Remember that we are working in a field and this equation must be satisfied at every point in the field. Now, we can neither guarantee that $\mathbf{dr}$ vanishes everywhere nor that there is orthogonality everywhere (so that at least one of the cosine terms in the inner products is cos(90°) = 0. Thus, we are forced to conclude that the only way we have of meeting the condition that $[(\underline{\mathbf{G}} - \underline{\mathbf{G}}^*) \cdot \mathbf{dr}] \cdot \mathbf{dr} = 0$ in all possible cases is to assert that $\underline{\mathbf{G}} - \underline{\mathbf{G}}^* = \underline{\mathbf{0}}$, where $\underline{\mathbf{0}}$ is the zero dyad $0\mathbf{ii} + 0\mathbf{ij} + 0\mathbf{ik} + 0\mathbf{jk} + \ldots$. In other words, we are forced into saying that the dyad $\underline{\mathbf{G}} - \underline{\mathbf{G}}^*$ vanishes everywhere in the field and then into drawing the obvious conclusion that $\underline{\mathbf{G}} = \underline{\mathbf{G}}^*$. In other words, the dyad $\underline{\mathbf{G}}$ is coordinate independent. Q.E.D.

We have already said that the components of $\underline{\mathbf{G}}$ are components of the metric tensor. The metric tensor is also known as the "fundamental tensor." This other name pertains to the broad role it plays throughout tensor analysis. To begin to understand this role, we will return to the dyad $\underline{\mathbf{G}}$ and determine the quantity $(\mathrm{d}s)^2$ yet once again, this time slightly altering the roles played by $\mathbf{i}$, $\mathbf{j}$, $\mathbf{k}$ and α, β, and χ.

Return to equation (120)

$$\mathbf{du} = (\alpha\,\mathrm{d}x)\mathbf{i} + (\beta\,\mathrm{d}y)\mathbf{j} + (\chi\,\mathrm{d}z)\mathbf{k} \tag{120}$$

and use the associative law to write

$$\mathbf{du} = (\mathrm{d}x)\mathbf{e_x} + (\mathrm{d}y)\mathbf{e_y} + (\mathrm{d}z)\mathbf{e_z} \tag{133}$$

where we have set $\mathbf{e}_x = \alpha\mathbf{i}$, $\mathbf{e}_y = \beta\mathbf{j}$, and $\mathbf{e}_z = \chi\mathbf{k}$. We will call $\mathbf{e}_x$, $\mathbf{e}_y$, and $\mathbf{e}_z$ base vectors (or basis vectors). Note that these base vectors now carry the metric information and also that we have surrendered the use of unit vectors in writing **du**. In the general cases dealt with by tensor analysis, unit vectors are seldom used; non-unit base vectors are used for convenience and expedience.

Now, let us find $(ds)^2$:

$$(ds)^2 = (dx)^2\,\mathbf{e}_x\cdot\mathbf{e}_x + (dy)^2\,\mathbf{e}_y\cdot\mathbf{e}_y + (dz)^2\,\mathbf{e}_z\cdot\mathbf{e}_z \tag{134}$$

It should be clear at this point that the components of $\underline{\mathbf{G}}$ may be represented in matrix form:

$$\underline{\mathbf{G}} = \begin{vmatrix} \mathbf{e}_x\cdot\mathbf{e}_x & 0 & 0 \\ 0 & \mathbf{e}_y\cdot\mathbf{e}_y & 0 \\ 0 & 0 & \mathbf{e}_z\cdot\mathbf{e}_z \end{vmatrix} \tag{135}$$

The off-diagonal terms are again all zero in this matrix. However, this time we can see that the reason they must all be zero is that the individual base vectors $\mathbf{e}_x$, $\mathbf{e}_y$, and $\mathbf{e}_z$ are all mutually orthogonal. Now, relax this condition and suppose that the axes (and therefore the base vectors) are not orthogonal. Look at a simple oblique two-dimensional coordinate system:

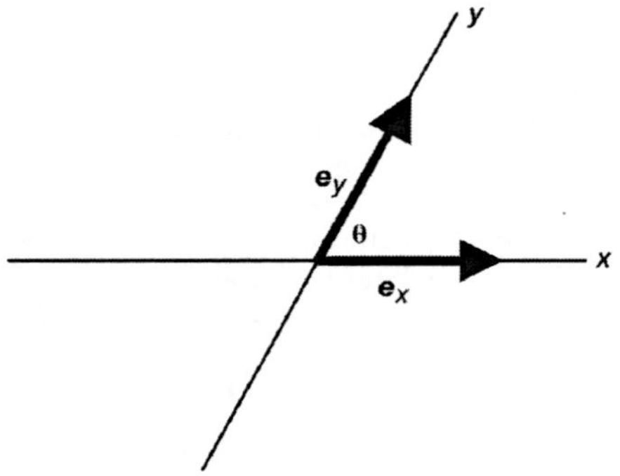

Note now that the cross terms $\mathbf{e}_x \cdot \mathbf{e}_y$ and $\mathbf{e}_y \cdot \mathbf{e}_x$ no longer vanish but have as their common value $e_x\, e_y \cos(\theta)$ (where e_x and e_y are the magnitudes of the respective base vectors). We never know when we will have to deal with such systems (e.g., in crystallography) so it pays at this point to generalize a bit. It is not a big stretch to return to three dimensions and to infer a more general form for $\underline{\mathbf{G}}$ as

$$\underline{\mathbf{G}} \rightarrow \begin{vmatrix} \mathbf{e}_x\cdot\mathbf{e}_x & \mathbf{e}_x\cdot\mathbf{e}_y & \mathbf{e}_x\cdot\mathbf{e}_z \\ \mathbf{e}_y\cdot\mathbf{e}_x & \mathbf{e}_y\cdot\mathbf{e}_y & \mathbf{e}_y\cdot\mathbf{e}_z \\ \mathbf{e}_z\cdot\mathbf{e}_x & \mathbf{e}_z\cdot\mathbf{e}_y & \mathbf{e}_z\cdot\mathbf{e}_z \end{vmatrix} \tag{136}$$

From this argument, it is now possible to infer another characteristic of the fundamental tensor itself: its symmetry. Since the inner product of vectors is commutative, we have the following relationships:

$$\begin{aligned} \mathbf{e}_x\cdot\mathbf{e}_y &= \mathbf{e}_y\cdot\mathbf{e}_x \\ \mathbf{e}_x\cdot\mathbf{e}_z &= \mathbf{e}_z\cdot\mathbf{e}_x \\ \mathbf{e}_y\cdot\mathbf{e}_z &= \mathbf{e}_z\cdot\mathbf{e}_y \end{aligned} \tag{137}$$

Any matrix with this property is called symmetric. Thus, the metric or fundamental tensor must be a symmetric tensor.

If we now replace the subscripts x, y, and z with the numbers 1, 2, and 3 and call the general term $\mathbf{e}_i \cdot \mathbf{e}_j = g_{ij}$, we may represent the components of $\underline{\mathbf{G}}$ in the classical form used to write the metric tensor:

$$\underline{\mathbf{G}} = \begin{vmatrix} g_{11} & g_{12} & g_{13} \\ g_{21} & g_{22} & g_{23} \\ g_{31} & g_{32} & g_{33} \end{vmatrix} \tag{138}$$

Now, the symmetry of $\underline{\mathbf{G}}$ is simply stated by noting that for all indices j and k, $g_{jk} = g_{kj}$.[13]

In addition to carrying metrical information in general coordinate systems, another important function of the metric tensor is to relate the covariant and contravariant components of a vector within a given coordinate system. However, before this comment can be elucidated further, we must return to a consideration of coordinate systems and base vectors.

Coordinate Systems, Base Vectors, Covariance, and Contravariance

It is time to give closer consideration to exactly how we chose the base vectors for a given coordinate system. Up to now, we have tacitly assumed that we could find unit vectors directed neatly along the axes of a Cartesian system, but matters are usually not so

[13]Two types of symmetry in tensor analysis are symmetry wherein the off-diagonal components are pairwise equal according to the rule $a_{mn} = a_{nm}$, and skew symmetry wherein the off-diagonal components are pairwise equal only after one of them has been multiplied by (−1), so that $a_{mn} = -a_{nm}$.

simple, such as in crystallography where the axes are not orthogonal and the base vectors are of different magnitudes or as in relativity where the axes are nonorthogonal and are usually bent or curved.

So, we will take a closer look at the base vectors. They are important for the same reason as the unit vectors **i**, **j**, and **k**: All the other vectors in the space are expressed as a linear combination of them. Thus, in the system where **i**, **j**, and **k** are the basis, any other vector **A** may be written as

$$\mathbf{A} = a_x\mathbf{i} + a_y\mathbf{j} + a_z\mathbf{k} \tag{139}$$

where a_x, a_y, and a_z are the components of **A** in directions **i**, **j**, and **k**, respectively.

Consider a Cartesian coordinate system. Two sets of geometrical entities are present to make up the system: the coordinate axes and the coordinate surfaces. We are already familiar with the coordinate axes; they are the lines that we have been labeling x, y, and z. What about the coordinate surfaces?

We know from our school geometry that two lines determine a plane. Therefore, there are three distinct planes in a Cartesian system generated by the three distinct pairs of coordinate axes; that is, the xy-, xz-, and yz-planes. These planes are the coordinate surfaces in the Cartesian system and are just as useful for specifying location and distance as are the coordinate axes. We have not concerned ourselves with the distinction between referring everything to the coordinate axes versus referring everything to the coordinate surfaces. So now, let us think about this distinction. Pick a point P away from the origin in our space and say that we wish to specify a vector **V** at P. How do we actually do so? To begin, we require a basis vector set at P. In a Euclidean space, this so-called local basis is seldom of concern since the basis vectors are the same everywhere throughout the space, but Euclidean space is a very particular space with some very nice properties (other types of spaces are not so well behaved). To prepare for these other cases, examine the Euclidean space with its Cartesian system and try to draw out some generalities.

If we are working at point P, we obviously wish to have a local coordinate system there, and we wish the local coordinate system to correlate readily with the global coordinate system of which it is a part. We specify the local system simply by specifying a local basis. We may specify our local basis at P in one of two ways:

1. We may construct a set of local axes at P using local coordinate curves belonging to the system at large. In a Cartesian system, these curves are straight lines parallel to the coordinate axes. Then, choose a set of base vectors such that there is one member of the set tangent to each of the local axes at P. Call this set $\mathbf{e}_1$, $\mathbf{e}_2$, and $\mathbf{e}_3$. The vectors need not be unit vectors but may be if we so desire. We may now specify **V** as a linear combination of these three vectors. The resulting components of **V** are said to be referred to the local axes and are called contravariant components of the vector; but if we are in a Cartesian system and have specified for our local basis the unit vectors **i**, **j**, and **k**, this additional verbiage may be omitted.
2. Alternatively, we may directly construct three local coordinate surfaces at P. (The intersections of the surfaces provide the local coordinate axes.) Then, choose a set of base vectors such that one member of the set is perpendicular to each of the coordinate surfaces at P. Call this set $\mathbf{e}_1^*, \mathbf{e}_2^*, \text{and } \mathbf{e}_3^*$. Again, the vectors need not be unit vectors but may be if we so desire. We may again specify **V** as a linear combination of these three vectors. The resulting components of **V** are said to be referred to the local coordinate surfaces and are called covariant components of the vector; but as before, if we are in a Cartesian system and have specified for our local basis the unit vectors **i**, **j**, and **k**, this additional verbiage may be omitted.

In the Cartesian system, the two sets of base vectors (i.e., contravariant and covariant) will be identical. However, in an oblique system, or in a curved system such as an elliptical coordinate system, the two sets will be distinct. One set is usually chosen over the other in such cases for simple expedience.

To recapitulate: the basis set tangent to the coordinate curves is called a contravariant basis set. The basis set perpendicular to the coordinate surfaces is called a covariant basis set. In the general case these sets are separate and distinct, though, as we will discover shortly, they are also related. The representation of the vector **V** using one set or the other is called either a contravariant or a covariant representation. Sometimes **V** is referred to as a contravariant or a covariant vector, and the implicit meaning is understood.

It is a well-known property of Euclidean geometry that two nonparallel lines with a common point of intersection determine a plane. The plane is said to be the product space of the two lines. If the lines are marked with coordinate intervals, then every point in the product space will possess a coordinate pair, one member of the pair deriving from each line.

The concept of product space is neither limited to lines nor to Euclidean geometry. Any two nonparallel curves intersecting at a point determine a unique product surface (two-dimensional space) in the same way that the two lines determined the plane. Thus, two circles with different radii, existing in perpendicular planes, and intersecting at a point determine a torus; also, two equal-radii circles intersecting at two points determine a sphere. Thus can two sets of curves be used to construct a curvilinear coordinate system in three-dimensional Euclidean space. Therein, the difference between covariant and contravariant components of a vector becomes very important.

In general, an n-dimensional space and an m-dimensional space may be used to determine a new and unique $(n+m)$-dimensional product space by an extension of the concepts briefly outlined herein for lines and curves.

We will now introduce a more formal notation for contravariant and covariant basis vectors. The contravariant set will be denoted by superscripts and the covariant set, by subscripts:

$$\mathbf{e}_1 \rightarrow \mathbf{e}^{(1)}$$
$$\mathbf{e}_2 \rightarrow \mathbf{e}^{(2)}$$
$$\mathbf{e}_3 \rightarrow \mathbf{e}^{(3)}$$
$$\mathbf{e}_1^* \rightarrow \mathbf{e}_{(1)}$$
$$\mathbf{e}_2^* \rightarrow \mathbf{e}_{(2)}$$
$$\mathbf{e}_3^* \rightarrow \mathbf{e}_{(3)}$$

We may write the vector **V** in its contravariant and its covariant forms as follows:

$$\begin{aligned}\mathbf{V} &= v^1\mathbf{e}^{(1)} + v^2\mathbf{e}^{(2)} + v^3\mathbf{e}^{(3)} \\ &= v_1\mathbf{e}_{(1)} + v_2\mathbf{e}_{(2)} + v_3\mathbf{e}_{(3)}\end{aligned} \tag{140}$$

Note the use of superscripts and subscripts on the contravariant and covariant vector components v^i and v_j, respectively, and on the basis vectors $\mathbf{e}^{(i)}$ and $\mathbf{e}_{(j)}$. These superscripts and subscripts are called indices. The component indices do not use parentheses, which are reserved for the basis vector indices only. The parenthesized indices on the basis vectors are not strictly tensor indices, but the indices on the vector components are.

Now let us try to discover some relationships between and within the two basis sets in a given coordinate system:

First, recall the dyad $\underline{\mathbf{G}}$. Its components were shown to be inner products of non-unit basis vectors like the general basis vectors $\mathbf{e}^{(j)}$ and $\mathbf{e}_{(k)}$ that have just been introduced. We now formally define the contravariant and covariant components of $\underline{\mathbf{G}}$ as follows:

1. Covariant $g_{jk} = \mathbf{e}^{(j)} \cdot \mathbf{e}^{(k)}$, where j and k individually take on the values 1, 2, 3
2. Contravariant $g^{jk} = \mathbf{e}_{(j)} \cdot \mathbf{e}_{(k)}$, where j and k individually take on the values 1, 2, 3[14]

Next, observe that the two sets of basis vectors (i.e., the contravariant set and the covariant set) are mutually orthogonal. Since the coordinate curves are contained in the coordinate surfaces (in the Cartesian system, the coordinate lines are contained in the coordinate planes) and the covariant basis vectors are perpendicular to these same surfaces, it follows that each covariant basis vector is perpendicular to two contravariant basis vectors, that is, the two that are tangent to the coordinate curves in the coordinate surface under consideration.

Let us agree on a labeling system for the coordinate curves and surfaces:

The coordinate plane perpendicular to the x-axis will be called the yz-plane.
The coordinate plane perpendicular to the y-axis will be called the xz-plane.
The coordinate plane perpendicular to the z-axis will be called the xy-plane.

Now, replace the designations x, y, z by 1, 2, 3 according to the following rule:

$$x \rightarrow 1$$
$$y \rightarrow 2$$
$$z \rightarrow 3$$

We may then restate the labeling system as

The coordinate plane perpendicular to the 1-axis will be called the 23-plane.
The coordinate plane perpendicular to the 2-axis will be called the 13-plane.

[14]Note that the covariant and contravariant components are derived from the superscripted and subscripted sets of unit vectors, respectively. This peculiarity arises from the transformation properties of the basis vectors when viewed from the standpoint of differential geometry.

The coordinate plane perpendicular to the 3-axis will be called the 12-plane.

So now we have that

$$\begin{aligned} &\mathbf{e}^{(1)} \perp \mathbf{e}_{(2)} \text{ and } \mathbf{e}_{(3)} && \mathbf{e}_{(1)} \perp \mathbf{e}^{(2)} \text{ and } \mathbf{e}^{(3)} \\ &\mathbf{e}^{(2)} \perp \mathbf{e}_{(1)} \text{ and } \mathbf{e}_{(3)} && \mathbf{e}_{(2)} \perp \mathbf{e}^{(1)} \text{ and } \mathbf{e}^{(3)} \\ &\mathbf{e}^{(3)} \perp \mathbf{e}_{(2)} \text{ and } \mathbf{e}_{(3)} && \mathbf{e}_{(3)} \perp \mathbf{e}^{(2)} \text{ and } \mathbf{e}^{(3)} \end{aligned}$$

Note that this listing says nothing about the three pairs of vectors $\mathbf{e}^{(1)}$ and $\mathbf{e}_{(1)}$, $\mathbf{e}^{(2)}$ and $\mathbf{e}_{(2)}$, $\mathbf{e}^{(3)}$ and $\mathbf{e}_{(3)}$. The reason is that these particular pairs are not usually perpendicular. They are either parallel as in the Cartesian system or meet at some angle $\theta < 90°$ as in the oblique system. At any rate, their inner products never vanish as do the inner products of such pairs as $\mathbf{e}^{(1)}$ and $\mathbf{e}_{(2)}$, $\mathbf{e}^{(2)}$ and $\mathbf{e}_{(3)}$, $\mathbf{e}_{(1)}$ and $\mathbf{e}^{(3)}$ and so on.

Finally, we may specify that the two sets of basis vectors must always be reciprocal sets. That is, when the inner product is formed between a covariant and a contravariant base vector in any order, the result will always be 0 or 1. Thus, we will choose the basis vectors so that the inner products of the three respective pairs $\mathbf{e}^{(1)}$ and $\mathbf{e}_{(1)}$, $\mathbf{e}^{(2)}$ and $\mathbf{e}_{(2)}$, $\mathbf{e}^{(3)}$ and $\mathbf{e}_{(3)}$ in any order are each equal to unity everywhere throughout the space. This requirement places a restriction on the choices of magnitude only, since the vector directions are already fixed by the local coordinate axes and surfaces. Again, this is done for expedience.

All this information about contravariant and covariant basis vectors may be summarized in a single equation. We must first introduce a peculiar symbol called Kronecker's delta (Leopold Kronecker, German algebraist, number theorist, and philosopher of mathematics, 1823–92). We will write this symbol as δ_k^j—a term that appears to mix covariant and contravariant indices (as, in fact, it does). We will specify that $\delta_k^j = 1$ only when $j = k$, and that $\delta_k^j = 0$ whenever $j \neq k$. Thus $\delta_1^1 = \delta_2^2 = \delta_3^3 = 1$; all other combinations of indices produce zero.

We may now summarize the relationships between contravariant and covariant base vectors as[15]

$$\mathbf{e}^{(j)} \cdot \mathbf{e}_{(k)} = \mathbf{e}_{(k)} \cdot \mathbf{e}^{(j)} = \delta_j^k \tag{141}$$

[15]Note again that the superscript j in the inner products becomes a covariant index in the delta and that the subscript k in the inner products becomes a contravariant index in the delta. This situation is reminiscent of what happened with the fundamental tensor.

It will turn out that the Kronecker delta represents the components of a rank 2 mixed tensor. In the following section, we will demonstrate coordinate independence.

Kronecker's Delta and the Identity Matrix

Look carefully at Kronecker's delta and write out its value for each pair of indices:

$$\begin{aligned} &\delta_1^1 = 1, && \delta_1^2 = 0, && \delta_1^3 = 0 \\ &\delta_2^1 = 0, && \delta_2^2 = 1, && \delta_2^3 = 0 \\ &\delta_3^1 = 0, && \delta_3^2 = 0, && \delta_3^3 = 1 \end{aligned}$$

Seen in this way, it should be apparent that Kronecker's delta may be thought of as representing the components of a 3×3 square matrix $\underline{\mathbf{I}}$:

$$\underline{\mathbf{I}} = \begin{vmatrix} \delta_1^1 & \delta_1^2 & \delta_1^3 \\ \delta_2^1 & \delta_2^2 & \delta_2^3 \\ \delta_3^1 & \delta_3^2 & \delta_3^3 \end{vmatrix} \tag{142}$$

Those familiar with matrices and linear algebra will immediately recognize that $\underline{\mathbf{I}}$ is the identity matrix. Recall that for any vector **A** or any matrix $\underline{\mathbf{M}}$, it is always true that

$$\underline{\mathbf{I}} \cdot \mathbf{A} = \mathbf{A} \cdot \underline{\mathbf{I}} = \mathbf{A} \tag{143}$$

and

$$\underline{\mathbf{I}} \cdot \underline{\mathbf{M}} = \underline{\mathbf{M}} \cdot \underline{\mathbf{I}} = \underline{\mathbf{M}} \tag{144}$$

and that, in general, for any n-ad $\underline{\mathbf{X}}$,

$$\underline{\mathbf{I}} \cdot \underline{\mathbf{X}} = \underline{\mathbf{X}} \cdot \underline{\mathbf{I}} = \underline{\mathbf{X}} \tag{145}$$

With these concepts in mind, we will now demonstrate the coordinate independence of Kronecker's delta by demonstrating the coordinate independence of the dyad $\underline{\mathbf{I}}$. Take any n-ad $\underline{\mathbf{T}}$ in the system K. We know that for $\underline{\mathbf{T}}$

$$\underline{\mathbf{I}} \cdot \underline{\mathbf{T}} = \underline{\mathbf{T}} \cdot \underline{\mathbf{I}} = \underline{\mathbf{T}} \tag{146}$$

It is sufficient to use only one of these relations, say $\underline{\mathbf{T}} \cdot \underline{\mathbf{I}} = \underline{\mathbf{T}}$. For $\underline{\mathbf{T}}$ in system K, we must have $\underline{\mathbf{T}}^*$ in system K^* and we specify that $\underline{\mathbf{T}}$ must be coordinate independent by writing $\underline{\mathbf{T}} = \underline{\mathbf{T}}^*$. This is the same as saying

$$\underline{\mathbf{T}} \cdot \underline{\mathbf{I}} = \underline{\mathbf{T}}^* \cdot \underline{\mathbf{I}}^* = \underline{\mathbf{T}} \cdot \underline{\mathbf{I}}^* \tag{147}$$

Then

$$\underline{\mathbf{T}} \cdot \underline{\mathbf{I}} - \underline{\mathbf{T}}^* \cdot \underline{\mathbf{I}}^* = \underline{\mathbf{T}} \cdot \underline{\mathbf{I}} - \underline{\mathbf{T}} \cdot \underline{\mathbf{I}}^* = \underline{\mathbf{T}} \cdot \left(\underline{\mathbf{I}} - \underline{\mathbf{I}}^*\right) = \underline{\mathbf{0}} \quad (148)$$

where $\underline{\mathbf{0}}$ is the zero n-ad of appropriate rank. Since $\underline{\mathbf{T}}$ is arbitrary, we must have

$$\underline{\mathbf{I}} - \underline{\mathbf{I}}^* = \underline{\mathbf{0}} \text{ or } \underline{\mathbf{I}} = \underline{\mathbf{I}}^* \quad (149)$$

The last expression is just what we require to establish the coordinate independence of $\underline{\mathbf{I}}$ and therefore of Kronecker's delta. Q.E.D.

Dyad Components: Covariant, Contravariant, and Mixed

Let us now reexamine what we have learned about dyads in the light of our new knowledge about covariant and contravariant vector components. In a typical dyad such as $\underline{\mathbf{D}} = \mathbf{AB}$, the vectors **A** and **B** may individually be

Covariant and covariant
Covariant and contravariant
Contravariant and covariant
Contravariant and contravariant

The same dyad $\underline{\mathbf{D}}$ may now be represented in four different ways: covariant, mixed, mixed, and contravariant. Using the indicial notation already introduced, we will display a typical term of $\underline{\mathbf{D}}$ for each case:

Covariant: $a_j b_k = c_{jk}$
Mixed: $a_j b^k = c_j^k$
Mixed: $a^j b_k = c_k^j$
Contravariant: $a^j b^k = c^{jk}$

The dyad is not changed by the choice of representation, even though the components are different in each case. Remember that the base vectors are also different in each case. Therefore, just as we had the covariant and contravariant representations of a vector, we may also have covariant, contravariant, and mixed representations of a dyad or of any of the higher order products, triad, quartad, and so forth. Similarly, since tensors are a subset of these different families of vector product, we may have tensors with covariant components, tensors with contravariant components, and tensors with mixed components. We usually simplify the grammar by simply saying covariant tensors, contravariant tensors, and mixed tensors.

Relationship Between Covariant and Contravariant Components of a Vector

Recall that the vector **V** in the coordinate system K may be represented in a contravariant or covariant form:

$$\begin{aligned}\mathbf{V} &= v^1\mathbf{e}^{(1)} + v^2\mathbf{e}^{(2)} + v^3\mathbf{e}^{(3)} \\ &= v_1\mathbf{e}_{(1)} + v_2\mathbf{e}_{(2)} + v_3\mathbf{e}_{(3)}\end{aligned} \quad (150)$$

We may now ask how the components v^j and v_k are related. To answer this question, we must invoke the rules of inner multiplication for the basis vectors $\mathbf{e}^{(j)}$ and $\mathbf{e}_{(k)}$. Those rules are restated here for the sake of completion:

$$\mathbf{e}^{(j)} \cdot \mathbf{e}^{(k)} = g_{jk}$$
$$\mathbf{e}_{(j)} \cdot \mathbf{e}_{(k)} = g^{jk}$$
$$\mathbf{e}^{(j)} \cdot \mathbf{e}_{(k)} = \mathbf{e}_{(k)} \cdot \mathbf{e}^{(j)} = \delta_j^k$$

We are now ready to determine how the two sets of vector components are related. When we have finished this determination, we will see that the fundamental tensor makes its presence felt. Perhaps you can already see how this is going to happen.

Form the inner product $\mathbf{V} \cdot \mathbf{e}^{(1)}$:

$$\begin{aligned}\mathbf{V} \cdot \mathbf{e}^{(1)} &= \left(v^1\mathbf{e}^{(1)} + v^2\mathbf{e}^{(2)} + v^3\mathbf{e}^{(3)}\right) \cdot \mathbf{e}^{(1)} \\ &= \left(v_1\mathbf{e}_{(1)} + v_2\mathbf{e}_{(2)} + v_3\mathbf{e}_{(3)}\right) \cdot \mathbf{e}^{(1)}\end{aligned} \quad (151)$$

When we distribute the inner product through the parentheses and simplify, we obtain the result that

$$v_1 = g_{11}v^1 + g_{12}v^2 + g_{13}v^3 \quad (152)$$

Similarly

$$v_2 = g_{21}v^1 + g_{22}v^2 + g_{23}v^3 \quad (153)$$

$$v_3 = g_{31}v^1 + g_{32}v^2 + g_{33}v^3 \quad (154)$$

and

$$v^1 = g^{11}v_1 + g^{12}v_2 + g^{13}v_3 \quad (155)$$

$$v^2 = g^{21}v_1 + g^{22}v_2 + g^{23}v_3 \quad (156)$$

$$v^3 = g^{31}v_1 + g^{32}v_2 + g^{33}v_3 \quad (157)$$

We might recognize that the two systems of equations are matrix products, which should be of no surprise at this point. Let us call $\underline{\mathbf{G}}_C$ the covariant fundamental dyad and $\underline{\mathbf{G}}^C$ the contravariant fundamental dyad. Similarly, introduce the column vector $\mathbf{V}_C$ as the column vector of covariant components and the column vector $\mathbf{V}^C$ as the column vector of contravariant components. Thus,

$$\mathbf{V}_C = \begin{vmatrix} v_1 \\ v_2 \\ v_3 \end{vmatrix}, \ \mathbf{V}^C = \begin{vmatrix} v^1 \\ v^2 \\ v^3 \end{vmatrix} \quad (158)$$

$$\underline{\mathbf{G}}_C = \begin{vmatrix} g_{11} & g_{12} & g_{13} \\ g_{21} & g_{22} & g_{23} \\ g_{31} & g_{32} & g_{33} \end{vmatrix}, \underline{\mathbf{G}}^C = \begin{vmatrix} g^{11} & g^{12} & g^{13} \\ g^{21} & g^{22} & g^{23} \\ g^{31} & g^{32} & g^{33} \end{vmatrix} \quad (159)$$

Using familiar notation from linear algebra, we can write the relationships in equations (152) through (157) as

$$\mathbf{V}_C = \underline{\mathbf{G}}_C \cdot \mathbf{V}^C \text{ and } \mathbf{V}^C = \underline{\mathbf{G}}^C \cdot \mathbf{V}_C \quad (160)$$

Equivalently, we may write

$$v_j = \Sigma_k g_{jk} v^k \text{ and } v^j = \Sigma_k g^{jk} v_k \quad (161)$$

Dr. Albert Einstein noticed that the summation sign Σ_k was redundant in these equations and all others like them since summation always occurred over a repeated index. Note that in each case above, summation is occurring over the index k, which is repeated once as a covariant index and once as a contravariant index in each term. Thus, in the severely abbreviated notation of tensor analysis, we have finally

$$v_j = g_{jk} v^k \text{ and } v^j = g^{jk} v_k \quad (162)$$

where summation over the index k is understood. This last convention is called Einstein's summation convention. In full, Einstein's summation convention states that

> In the notation of tensors, summation always takes place over a repeated pair of indices, one covariant and the other contravariant. The repeated indices are called bound or dummy indices. The nonrepeated indices are called free indices and indicate actual tensor rank and type.

To work with an equation such as $v_j = g_{jk}v^k$, first observe where the repeated indices fall. Since these indices indicate summation, expand along these indices first:

$$v_j = g_{j1}v^1 + g_{j2}v^2 + g_{j3}v^3 \quad (163)$$

Next, remember that the free index j must take on all possible values sequentially. Since j ranges in value over 1, 2, and 3, expand the free index (or indices) next:

$$v_1 = g_{11}v^1 + g_{12}v^2 + g_{13}v^3 \quad (164)$$

$$v_2 = g_{21}v^1 + g_{22}v^2 + g_{23}v^3 \quad (165)$$

$$v_3 = g_{31}v^1 + g_{32}v^2 + g_{33}v^3 \quad (166)$$

When done, the information stored in the compact tensor notation is ready and available for you to work with.

It is worthwhile here to demonstrate the expedience of tensor notation. Let us repeat the argument that we just went through in "longhand" but this time use strict tensor notation.

The vector $\mathbf{V}$ can be stated in terms of its contravariant components and its covariant components as

$$\mathbf{V} = v^i \mathbf{e}_{(i)} = v_j \mathbf{e}^{(j)} \quad (167)$$

Note that we do not use i as an index in both equations; we choose different letters. Now, form the inner product $\mathbf{V} \cdot \mathbf{e}^{(k)}$:

$$\mathbf{V} \cdot \mathbf{e}^{(k)} = v^i \mathbf{e}_{(i)} \cdot \mathbf{e}^{(k)} = v_j \mathbf{e}^{(j)} \cdot \mathbf{e}^{(k)} \quad (168)$$

The second equality simplifies as

$$v^i g_{ik} \left(= g_{ik} v^i\right) = v_j \delta_k^j = v_k \qquad (169)$$

where in the term $v_j \delta_k^j$, summation is over the index j.

A similar argument may be formed for $\mathbf{V} \cdot \mathbf{e}_{(m)}$. If nothing else, you see the compactness of the notation and the capability it provides for manipulating large amounts of information with only a few symbols.

Relation Between g_{ij}, g^{st}, and δ_w^s

Now we will use our new Einstein notation to establish the relationship

$$g^{ij} g_{jk} = g_{jk} g^{ij} = \delta_k^i \qquad (170)$$

Begin by recalling that for any vector **V** with covariant components v_i and contravariant components v^j, we can write

$$v_i = g_{ik} v^k \text{ and } v^k = g^{kp} v_p \qquad (171)$$

Substituting the second equation into the first, we find that

$$v_i = g_{ik} g^{kp} v_p \qquad (172)$$

And we can always write the trivial identity[16]

$$v_i = \delta_i^p v_p \qquad (173)$$

Subtracting these two equations, we obtain

$$\begin{aligned}&\left(g_{ik} g^{kp} v_p - \delta_i^p v_p\right) = 0 \\ &\qquad \rightarrow \left(g_{ik} g^{kp} v_p - \delta_i^p\right) v_p = 0\end{aligned} \qquad (174)$$

But v_p is an arbitrary vector so that we cannot assume that $v_p = 0$. Therefore, this equation can only be true provided that

$$g_{ik} g^{kp} = \delta_i^p \qquad (175)$$

An identical argument (starting with $v^k = g^{kp} g_{pm} v^m$) permits us to establish that $g^{kp} g_{pm} = \delta_m^k$. With these two identities, we can then write

$$g^{ij} g_{jk} = g_{jk} g^{ij} = \delta_k^i \text{ Q.E.D.} \qquad (176)$$

NOTE: We never divide out terms as we do in algebra. Division is not defined for tensors. However, because division is a process of repeated subtractions, we do use subtraction as we just did in the example above and in other examples throughout this text.

Inner Product as an Operation Involving Mixed Indices

Now we return to the inner product of two vectors. Recall that any vector **V** has two representations within a given system: a contravariant and a covariant:

$$\begin{aligned}\mathbf{V} &= v^1 \mathbf{e}^{(1)} + v^2 \mathbf{e}^{(2)} + v^3 \mathbf{e}^{(3)} \\ &= v_1 \mathbf{e}_{(1)} + v_2 \mathbf{e}_{(2)} + v_3 \mathbf{e}_{(3)}\end{aligned} \qquad (177)$$

Take this vector and another vector

$$\begin{aligned}\mathbf{U} &= u^1 \mathbf{e}^{(1)} + u^2 \mathbf{e}^{(2)} + u^3 \mathbf{e}^{(3)} \\ &= u_1 \mathbf{e}_{(1)} + u_2 \mathbf{e}_{(2)} + u_3 \mathbf{e}_{(3)}\end{aligned} \qquad (178)$$

and form their inner product $\mathbf{V} \cdot \mathbf{U}$ in the following ways:

Covariant · covariant
Covariant · contravariant
Contravariant · covariant
Contravariant · contravariant

We will do each combination in turn and look at the results.

Covariant · covariant:

$$\begin{aligned}&\left(v_1 \mathbf{e}_{(1)} + v_2 \mathbf{e}_{(2)} + v_3 \mathbf{e}_{(3)}\right) \cdot \left(u_1 \mathbf{e}_{(1)} + u_2 \mathbf{e}_{(2)} + u_3 \mathbf{e}_{(3)}\right) \\ &= v_1 u_1 g^{11} + v_1 u_2 g^{12} + \ldots (7 \text{ additional terms})\end{aligned} \qquad (179)$$

Covariant · contravariant:

[16]A trivial identity in algebra is any identity of the type $1 \times a = a \times 1 = a$ or $0 + x = x + 0 = x$. These identities are important in applications such as the one with which we are dealing and will be used many times more throughout this text.

$$\left(v_1\mathbf{e}_{(1)} + v_2\mathbf{e}_{(2)} + v_3\mathbf{e}_{(3)}\right)\cdot\left(u^1\mathbf{e}^{(1)} + u^2\mathbf{e}^{(2)} + u^3\mathbf{e}^{(3)}\right) = v_1u^1 + v_2u^2 + v_3u^3 \quad (180)$$

Contravariant · covariant:

$$\left(v^1\mathbf{e}^{(1)} + v^2\mathbf{e}^{(2)} + v^3\mathbf{e}^{(3)}\right)\cdot\left(u_1\mathbf{e}_{(1)} + u_2\mathbf{e}_{(2)} + u_3\mathbf{e}_{(3)}\right) = v^1u_1 + v^2u_2 + v^3u_3 \quad (181)$$

Contravariant · contravariant:

$$\left(v^1\mathbf{e}^{(1)} + v^2\mathbf{e}^{(2)} + v^3\mathbf{e}^{(3)}\right)\cdot\left(u^1\mathbf{e}^{(1)} + u^2\mathbf{e}^{(2)} + u^3\mathbf{e}^{(3)}\right) = v^1u^1g_{11} + v^1u^2g_{12} + \ldots(\text{7 additional terms}) \quad (182)$$

It should be clear that two of the four combinations yield simpler results than the other two. The combinations covariant · covariant and contravariant · contravariant yield nine separate terms, each involving the component values and the components g_{ij} or g^{mn}. The combinations covariant · contravariant and contravariant · covariant yield three separate terms, each without the components g_{ij} or g^{mn} and look much the same as the form for the inner product that we first memorized in basic calculus. Therefore, we will adopt the convention that the inner product of two vectors must always involve the covariant representation of one and the contravariant representation of the other.

Note: In adopting this convention for the inner product of two vectors, we were led by the form for the inner product that we memorized in basic calculus. It is important to always remember that in extending any mathematical system into new territory (i.e., territory differing from what has already been established), we must also take care to establish firm tie-ins with what has already been established so that a two-way road exists between the old and the new. In this way, the growing body of mathematics remains a seamless whole, much like the great system of highways that crisscross our Nation.

Using Einstein's notation, we formally define the inner product of the tensors v_j and u^k as

$$v_ju^j = u^jv_j \quad (183)$$

The following will show that the other three possibilities readily derive from equation (183):

1. The covariant v_j is related to the contravariant v^s via the expression $v_j = g_{js}v^s$. Making the appropriate substitution yields

$$v_ju^j = g_{js}v^su^j \quad (184)$$

which is the same result found for contravariant · contravariant.

2. The contravariant u^j is related to the covariant u_t by $u^j = g^{jt}u_t$. Thus

$$v_ju^j = v_jg^{jt}u_t = g^{jt}v_ju_t \quad (185)$$

which is the same result found for covariant · covariant.

3. Using both relations together yields

$$v_ju^j = \left(g_{js}v^s\right)\left(g^{jt}u_t\right) = g_{js}g^{jt}v^su_t = \delta^t_sv^su_t = v^tu_t \quad (186)$$

which is the same result found for contravariant · covariant. These last calculations continue to demonstrate the manipulation of the tensor indices. Again, you should be able to see how effective the shorthand of tensor analysis is when performing these types of calculations and (hopefully) why it is very worth your time to practice it carefully.

General Mixed Component: Raising and Lowering Indices

Now, imagine the general n-ad $\underline{\mathbf{R}}$ with mixed components written as

$$R^{ijk\ldots}_{stu\ldots} \quad (187)$$

The covariant components are s, t, u,... and the contravariant components are i, j, k,... . Now, if we wish to represent this quantity using the contravariant form for the s component rather than the covariant form, we multiply by g^{wz} to form a new term:

$$g^{wz}R^{ijk\ldots}_{stu\ldots} \quad (188)$$

Next, we set the index $z = s$ and sum over the repeated index s to obtain the new representation:

$$g^{wz} R^{ijk\ldots}_{stu\ldots} \to g^{ws} R^{ijk\ldots}_{stu\ldots} = R^{iwjk\ldots}_{tu\ldots} \qquad (189)$$

The term for this process is "raising an index." Similarly, we may use g_{qv} to lower a contravariant index. What must be done is to switch a contravariant component for a covariant one or vice verse. The overall term is not affected by this manipulation.

In the dyad notation that we have become accustomed to using, this same calculation would appear as follows. Let

$$\underline{\mathbf{R}} = \mathbf{I}^C \mathbf{J}^C \mathbf{K}^C \ldots \mathbf{S}_C \mathbf{T}_C \mathbf{U}_{C\ldots} \qquad (190)$$

where the individual vectors are now represented by the same letters as those used for their respective indices in $R^{ijk\ldots}_{stu\ldots}$, and the superscripted and subscripted capital "Cs" indicate contravariance and covariance. Now, if we wish to use the contravariant representation of **S** rather than its covariant representation, we first left-multiply the n-ad $\underline{\mathbf{R}}$ by $\underline{\mathbf{G}}^C$:

$$\underline{\mathbf{G}}^C \underline{\mathbf{R}} = \underline{\mathbf{G}}^C \mathbf{I}^C \mathbf{J}^C \mathbf{K}^C \ldots \mathbf{S}_C \mathbf{T}_C \mathbf{U}_C \ldots \qquad (191)$$

Note that the dot signifying inner product has not been placed. At this time, we select the location for the dot and write accordingly

$$\begin{aligned} \underline{\mathbf{G}}^C \cdot \underline{\mathbf{R}} &= \mathbf{I}^C \mathbf{J}^C \mathbf{K}^C \ldots \left(\underline{\mathbf{G}}^C \cdot \mathbf{S}_C \right) \mathbf{T}_C \mathbf{U}_C \ldots \\ &= \mathbf{I}^C \mathbf{J}^C \mathbf{K}^C \ldots \mathbf{S}^C \mathbf{T}_C \mathbf{U}_C \ldots \end{aligned} \qquad (192)$$

This last result is the one sought. The new n-ad has as its components the terms $R^{iwjk\ldots}_{tu\ldots}$.

Why raise and lower indices? For expedience. For example, consider the dyad $\underline{\mathbf{M}}$ with covariant components m_{jk}. We wish to find its trace.[17] Can we just add the terms $m_{11} + m_{22} + m_{33}$? No, we cannot because a greater degree of caution is required when working with covariant, contravariant, and mixed terms.

Therefore, what exactly is the definition of the trace of a matrix? The trace of a matrix is a solution λ (a scalar) to the so-called characteristic equation of a matrix:

$$\underline{\mathbf{M}} \cdot \mathbf{X} = \lambda \mathbf{X} \qquad (193)$$

where $\mathbf{X}$ ($\neq \mathbf{0}$) is a vector. We can rewrite this equation in tensor notation, assuming that we are free to use the covariant form of $\underline{\mathbf{M}}$:

$$m_{jk} x^k = \lambda x^j \qquad (194)$$

Note that an immediate problem here is that the free index j on x^j is contravariant whereas the corresponding index j on m_{jk} is covariant. We are asserting that a covariant vector $m_{jk}x^k$ is identical to a contravariant vector λx^j, which in the general case, we have no right to do. So, evidently, the use of a covariant $\underline{\mathbf{M}}$ is not appropriate here.

Let us examine our situation further: the summation index k in $m_{jk}x^k$ seems to be properly arranged. Therefore, if we were to use a mixed form of $\underline{\mathbf{M}}$ with a contravariant index j, everything would be in proper order. Write[18]

$$m^j_k x^k = \lambda x^j \qquad (195)$$

which is indeed a legitimate equation. Next, proceed as before by subtracting λx^j from both sides:

$$m^j_k x^k - \lambda x^j = 0 \qquad (196)$$

Simplify further by noting that $x^j = \delta^j_k x^k$ and then substitute and factor out common terms:

$$\left(m^j_k - \lambda \delta^j_k \right) x^k = 0 \qquad (197)$$

Since x^j is an arbitrary vector, we must have

$$m^j_k = \lambda \delta^j_k \qquad (198)$$

But $\lambda \delta^j_k$ is zero unless $j = k$. So, let us set $j = k = s$ and sum:[19]

[17]When the dyad is represented as a Cartesian matrix, the trace is the sum of the diagonal terms.

[18]Recall that $m^j_k = g^{js} m_{sk}$. Therefore, if we have the fundamental tensor, then we also have the means of obtaining the necessary mixed components of $\underline{\mathbf{M}}$ from the given covariant components.

[19]We say that $\delta^j_k = 0$ unless $j = k$ for which case $\delta^j_k = 1$. We are here speaking of the individual terms in δ^j_k without summation. Setting $j = k$

$$\text{Trace of } \underline{\mathbf{M}} \rightarrow m_s^s = 3\lambda \qquad (199)$$

The direct approach to the problem of finding the trace of the matrix $\underline{\mathbf{M}}$ given its covariant components is as follows: Given m_{jk}, first raise one of the two covariant indices (it does not matter which); then set the values of the new indices equal and sum over the repeated index. Thus,

$$m_{jk} \rightarrow g^{st} m_{jk} \rightarrow g^{sj} m_{jk} \rightarrow m_k^s \qquad (200)$$

and

$$m_k^s \rightarrow m_u^u = m_1^1 + m_2^2 + m_3^3 \rightarrow \text{trace of } \underline{\mathbf{M}} \qquad (201)$$

At this point, you might again be wondering why covariance and contravariance never occurred before in college mathematics. Remember that mathematics, as it relates to physics and engineering, assumes Euclidean space with Cartesian coordinates almost exclusively. In Cartesian coordinates, the covariant and the contravariant components are one and the same, and the fundamental tensor is merely the identity tensor.

When other coordinate systems are used, such as spherical or cylindrical coordinate systems, the covariant and contravariant components are still one and the same, provided that unit vectors are used as basis vectors. However, the fundamental tensor has some diagonal terms other than unity. The full machinery of tensor analysis with all its distinctions and carefully crafted terminology is simply not necessary to handle such things, so the distinctions remained hidden.

Herein, we are introducing a branch of mathematics that deals with what happens in cases that are more general than those studied in college. In fact, we are developing a mathematical system so general that it can be used in any type of space, with any type of curvature, and with any number of dimensions. This point is evident in the fact that although we are tacitly assuming the space of familiarity (Euclidean three-space), we are making no specific caveats about the actual space under consideration or about its dimensionality. Thus, what we are saying is not limited to Euclidean three-space or to anything else. This fact alone does not prove the generality of tensor analysis, but for our purposes, it at least points very strongly towards it.

and summing yields $\delta_1^1 + \delta_2^2 + \delta_3^3 = 1 + 1 + 1 = 3$. (In an n-dimensional space, we would have $\delta_1^1 + \delta_2^2 + \ldots + \delta_n^n = 1 + 1 + \ldots + 1 = n$.) Remember that when using tensor notation, be very specific in defining everything. Specificity is the price we must pay for the great generality and convenience the notation affords.

Tensors: Formal Definitions

Tensors are coordinate-independent objects. Because they possess this important property, they are ideally suited for constructing models and theories in physics and engineering. The components of the physical world are also coordinate independent, that is, they do not depend for their existence or for their properties on what we think about them or on the direction in which we view them.[20]

The components of tensors are the equivalent of projections of the tensor onto the coordinate axes. This statement has explicit meaning for vectors only. It has only heuristic meaning in all other cases and serves as a guide to thinking. The components are therefore coordinate dependent in the sense that the angle at which we view a house or a car is dependent on our location relative to the house or the car.

Coordinate independence is best expressed mathematically by writing down a system of equations that relate the components seen in one arbitrarily chosen coordinate system (which we have been calling K) to those seen in another arbitrarily chosen coordinate system (which we have been calling K^*). Such a system of equations is called a transformation. The transformations that are used to define tensors are subject to the restriction that the tensors themselves must be coordinate independent; that is, they must possess a kind of physical reality.

Now, specific mathematical shape will be given to these ideas. We have already written coordinate transformations in integral form:

$$x^* = x^*(x, y, z) \qquad (202)$$

$$y^* = y^*(x, y, z) \qquad (203)$$

$$z^* = z^*(x, y, z) \qquad (204)$$

Now switch from using these expressions to using the equivalent differential forms. Doing so involves the use of differential calculus and actually represents the

[20]This situation is characteristic of classical and relativistic models; it is replaced in quantum mechanics with the uncertainty principle.

beginnings of differential geometry, the work developed by Riemann and others (Bell, 1945) in the 19th century and used so effectively by Einstein in the 20th century. Differential geometry is at the basis of tensor analysis and therefore of both theories of relativity.

In differential form, the transformation equations are

$$\mathrm{d}x^* = \left(\frac{\partial x^*}{\partial x}\right)\mathrm{d}x + \left(\frac{\partial x^*}{\partial y}\right)\mathrm{d}y + \left(\frac{\partial x^*}{\partial z}\right)\mathrm{d}z \quad (205)$$

$$\mathrm{d}y^* = \left(\frac{\partial y^*}{\partial x}\right)\mathrm{d}x + \left(\frac{\partial y^*}{\partial y}\right)\mathrm{d}y + \left(\frac{\partial y^*}{\partial z}\right)\mathrm{d}z \quad (206)$$

$$\mathrm{d}y^* = \left(\frac{\partial y^*}{\partial x}\right)\mathrm{d}x + \left(\frac{\partial y^*}{\partial y}\right)\mathrm{d}y + \left(\frac{\partial y^*}{\partial z}\right)\mathrm{d}z \quad (207)$$

These expressions should appear familiar since they are nothing more than an application of the chain rule for partial derivatives to the differentials of x^*, y^*, and z^* in turn.

We have already argued that the vector **dr** = dx**i** + dy**j** + dz**k** (the differential displacement vector) is coordinate independent. We further note that the terms dx, dy, and dz are the components of the differential position vector in a coordinate system K and that the terms dx^*, dy^*, and dz^* are the components of that same vector in another system K^*. Therefore, the three differential equations (205) to (207) represent an actual transformation between the K and K^* systems. Moreover, they represent the transformation that we are seeking for the specific case of the vector **dr**.

The equations are linear with respect to the coordinate differentials dx, dy, and dz, which are combined in turn with the derivatives $(\partial x^*/\partial x)$, $(\partial x^*/\partial y)$, and $(\partial x^*/\partial z)$, and so forth, to give the terms dx^*, dy^*, and dz^*. The original coordinate transformations

$$x^* = x^*(x,y,z) \quad (208)$$

$$y^* = y^*(x,y,z) \quad (209)$$

$$z^* = z^*(x,y,z) \quad (210)$$

enter into the picture through these derivatives.

Since, in a Cartesian system, the unit vectors **i**, **j**, and **k** are both covariant and contravariant without distinction, it appears that we are free to specify which type of tensor we wish **dr** to be. We assert that whatever it is in one coordinate system, it will be in all coordinate systems. Let us choose to make it the prototypical contravariant tensor. This choice makes sense because for the vanishing of dy and dz, **dr** = dx**i**, a vector tangent to the x-axis (similarly for the vanishing of dx and dz and dx and dy). To reiterate, select the vector **dr** to represent the prototypical contravariant vector. All other vectors that transform according to the rule established for **dr** will be called contravariant vectors. That is, all other vectors whose components transform like

$$\mathrm{d}x^* = \left(\frac{\partial x^*}{\partial x}\right)\mathrm{d}x + \left(\frac{\partial x^*}{\partial y}\right)\mathrm{d}y + \left(\frac{\partial x^*}{\partial z}\right)\mathrm{d}z \quad (211)$$

$$\mathrm{d}y^* = \left(\frac{\partial y^*}{\partial x}\right)\mathrm{d}x + \left(\frac{\partial y^*}{\partial y}\right)\mathrm{d}y + \left(\frac{\partial y^*}{\partial z}\right)\mathrm{d}z \quad (212)$$

$$\mathrm{d}z^* = \left(\frac{\partial z^*}{\partial x}\right)\mathrm{d}x + \left(\frac{\partial z^*}{\partial y}\right)\mathrm{d}y + \left(\frac{\partial z^*}{\partial z}\right)\mathrm{d}z \quad (213)$$

In matrix form, the same transformation equations become

$$\mathrm{d}\mathbf{r}^* = \begin{vmatrix} \left(\frac{\partial x^*}{\partial x}\right) & \left(\frac{\partial x^*}{\partial y}\right) & \left(\frac{\partial x^*}{\partial z}\right) \\ \left(\frac{\partial y^*}{\partial x}\right) & \left(\frac{\partial y^*}{\partial y}\right) & \left(\frac{\partial y^*}{\partial z}\right) \\ \left(\frac{\partial z^*}{\partial x}\right) & \left(\frac{\partial z^*}{\partial y}\right) & \left(\frac{\partial z^*}{\partial z}\right) \end{vmatrix} \mathrm{d}\mathbf{r} \quad (214)$$

If we now make the formal notational changes d$x \to$ dx^1, d$y \to$ dx^2, and d$z \to$ dx^3; d$x^* \to$ dx^1*, d$y^* \to$ dx^2*, and d$z^* \to$ dx^3* and substitute, we observe that this entire set of expressions can be written in tensor format as

$$\mathrm{d}x^{i*} = \left(\frac{\partial x^{i*}}{\partial x^k}\right)\mathrm{d}x^k \quad (215)$$

where summation takes place over the repeated index k. This expression is the prototype for contravariant vectors. Since all contravariant vectors must behave the same way, we are now in a position to state the general definition of a contravariant vector or tensor of rank 1:

> Any vector having components A^i in K and A^j* in $K*$ is a contravariant tensor of rank 1 if its components transform according to the rule

$$A^i* = \left(\frac{\partial x^i*}{\partial x^k}\right) A^k \tag{216}$$

Now, we will do the same type of exercise for the covariant vector or covariant tensor of rank 1. Only this time, we will dive immediately into Einstein's shorthand notation.

We have already said that contravariant basis vectors are basis vectors that are tangent to the coordinate curves. Also, covariant basis vectors are basis vectors that are perpendicular to the coordinate surfaces. We know that for any surface corresponding to a scalar function of the form $\phi(x, y, z)$ = constant, a vector perpendicular to ϕ is the gradient $\nabla\phi$ where ∇ is the differential operator:

$$\nabla = \left(\frac{\partial}{\partial x}\right)\mathbf{i} + \left(\frac{\partial}{\mathrm{d}y}\right)\mathbf{j} + \left(\frac{\partial}{\mathrm{d}z}\right)\mathbf{k} \tag{217}$$

Let us demonstrate the coordinate independence of $\nabla\phi$. We know from beginning calculus that

$$\nabla\phi \cdot \mathbf{dr} = \mathrm{d}\phi \tag{218}$$

and therefore,

$$\nabla*\phi*\cdot\mathbf{dr}* = \mathrm{d}\phi* \tag{219}$$

But since ϕ and therefore $\mathrm{d}\phi$ are scalars, we also have $\mathrm{d}\phi = \mathrm{d}\phi*$. Furthermore, we have also established that $\mathbf{dr} = \mathbf{dr}*$. Therefore,

$$\begin{aligned} \mathrm{d}\phi &= \nabla\phi\cdot\mathbf{dr} \\ &= \nabla*\phi*\cdot\mathbf{dr} \rightarrow (\nabla\phi - \nabla*\phi*)\cdot\mathbf{dr} = 0 \end{aligned} \tag{220}$$

Since $\mathbf{dr}$ is an arbitrary tensor, this equation is everywhere satisfied only if $\nabla\phi = \nabla*\phi*$. Q.E.D.

In index notation, the gradient of ϕ is simply written $\partial\phi/\partial x^s$ in K and $\partial\phi*/\partial x^t*$ in $K*$. By the chain rule for partial derivatives, we have

$$\frac{\partial\phi*}{\partial x^t*} = \left(\frac{\partial x^s}{\partial x^t*}\right)\left(\frac{\partial\phi}{\partial x^s}\right) \tag{221}$$

where summation occurs over the repeated index s.

Using arguments analogous to those used for the contravariant case, we take this expression to be the prototype transformation for covariant vectors. Since all covariant vectors must behave the same way, we are now in a position to state the general definition of a covariant vector or tensor of rank 1:

> Any vector having components A_i in K and A_j* in $K*$ is a covariant tensor of rank 1 if its components transform according to the rule

$$A_i^* = \left(\frac{\partial x^k}{\partial x^i*}\right) A_k \tag{222}$$

To reiterate, the covariant and contravariant vectors of rank 1 tensors are formally defined by their transformation rules:

$$\text{Covariant} \qquad A_i^* = \left(\frac{\partial x^k}{\partial x^i*}\right) A_k \tag{223}$$

$$\text{Contravariant} \qquad A^{i*} = \left(\frac{\partial x^i*}{\partial x^k}\right) A^k \tag{224}$$

Many (if not most) texts on tensors begin by stating these definitions without offering any background. What this monograph has attempted to do is build a bridge from what is considered a sound knowledge of vectors (i.e., a knowledge common to all students of physics and engineering) up to this point so that the natural flow of thought, the natural connectivity of mathematical ideas, does not appear interrupted when tensors are first encountered.

From this point, we may proceed at once to write down the law for the general rank n mixed tensor $R^{ijl\ldots}_{stu\ldots}$. Since this tensor is equivalent to an n-ad made up of covariant and contravariant vectors, let us simply note that the same laws apply for those vectors when "locked up in combination" in an n-ad as when they are free to stand alone. So, using what we have just done, we can write the general definition of the transformation law directly:

Any quantity $R^{ijl\ldots}_{stu\ldots}$ is a rank n mixed tensor provided that its components transform according to the rule

$$R*^{\alpha\beta\chi\ldots}_{\lambda\mu\nu\ldots} = \left(\frac{\partial x^{\alpha}*}{\partial x^{i}}\right)\left(\frac{\partial x^{\beta}*}{\partial x^{j}}\right)\left(\frac{\partial x^{\chi}*}{\partial x^{k}}\right) \ldots\left(\frac{\partial x^{s}}{\partial x^{\lambda}*}\right)\left(\frac{\partial x^{t}}{\partial x^{\mu}*}\right)\left(\frac{\partial x^{u}}{\partial x^{\nu}*}\right) \ldots R^{ijk\ldots}_{stu\ldots} \tag{225}$$

Study this rule carefully until you begin to see its structure and rhythm. Note that there are bound and free indices. The free indices are represented by Greek letters to make them more distinctive; however, these are not summation indices. The bound indices are represented by Roman letters, and they *are* summation indices. The term on the right is a multiple summation; in other words, summation occurs first over the index i, then the result is summed over the index j, then *that* result is summed over the index k, and so on. Perhaps now you can begin to appreciate anew the efficacy of tensor analysis' beautiful, if somewhat severe, shorthand notation.

Is the Position Vector a Tensor?

Assume two linear two-dimensional coordinate systems K and K^* in the plane. Let the coordinates in K be designated (x, y) and the coordinates in K^* be designated (x^*, y^*). Since both systems comprise straight lines, we may write[21]

$$x^* = a(x+h) + b(y+k) \tag{226}$$

$$y^* = c(x+h) + d(y+k) \tag{227}$$

In index notation, these same equations become

$$x^1* = a(x^1+h) + b(x^2+k) \tag{228}$$

$$x^2* = c(x^1+h) + d(x^2+k) \tag{229}$$

Assume that the components of the position vectors are contravariant components; therefore, we must have

$$x^1* = \left(\frac{\partial x^1*}{\partial x^1}\right)x^1 + \left(\frac{\partial x^1*}{\partial x^2}\right)x^2 \tag{230}$$

$$x^2* = \left(\frac{\partial x^2*}{\partial x^1}\right)x^1 + \left(\frac{\partial x^2*}{\partial x^2}\right)x^2 \tag{231}$$

But, since

$$\left(\frac{\partial x^1*}{\partial x^1}\right) = a \tag{232}$$

$$\left(\frac{\partial x^1*}{\partial x^2}\right) = b \tag{233}$$

$$\left(\frac{\partial x^2*}{\partial x^1}\right) = c \tag{234}$$

$$\left(\frac{\partial x^2*}{\partial x^2}\right) = d \tag{235}$$

this obviously cannot be the case unless $h = k = 0$, that is, unless the origins coincide.

There is another argument, for those who might have some trouble with the one just advanced. From the theory of differential equations for the general case, write

$$\mathrm{d}x^* = \left(\frac{\partial x^*}{\partial x}\right)\mathrm{d}x + \left(\frac{\partial x^*}{\partial y}\right)\mathrm{d}y \tag{236}$$

$$\mathrm{d}y^* = \left(\frac{\partial y^*}{\partial x}\right)\mathrm{d}x + \left(\frac{\partial y^*}{\partial y}\right)\mathrm{d}y \tag{237}$$

However, except under certain very specialized conditions, we are not permitted to write

$$x^* = \left(\frac{\partial x^*}{\partial x}\right)x + \left(\frac{\partial x^*}{\partial y}\right)y \tag{238}$$

$$y^* = \left(\frac{\partial y^*}{\partial x}\right)x + \left(\frac{\partial y^*}{\partial y}\right)y \tag{239}$$

[21]We might also have written $x^* = sx + ty + x_0^*$ and $y^* = mx + py + y_0^*$ where (x_0^*, y_0^*) is the location of the K^* origin as seen from K. If we set $x_0^* = sh + tk$ and $y_0^* = mh + pk$, then we acquire the form of the equations presented in the text, namely, $x^* = s(x + h) + t(y + k)$ and $y^* = m(x + h) + p(y + k)$.

This second argument aptly demonstrates that the differential position vector is a rank 1 tensor in the general case, but the position vector itself is not.

The Equivalence of Coordinate Independence With the Formal Definition for a Rank 1 Tensor (Vector)

Recall that earlier, we provisionally defined a rank 1 tensor as any quantity with direction and magnitude that satisfied the relationship **V** = **V*** when viewed respectively from reference systems K and K^*. We will now argue that this provisional definition is equivalent to the formal definition we have just set down in terms of vector components.

Let a Riemannian n-space R^n have two coordinate systems K and K^*. Let **V** be a vector in R^n as seen from the system K and **V*** be the same vector as seen from the system K^*. To show equivalence of the expression **V** = **V*** for the total vector and the expression $v^i(\partial x^{*j}/\partial x^i) = v^{*j}$ for the contravariant components, we must demonstrate that

$$\{\mathbf{V} = \mathbf{V}^*\} \Leftrightarrow \left\{ v^i = \left(\frac{\partial x^i}{\partial x^{*j}}\right) v^{*j} \right\} \tag{240}$$

First: Necessity (⇐).—Assume that

$$v^i = \left(\frac{\partial x^i}{\partial x^{*j}}\right) v^{*j} \tag{241}$$

Then

$$\mathbf{V} = v^i \mathbf{e}^{(i)} = \left(\frac{\partial x^i}{\partial x^{*j}}\right) v^{*j}\, \mathbf{e}^{(i)} = v^{*j} \left[\left(\frac{\partial x^i}{\partial x^{*j}}\right) \mathbf{e}^{(i)}\right] = v^{*j}\, \mathbf{e}^{*(j)} = \mathbf{V}^* \tag{242}$$

Therefore,

$$\left\{ v^i = \left(\frac{\partial x^i}{\partial x^{*j}}\right) v^{*j} \right\} \Rightarrow \{\mathbf{V} = \mathbf{V}^*\} \tag{243}$$

Next: Sufficiency (⇒).—Assume that **V** = **V***. Then

$$v^i \mathbf{e}^{(i)} = v^{*j}\, \mathbf{e}^{*(j)} \tag{244}$$

Consider the point P at which the vector is located in R^n. Set up local axes at P for both K and K^*. These axes must all intersect at P.

Now embed R^n into a Euclidean space E^{n+1} with an (n+1)-dimensional Cartesian coordinate system. In E^{n+1}, the base vectors $\mathbf{e}^{(i)}$ and $\mathbf{e}^{*(j)}$ are tangent to the coordinate axes in their respective coordinate systems K and K^* in R^n. Also, in E^{n+1}, the space R^n is a hypersurface on which every point in R^n may be located by a position vector **r** in E^{n+1}.

The base vectors $\mathbf{e}^{(i)}$ and $\mathbf{e}^{*(j)}$ are tangent to the coordinate axes in K and K^*, respectively. Let these axes be labeled x^i in K and x^{*j} in K^*. Then

$$\mathbf{e}^{(i)} = \frac{\partial \mathbf{r}}{\partial x^i} \quad \text{and} \quad \mathbf{e}^{*(j)} = \frac{\partial \mathbf{r}}{\partial x^{*j}} \tag{245}$$

But, from the theory of differential equations, we have

$$\mathbf{e}^{(i)} = \frac{\partial \mathbf{r}}{\partial x^i} = \left(\frac{\partial \mathbf{r}}{\partial x^{*j}}\right)\left(\frac{\partial x^{*j}}{\partial x^i}\right) = \mathbf{e}^{*(j)}\left(\frac{\partial x^{*j}}{\partial x^i}\right) = \left(\frac{\partial x^{*j}}{\partial x^i}\right)\mathbf{e}^{*(j)} \tag{246}$$

that is, $\mathbf{e}^{(i)} = (\partial x^{*j}/\partial x^i)\mathbf{e}^{*(j)}$.

Substitution of this result into $v^i\mathbf{e}^{(i)} = v^{*j}\mathbf{e}^{*(j)}$ gives

$$v^i \mathbf{e}^{(i)} = v^i\left(\frac{\partial x^{*j}}{\partial x^i}\right)\mathbf{e}^{*(j)} = \left[v^i\left(\frac{\partial x^{*j}}{\partial x^i}\right)\right]\mathbf{e}^{*(j)} = v^{*j}\,\mathbf{e}^{*(j)} \tag{247}$$

We conclude that $v^i(\partial x^{*j}/\partial x^i) = v^{*j}$. Therefore,

$$\{\mathbf{V} = \mathbf{V}^*\} \Rightarrow \left\{ v^i = \left(\frac{\partial x^i}{\partial x^{*j}}\right) v^{*j} \right\} \tag{248}$$

Thus, the equation **V** = **V*** is both necessary and sufficient to ensure that $v^i(\partial x^{*j}/\partial x^i) = v^{*j}$. The two expressions are equivalent. Q.E.D.

Coordinate Transformation of the Fundamental Tensor and Kronecker's Delta

It is worthwhile to write down the coordinate transformations of the covariant and contravariant components of the fundamental tensors as practice and also for future reference. We will simply specialize the general rule, equation (225).

For the covariant fundamental tensor, we have

$$g^*_{jk} = \left(\frac{\partial x^s}{\partial x^{j*}}\right)\left(\frac{\partial x^t}{\partial x^{k*}}\right) g_{st} \tag{249}$$

For the contravariant fundamental tensor, we have

$$g^{jk*} = \left(\frac{\partial x^{j*}}{\partial x^s}\right)\left(\frac{\partial x^{k*}}{\partial x^t}\right) g^{st} \tag{250}$$

Finally, we know that the components of Kronecker's delta may be represented in terms of the components of the fundamental tensor as

$$\delta^i_k = g^{ij} g_{jk} \tag{251}$$

We may use the two expressions just given to write

$$\delta^{*i}_k = \left(\frac{\partial x^{i*}}{\partial x^s}\right)\left(\frac{\partial x^t}{\partial x^{k*}}\right) \delta^s_t \tag{252}$$

Please study these expressions in relation to the general transformation formula to make certain that you understand how they were obtained so that you are able to write similar expressions.

Two Examples From Solid Analytical Geometry

We take our space to be the usual Euclidean three-space of our college analytical geometry and use different sets of coordinate systems to map this space. Within these systems, we will begin to see how the ideas about tensors may be applied on a rudimentary level.

Example 1: Cartesian coordinates.—We begin with the most familiar system of all, the three-dimensional Cartesian coordinate system. We will place this system into our space and call it K. This system comprises three mutually perpendicular straight lines intersecting at a common point called the origin. The unit interval is usually taken as a unit of distance and is the same on all three of the axes x, y, and z. In K, $(\mathrm{d}s)^2 = (\mathrm{d}x)^2 + (\mathrm{d}y)^2 + (\mathrm{d}z)^2$.

Now, let us show the tensor character of ds by showing that ds = ds*. Let us place a second system into our space such that its origin is displaced from the origin of K and the system itself is at some arbitrary angle to K. Call this new system K*. In K*, $(\mathrm{d}s^*)^2 = (\mathrm{d}x^*)^2 + (\mathrm{d}y^*)^2 + (\mathrm{d}z^*)^2$. The coordinate transformations from K to K* are the linear equations

$$x^* = l_1(x - x_0) + m_1(y - y_0) + n_1(z - z_0) \tag{253}$$

$$y^* = l_2(x - x_0) + m_2(y - y_0) + n_2(z - z_0) \tag{254}$$

$$y^* = l_3(x - x_0) + m_3(y - y_0) + n_3(z - z_0) \tag{255}$$

where (x_0, y_0, z_0) is the location of the K* origin in K, and (l_1, m_1, n_1), (l_2, m_2, n_2), (l_3, m_3, n_3) are the direction cosines of the x*-, y*-, and z*-axes, respectively, measured with respect to the x-, y-, and z-axes in K. If we now form the coordinate differentials, we find that

$$\mathrm{d}x^* = l_1\,\mathrm{d}x + m_1\,\mathrm{d}y + n_1\,\mathrm{d}z \tag{256}$$

$$\mathrm{d}y^* = l_2\,\mathrm{d}x + m_2\,\mathrm{d}y + n_2\,\mathrm{d}z \tag{257}$$

$$\mathrm{d}z^* = l_3\,\mathrm{d}x + m_3\,\mathrm{d}y + n_3\,\mathrm{d}z \tag{258}$$

and

$$\begin{aligned}(\mathrm{d}s^*)^2 &= (\mathrm{d}x^*)^2 + (\mathrm{d}y^*)^2 + (\mathrm{d}z^*)^2 \\ &= \left(l_1^2 + l_2^2 + l_3^2\right)(\mathrm{d}x)^2 + \left(m_1^2 + m_2^2 + m_3^2\right)(\mathrm{d}y)^2 \\ &\quad + \left(n_1^2 + n_2^2 + n_3^2\right)(\mathrm{d}z)^2\end{aligned} \tag{259}$$

Since the direction cosines must satisfy $\left(l_1^2 + l_2^2 + l_3^2\right) = \left(m_1^2 + m_2^2 + m_3^2\right) = \left(n_1^2 + n_2^2 + n_3^2\right) = 1$, we have that

$$\begin{aligned}(\mathrm{d}s^*)^2 &= (\mathrm{d}x^*)^2 + (\mathrm{d}y^*)^2 + (\mathrm{d}z^*)^2 \\ &= (\mathrm{d}x)^2 + (\mathrm{d}y)^2 + (\mathrm{d}z)^2 = (\mathrm{d}s)^2\end{aligned} \tag{260}$$

as we were to show. Q.E.D. This calculation reaffirms the rank 0 tensor characteristic of ds.

> Remember, if a quantity is shown to be a tensor in one particular system, then it is a tensor in all systems.

Sometimes, the proof of tensor character may be greatly simplified by keeping this rule in mind and choosing a particular coordinate system in which to demonstrate tensor character.

Next, let us determine the fundamental tensor in K. We know, in general, that $\mathrm{d}s^2 = g_{jk}\mathrm{d}x^j\mathrm{d}x^k$. In the case of system K, we have $(ds)^2 = (dx)^2 + (dy)^2 + (dz)^2 = (1)(dx)(dx) + (1)(dy)(dy) + (1)(dz)(dz) = (1)dx^1dx^1 + (1)dx^2dx^2 + (1)dx^3dx^3$, where the superscripted variables have been substituted for x, y, and z. We must conclude that

$$g_{11} = g_{22} = g_{33} = 1 \tag{261}$$

$$g_{jk}\left(j \neq k\right) = 0 \tag{262}$$

Equivalently, we have

$$\underline{\mathbf{G}} = \begin{vmatrix} 1 & 0 & 0 \\ 0 & 1 & 0 \\ 0 & 0 & 1 \end{vmatrix} \tag{263}$$

That is, the fundamental tensor in this case is none other than the identity tensor whose components are given by Kronecker's delta.

Since the components that we are looking at are the subscripted g_{jk}, we conclude that this tensor is the covariant fundamental tensor. What about the contravariant fundamental tensor? Well, we have just shown that $\underline{\mathbf{G}}_C = \underline{\mathbf{I}}$. Let $\underline{\mathbf{G}}^C = \underline{\mathbf{A}}$ and invoke the rule $\underline{\mathbf{G}}_C \cdot \underline{\mathbf{G}}^C = \underline{\mathbf{I}}$. Substituting, we see immediately that we have

$$\underline{\mathbf{I}} \cdot \underline{\mathbf{A}} = \underline{\mathbf{I}} \tag{264}$$

There is only one tensor $\underline{\mathbf{A}}$ that will satisfy this relationship, and that is $\underline{\mathbf{A}} = \underline{\mathbf{I}}$. So the covariant and the contravariant fundamental tensor are one and the same in K (and by extension, in K^*, also). This identity is the reason that covariance and contravariance do not appear as distinct cases in a Cartesian system in Euclidean three-space. They are indistinguishable.

Example 2: Spherical coordinates.—Let us leave Cartesian coordinates now and go to something a little more interesting. The spherical coordinate system comprises the same three axes as the Cartesian system with the addition of concentric spheres centered on the origin. The coordinates used to locate a point in space with spherical coordinates are (1) its distance ρ from the origin (i.e., the radius of the sphere on which it lies); (2) the angle ϕ that the line from the origin to the point makes with the z-axis; and (3) the angle θ that the projection of the same line in the x,y-plane makes with the x-axis.

Let us erase the previous Cartesian systems and begin again. We place a spherical coordinate system in our space and call it K. We have learned in our basic calculus that in K, $(ds)^2 = (d\rho)^2 + (\rho d\phi)^2 + (\rho \sin\phi d\theta)^2$. We have already shown the tensor character of ds in the Cartesian system, so there is no need to show it again here. It is apparent, however, that if we did, the calculation would be messier than before.

Let us determine the fundamental tensor in K. First, we must recognize that the coordinate differentials are $d\rho$, $d\phi$, and $d\theta$. Setting $x^1 = \rho$, $x^2 = \phi$, and $x^3 = \theta$, we discover that

$$g_{11} = 1, g_{22} = \left(\rho\right)^2, g_{33} = \left(\rho \sin\phi\right)^2 \tag{265}$$

$$g_{jk}\left(j \neq k\right) = 0 \tag{266}$$

This time, the tensor $\underline{\mathbf{G}}_C$ takes on a more interesting aspect:

$$\underline{\mathbf{G}}_C = \begin{vmatrix} 1 & 0 & 0 \\ 0 & \left(\rho\right)^2 & 0 \\ 0 & 0 & \left(\rho \sin\phi\right)^2 \end{vmatrix} \tag{267}$$

This time, the contravariant fundamental will not be a mere repeat of the covariant fundamental tensor. Again using the rule $\underline{\mathbf{G}}_C \cdot \underline{\mathbf{G}}^C = \underline{\mathbf{I}}$, we discover that

$$\underline{\mathbf{G}}^C = \begin{vmatrix} 1 & 0 & 0 \\ 0 & \left(\rho\right)^{-2} & 0 \\ 0 & 0 & \left(\rho \sin\phi\right)^{-2} \end{vmatrix} \tag{268}$$

In this case, there is a difference between covariance and contravariance. Using $v_s = g_{sk}v^k$, write the relationship between contravariant and covariant components of a vector in spherical coordinates:

$$v_1 = v^1 \tag{269}$$

$$v_2 = \left[\left(\rho\right)^2\right]v^2 \tag{270}$$

$$v_3 = \left[\left(\rho \sin\phi\right)^2\right]v^3 \tag{271}$$

These equations are not overly exciting (since there are no off-diagonal terms in the matrix to "spice things up"), but they do illustrate the essential role played by the fundamental tensor and the difference between covariant and contravariant components of a vector in a familiar space using familiar coordinate systems.

Calculus

Statement of Core Idea

In general, base vectors have nonzero derivatives with respect to space and time. These nonzero derivatives enable us to model two very important but independent mechanical ideas:

1. The pseudoforces that are observed in accelerated coordinate systems (gravitational, centrifugal, and Coriolis)
2. The curvature or non-Euclidean characteristics of space and time as measured by real physical instruments

In tensor analysis, the base vector derivatives have a very specific mathematical form.

First Steps Toward a Tensor Calculus: An Example From Classical Mechanics

Now that we have acquired a formal definition of tensor as a quantity that possesses certain prescribed transformation properties (i.e., is coordinate independent) and a beginning grasp of tensor algebra, we may proceed directly to develop a tensor calculus.

The calculus that we learned in college is a body of mathematics that enables us to deal with continuous fields. Classical mechanics and relativity both are concerned with fields: flow, gravitational and electric, magnetic, and so on. We have already learned that prescribing coordinate independence to tensors provides us with an ideal tool for building physical theories, the correlation being that physical objects and events also are coordinate independent.

This correlation is worth noting again and again. It provides an important clue to understanding applied mathematics in general. All too often, students learn bare problem-solving techniques without ever learning what their solutions are telling them about the world at large. If the concepts of mathematics are not as familiar as the concepts of language and as easily expressed and interpreted, the value of the students' mathematical knowledge is at best questionable.

Applied mathematics has its roots in the study of the world at large. As complex as that world may seem, it provides us with certain comprehensible themes that are repeated over and over in an almost bewildering array of diverse phenomena. Thus, we speak of the flow of ocean currents as easily as we speak of the flow of electrical currents in a wire or in space or the flow of pulverized pyroclastic material from an erupting volcano. The common denominator here is the concept of flow.

The theory of fields involves flow. In a velocity field, we speak of a continuously moving medium, air perhaps or water whose velocity at every point in the field is represented by the vector at that point. In magnetic and electric fields, we speak of magnetic and electric flux (from the Latin fluxit, flow) and flux density (flow per unit area). Classically, the electric and magnetic fluxes were thought to be a class of imponderable fluids. Although the concept of imponderable fluids is no longer used in physics, the idea of flux remains.

The concept of flow leads directly to the calculus. Consider the flow of water from a faucet. If everything is working properly, the flow is both smooth and continuous. However, to describe the flow, we use ratios formed from discontinuous "chunks" of space and time. It seems that we have no choice in the matter. We speak of liters per second or gallons per minute, but this description applies equally well to a liter "slug" dropping once every second as it does a continuous flow. We divide the flow into discreet spatiotemporal portions to express its smoothness and continuity.

Realizing the incongruity here, we might attempt to correct our description by choosing a smaller unit of time and a correspondingly smaller unit of volume. Thus, we might speak of milliliters per millisecond, but the idea of a slug of material is still present, although each slug is a thousand times smaller and the slugs are a thousand times more frequent in their appearance. We may in imagination continue this process of subdividing indefinitely until we approach the limit of an infinitesimal time unit and a correspondingly infinitesimal unit of volume. This concept of limit lies at the very heart of the calculus.

In the calculus, we learn to form ratios such as the one described above and to take the limit as the denominator term "tends to zero." Such a ratio is called, in the limit, a derivative. In college, we spoke of total and partial derivatives. In tensor calculus, we will speak of an absolute and a covariant derivative as natural generalizations of total and partial derivatives. We will learn to differentiate a vector and then by extension how to differentiate a general mixed tensor. We will approach these concepts via classical mechanics so that the abstractions of tensor calculus become founded in real-world considerations.

Sir Isaac Newton (1642–1727) first developed classical mechanics as we know it today. Newton was not the first to create classical mechanics, but he synthesized ideas that were replete during his lifetime. He once admitted that if he had seen farther than most, it was because he stood on the shoulders of giants. Newton certainly realized the debt he owed to the great minds who preceded him.

Newton set down his great work in a volume that is today commonly called the Principia.[22] His theoretical framework was not without problems, and his ideas were reformulated and refined in various ways during the years following his initial work. One such refinement is attributed to Professor Ernst Mach (1838–1916), a German physicist and philosopher who specifically addressed Newton's ideas about absolute space. Recall that we just spoke of a correlation between theoretical ideas and the real world. Mach sought such a correlation: an astronomical interpretation of Newton's absolute space.

Mach suggested that the fixed stars provided the stationary reference that Newton required. We know today that the concept of fixed stars is a fiction and that no such stationary reference exists in nature. But Mach's ideas are nonetheless an important part of modern physics. Einstein strongly favored the fixed star point of view and attempted without success to make it follow from the equations of general relativity. In keeping with the astronomical understanding of his time, Einstein substituted the somewhat more vague notion of "total distant matter" for fixed stars and called the resultant statement Mach's principle.

Because relativity radically revised the foundations of physics laid down by Newton, it is essential that we understand something about them. Paramount among these foundations are the concepts of absolute space and absolute time. We begin by quoting Newton's own words (Hawking, 2002):

> Absolute space, in its own nature, without regard to anything external, remains always similar and immovable… . Absolute, true, and mathematical time, of itself, and from its own nature flows equably without regard to anything external… .

Space for Newton was strictly Euclidean and three-dimensional. In Newton's day, the so-called non-Euclidean geometries had not been conceived. It was generally accepted among philosophers that there was one and only one legitimate geometry of the world. Straight lines could be extended throughout the known universe and their various relationships written down without ever asking precisely what such extension might mean physically. (Note that the precise correlations between the Euclidean straight line and its physical realization are being ignored here.) Perhaps such questions were just not considered important.[23]

For Newton, time was a quantity independent and different from space. Like space, it was rigid and absolute; unlike space, the same instant (or point) of time could be simultaneously present to observers everywhere—could be occupied by observers everywhere—whereas spatial points were spread out so that the same point could not be occupied by more than one observer at a time. Under these conditions, Newton assumed that information could be transferred throughout space instantaneously regardless of the spatial separation between the points or regions involved.[24]

Newton was uncomfortable with his absolutes but had nothing better to replace them with. For him, physical objects such as pebbles, boulders, or planets existed in space much as actors existed on the stage. Remove or change the actors and the stage remained behind unaltered. The Newtonian stage was the framework of absolute space and time. He developed his mechanics to describe how and why the actors moved about as they did on the stage. In the mathematical formulation, the actors were represented by Euclidean points called mass points (geometrical

---

[22]The entire title is Philosophiae Naturalis Principia Mathematica (The Mathematical Principles of Natural Philosophy). In Newton's day, the science that we call physics was referred to as natural philosophy.

[23]But it was by asking just such a question that Einstein was first led to develop relativity. The classical straight line may be represented physically by a pencil of light or as we might say today, by an ideal laser beam that propagates with no divergence. Einstein specifically asked how such a pencil would appear to an observer running abreast of it. The implication is that to do so, the observer must run away from the light source at 3×10^8 m/s to keep pace with a single wave front of the light pencil. The answer to his question is surprising: to such an observer, the pencil would still outpace her at a speed of 3×10^8 m/s, exactly the same as if she were standing still next to the source. This result led Einstein to a complete redefinition of the notions of space and time.

[24]We might argue in favor of this point as follows: Suppose that there is a supermassive star somewhere in our spatial vicinity. We may not be able to see the star, but we have instruments that indicate its local gravitational influence. Now, at some time t_0 the star ceases to exist. Since we and the star both simultaneously occupy the time t_0, we know immediately that something has happened because our instruments register the change. In relativity, we have no way of knowing that anything has happened to the star until at least the time $t_0 + x/c$ where x is the spatial distance of the star from us and c is the speed of light. In relativity, we say that a gravitational wave has propagated from the site of the vanished star and that its passage is what our instruments actually registered.

points with a mass in kilograms associated with them). The actors in turn were acted upon by contact forces that were the agents which produced changes in their state of motion or rest.

The use of mass points to represent extended objects required some care in their selection. If a single point were to be used, it was typically the center of mass, center of gravity, center of percussion, or some other equivalent center. There were rules and mathematical methods for locating these points given the shape and mass distribution of the object being represented. The center always moved along a well-defined trajectory even though the object itself might be tumbling or gyrating in some way. It was the trajectory of the center that was predicted by the equations of mechanics. In some cases, more than one point was required to represent an extended mass; for example, two points were required when forces of rotation (called torques or couples) were involved.

Newtonian mechanics was governed by three laws of motion:

1. An object will persist in its state of absolute rest or motion along a straight line unless acted upon by an outside force.
2. The force acting on an object is equal to its time rate of momentum.
3. Internal forces, forces of action and reaction, occur in equal and opposite pairs.

For rotational motion, the word "force" in the above statements may be replaced by the word "torque." There were also conserved quantities for which strict accounts were required to be bookkept. These quantities included mass, electrical charge, energy, linear momentum, and angular momentum.

In dealing with planetary motions and those of the Moon and the tides, Newton had to establish one more law for noncontact forces, specifically for the noncontact force of gravity.[25] This "action at a distance"[26] operation of gravity (i.e., action that involved neither contact nor an intervening medium) was particularly uncomfortable for Newton, but it certainly appeared to occur in nature and had to be accommodated in his theory. The law of gravity states that the force acting between any two objects is proportional to the product of their respective masses and is inversely proportional to the square of the distance between their centers.

The mathematics used to express classical mechanics is the vector calculus. Locations, velocities, accelerations, forces, and momentums are all vectors. Some of these vectors appear as derivatives of others. It is at this point that our development of tensor calculus may begin.

First, let us write the basic equations that describe the motion of a mass point in Euclidean three-space. We will use a Cartesian coordinate system that is unaccelerated, that is, an inertial frame of reference. (Such a coordinate system is also called an Eulerian frame if it is fixed.[27]) Here is the general procedure that we will follow:

1. Locate the mass point at any time t by using a position vector $\mathbf{r}(t)$. Since the point is moving through the space mapped by the coordinate system, $\mathbf{r}(t)$ will have a magnitude and direction dependent upon the time of observation. This dependency is noted by the symbol (t) immediately following the symbol $\mathbf{r}$.
2. The velocity of the point will be the time derivative $\mathrm{d}\mathbf{r}(t)/\mathrm{d}t$. Strictly speaking, even though $\mathrm{d}\mathbf{r}$ is a tensor, the velocity $\mathrm{d}\mathbf{r}/\mathrm{d}t$ is not[28] because if viewed from another coordinate system K^* in uniform (i.e., unaccelerated) motion $\mathbf{V}_{\mathrm{REL}}$ relative to the first, the velocity of the point as viewed in K^* is $\mathrm{d}\mathbf{r}(t)/\mathrm{d}t + \mathbf{V}_{\mathrm{REL}}$. Thus, $\mathrm{d}\mathbf{r}^*(t)/\mathrm{d}t \neq \mathrm{d}\mathbf{r}(t)/\mathrm{d}t$; that is, it is not strictly coordinate independent.
3. The acceleration of the point will be the time derivative of the velocity $\mathrm{d}^2\mathbf{r}(t)/\mathrm{d}t^2$. Interestingly, for coordinate systems in uniform relative motion, acceleration is a tensor; that is, $\mathrm{d}^2\mathbf{r}^*/\mathrm{d}t^2 = \mathrm{d}^2\mathbf{r}/\mathrm{d}t^2$. This relationship does not hold, however, when one or both of the coordinate systems themselves are accelerated.[29]

Let us use the now familiar form $\mathbf{r} = x\mathbf{i} + y\mathbf{j} + z\mathbf{k}$ to represent position. We then have the following system of equations:

[25] Post-Newtonian developments include similar laws of force between isolated electric charges and individual magnetic poles.

[26] In modern physics, the idea of action at a distance is replaced by the field. The object in question does not mysteriously respond to the influence of some other distant object but to the field conditions in its immediate vicinity. The field is set up by the distant object. Changes in the field propagate at the speed of light.

[27] The term "fixed" is applied either in the sense of Newton's absolute space or Mach's fixed stars frame of reference. In modern physics, the concept of a fixed frame loses all meaning.

[28] The differential time $\mathrm{d}t$ is the component of a so-called four-vector in special relativity. Thus, the ratio $\mathrm{d}\mathbf{r}/\mathrm{d}t$ is not strictly the ratio of a vector and a scalar. Einstein corrected this lack by using the spacetime metric $\mathrm{d}s$ in place of the differential time $\mathrm{d}t$ in special relativity. Thus, he essentially redefined velocity as $\mathrm{d}\mathbf{r}/\mathrm{d}s$, which is a tensor.

[29] Again, the problem is more subtle than presented here. Refer to comments about $\mathrm{d}t$ and $\mathrm{d}s$ in footnote 28.

Position

$$\mathbf{r} = x\mathbf{i} + y\mathbf{j} + z\mathbf{k} \tag{272a}$$

Velocity

$$\mathbf{v} = \frac{d\mathbf{r}}{dt} = \left(\frac{dx}{dt}\right)\mathbf{i} + \left(\frac{dy}{dt}\right)\mathbf{j} + \left(\frac{dz}{dt}\right)\mathbf{k} \tag{272b}$$

Acceleration

$$\mathbf{a} = \frac{d^2\mathbf{r}}{dt^2} = \left(\frac{d^2x}{dt^2}\right)\mathbf{i} + \left(\frac{d^2y}{dt^2}\right)\mathbf{j} + \left(\frac{d^2z}{dt^2}\right)\mathbf{k} \tag{272c}$$

Do you notice anything peculiar about these equations? Probably not at first glance. They are easily recognizable from a basic physics text. But you might have asked, Whatever happened to the derivatives of the base vectors **i**, **j**, and **k**? We know from basic calculus that the derivative of a product (uv) always goes according to the rule: $d(uv) = u dv + v du$. So why do we not apply this rule in forming the velocity and acceleration vectors above; that is, $d(x\mathbf{i}) = (dx)\mathbf{i} + x(d\mathbf{i})$ and so on for the other terms?

The answer is obvious: the derivatives of the base vectors are all equal to zero, so there is no point in writing them. Why are they all equal to zero? The coordinate systems are all inertial coordinate systems that are unaccelerated relative to absolute space. Even though the base vectors of K^* are in motion as viewed from K (and vice versa), they change neither their magnitude (which remains unity) nor their direction (they translate but do not rotate).

What if the coordinate system K^* were to accelerate relative to the inertial coordinate system K? This question can most easily be answered by selecting a test case and working it through. Make K^* an accelerated coordinate system and then introduce a mass point whose motion in K^* we will examine.

First, let us introduce a slight change in terminology: we will refer to a coordinate system as a frame of reference (this usage was already hinted at a few paragraphs ago). This terminology is better in keeping with that used in classical mechanics, the theory of relativity, electrodynamics, and those disciplines of physics and engineering most likely to use tensor analysis.

Now, what type of acceleration should we choose for K^*? Let us make it a rotating frame of reference. It will rotate uniformly about its origin as seen from K. Where shall we locate K^* relative to K? Well, since we can place the origin of K^* anywhere we like in K, let us place it right at the origin of K for ease in visualization and in writing equations.

We will also assume that the z- and the z^*-axes coincide and that the rotation of K^* is about the z-axis. Doing so actually reduces the calculation to two dimensions for the most part (in the xy-plane). The motion of the mass point will be confined to this plane for the remainder of this discussion, and the z-axis will be invoked only as necessary to specify the rotation vector that lies along the z-axis in the present scheme. The following sketch illustrates the foregoing discussion.

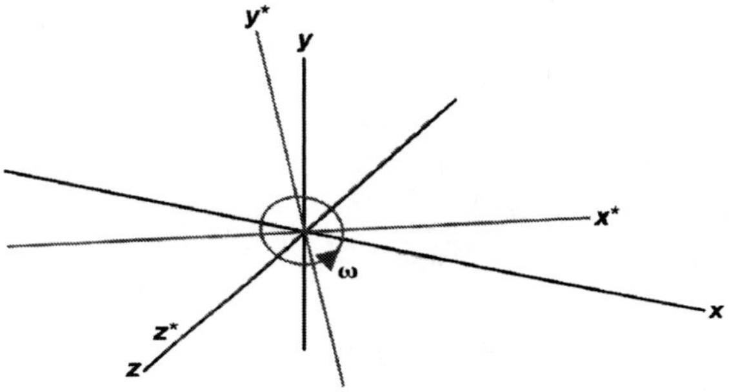

The Greek letter ω represents the angular velocity of K^* relative to K. Its units are radians per second (s^{-1}). If K^* is rotating at υ revolutions per second, then by definition $\omega = 2\pi\upsilon$. (ω is also called the angular frequency in some cases. Note that this particular choice for ω gives the very desirable result that one complete revolution corresponds to 2π radians.) As a vector, we may choose $\boldsymbol{\omega} = \pm\omega\mathbf{k}$. We will take counterclockwise rotation (as viewed from positive z in K) to be positive rotation. In this case, $\boldsymbol{\omega} = +\omega\mathbf{k}$ and points along the positive z-axis.

Now, ignoring the z-direction for the moment, concentrate on what is happening in the xy-plane. First, there are the basis (unit) vectors **i** and **j** in K and **i*** and **j*** in K^*. Perhaps you recall that with K^* rotating in the manner we have selected, they are related by the linear system of equations:

$$\mathbf{i}^*(t) = \mathbf{i}\cos(\omega t) + \mathbf{j}\sin(\omega t) \tag{273a}$$

$$\mathbf{j}^*(t) = -\mathbf{i}\sin(\omega t) + \mathbf{j}\cos(\omega t) \tag{273b}$$

where t is time in seconds. Note that the unit vectors in K^* are time variable, at least with regard to their direction. Therefore, their time derivatives possess nonzero values:

Position

$$\mathbf{r}^* = x^*\mathbf{i}^* + y^*\mathbf{j}^* \qquad (274a)$$

Velocity

$$\mathbf{v}^* = \left(\frac{\mathrm{d}x^*}{\mathrm{d}t}\right)\mathbf{i}^* + \left(\frac{\mathrm{d}y^*}{\mathrm{d}t}\right)\mathbf{j}^* + x^*\left(\frac{\mathrm{d}\mathbf{i}^*}{\mathrm{d}t}\right) + y^*\left(\frac{\mathrm{d}\mathbf{j}^*}{\mathrm{d}t}\right) \qquad (274b)$$

Acceleration

$$\mathbf{a}^* = \left(\frac{\mathrm{d}^2 x^*}{\mathrm{d}t^2}\right)\mathbf{i}^* + \left(\frac{\mathrm{d}^2 y^*}{\mathrm{d}t^2}\right)\mathbf{j}^* + 2\left[\left(\frac{\mathrm{d}x^*}{\mathrm{d}t}\right)\left(\frac{\mathrm{d}\mathbf{i}^*}{\mathrm{d}t}\right) + \left(\frac{\mathrm{d}y^*}{\mathrm{d}t}\right)\left(\frac{\mathrm{d}\mathbf{j}^*}{\mathrm{d}t}\right)\right] + x^*\left(\frac{\mathrm{d}^2\mathbf{i}^*}{\mathrm{d}t^2}\right) + y^*\left(\frac{\mathrm{d}^2\mathbf{j}^*}{\mathrm{d}t^2}\right) \qquad (274c)$$

These expressions may be simplified by choosing a less cumbersome notation. For the velocity terms, let $v_x^* = \mathrm{d}x^*/\mathrm{d}t$, and so forth and for the acceleration terms, $a_x^* = \mathrm{d}^2 x^*/\mathrm{d}t^2$, and so forth. Then we can write

Position

$$\mathbf{r}^* = x^*\mathbf{i}^* + y^*\mathbf{j}^* \qquad (275a)$$

Velocity

$$\mathbf{v}^* = v_x^*\mathbf{i}^* + v_y^*\mathbf{j}^* + x^*\left(\frac{\mathrm{d}\mathbf{i}^*}{\mathrm{d}t}\right) + y^*\left(\frac{\mathrm{d}\mathbf{j}^*}{\mathrm{d}t}\right) \qquad (275b)$$

Acceleration

$$\mathbf{a}^* = a_x^*\mathbf{i}^* + a_y^*\mathbf{j}^* + 2\left[v_x^*\left(\frac{\mathrm{d}\mathbf{i}^*}{\mathrm{d}t}\right) + v_y^*\left(\frac{\mathrm{d}\mathbf{j}^*}{\mathrm{d}t}\right)\right] + x^*\left(\frac{\mathrm{d}^2\mathbf{i}^*}{\mathrm{d}t^2}\right) + y^*\left(\frac{\mathrm{d}^2\mathbf{j}^*}{\mathrm{d}t^2}\right) \qquad (275c)$$

This presentation is somewhat more easily read than the previous one. Let us go one step farther and define more new terms:

$$\mathbf{V}^* = v_x^*\mathbf{i}^* + v_y^*\mathbf{j}^* \qquad (276a)$$

$$\mathbf{A}^* = a_x^*\mathbf{i}^* + a_y^*\mathbf{j}^* \qquad (276b)$$

$$\underline{\mathbf{E}}^* = \mathbf{i}^*\left(\frac{\mathrm{d}\mathbf{i}^*}{\mathrm{d}t}\right) + \mathbf{j}^*\left(\frac{\mathrm{d}\mathbf{j}^*}{\mathrm{d}t}\right) \qquad (276c)$$

$$\underline{\mathbf{F}}^* = \mathbf{i}^*\left(\frac{\mathrm{d}^2\mathbf{i}^*}{\mathrm{d}t^2}\right) + \mathbf{j}^*\left(\frac{\mathrm{d}^2\mathbf{j}^*}{\mathrm{d}t^2}\right) \qquad (276d)$$

With these new terms, we are able to write

Position

$$\mathbf{r}^* = x^*\mathbf{i}^* + y^*\mathbf{j}^* \qquad (277a)$$

Velocity

$$\mathbf{v}^* = \mathbf{V}^* + \left(\mathbf{r}^* \cdot \underline{\mathbf{E}}^*\right) \qquad (277b)$$

Acceleration

$$\mathbf{a}^* = \mathbf{A}^* + \left(2\mathbf{V}^* \cdot \underline{\mathbf{E}}^* + \mathbf{r}^* \cdot \underline{\mathbf{F}}^*\right) \qquad (277c)$$

Note that for unaccelerated motion, $\underline{\mathbf{E}}^* = \underline{\mathbf{F}}^* = \underline{\mathbf{0}}$ (the zero dyad), and the three equations reduce to the same form that they have in *K*. It is easily shown that the two "extra" terms in the equation for acceleration (i.e., $2\mathbf{V}^* \cdot \underline{\mathbf{E}}^*$ and $\mathbf{r}^* \cdot \underline{\mathbf{F}}^*$) are the Coriolis and centrifugal accelerations, respectively, and are pseudo-accelerations observed by an observer who is stationary in *K** (and therefore rotating relative to *K*).

When the mass point is introduced into the picture, the peculiarities inherent in our description will be perceived. First, assume that its path in *K* is rectilinear; that is, no external forces are acting on the mass point, which is in conformity with Newton's first law of motion. In this simplest of all cases, we have (in *K*) $\mathbf{v} = \mathbf{constant}$ and $\mathbf{a} = \mathbf{0}$.

However, in *K**, another situation prevails: $\mathbf{v}^* = \mathbf{v}^*(t)$ and $\mathbf{a}^* \neq \mathbf{0}$. The path of the mass point in *K** is seen as a curve along which the mass point is accelerating. The accelerations seen in *K** are none other than the Coriolis and centrifugal accelerations that are nonzero in all rotating frames of reference.

The nonzero derivatives of the base vectors in *K** correspond to the appearance of the Coriolis and centrifugal accelerations in *K**. It is important, therefore, to keep track of the base vector derivatives, for they tell us how mass points behave in our particular frame of reference. This situation will arise again when we examine Einstein's view of the gravitational field.

Let us carefully examine the acceleration given above:

$$\mathbf{a}^* = \mathbf{A}^* + \left(2\mathbf{V}^* \cdot \underline{\mathbf{E}}^* + \mathbf{r}^* \cdot \underline{\mathbf{F}}^*\right) \qquad (277c)$$

We will ignore the term $\mathbf{A}^*$ for the moment and consider just the terms $2\mathbf{V}^* \cdot \underline{\mathbf{E}}^*$ and $\mathbf{r}^* \cdot \underline{\mathbf{F}}^*$. We must proceed with care. First, consider just the term $2\mathbf{V}^* \cdot \underline{\mathbf{E}}^*$. Since we have

$$\mathbf{i}^*(t) = \mathbf{i}\cos(\omega t) + \mathbf{j}\sin(\omega t) \qquad (278a)$$

$$\mathbf{j}^*(t) = -\mathbf{i}\sin(\omega t) + \mathbf{j}\cos(\omega t) \qquad (278b)$$

the unit vector derivatives contained in $\mathbf{E}^*$ must be

$$\frac{\mathrm{d}\mathbf{i}^*}{\mathrm{d}t} = -\mathbf{i}\omega\sin(\omega t) + \mathbf{j}\omega\cos(\omega t) = \omega\mathbf{j}^* \qquad (279a)$$

$$\frac{\mathrm{d}\mathbf{j}^*}{\mathrm{d}t} = -\mathbf{i}\omega\cos(\omega t) - \mathbf{j}\omega\sin(\omega t) = -\omega\mathbf{i}^* \qquad (279b)$$

We have $\mathbf{V}^*$, so let us put the pieces together:

$$\begin{aligned} 2\mathbf{V}^* \cdot \underline{\mathbf{E}}^* &= -2v_x^*\omega\mathbf{i}^* + 2v_y^*\omega\mathbf{j}^* \\ &= 2\omega\mathbf{k}^* \times \mathbf{V}^* = 2\boldsymbol{\omega} \times \mathbf{V}^* \end{aligned} \qquad (280)$$

Save this result for a moment and proceed. Next, consider just the term $\mathbf{r}^* \cdot \underline{\mathbf{F}}^*$. Using the derivatives previously obtained, we find that

$$\frac{\mathrm{d}^2\mathbf{i}^*}{\mathrm{d}t^2} = -\mathbf{i}\omega^2\cos(\omega t) - \mathbf{j}\omega^2\sin(\omega t) = -\omega^2\mathbf{i}^* \qquad (281a)$$

$$\frac{\mathrm{d}^2\mathbf{j}^*}{\mathrm{d}^2 t} = \mathbf{i}\omega^2\sin(\omega t) - \mathbf{j}\omega^2\cos(\omega t) = -\omega^2\mathbf{j}^* \qquad (281b)$$

so that

$$\mathbf{r}^* \cdot \underline{\mathbf{F}}^* = x^*\left(-\omega^2\mathbf{i}^*\right) + y^*\left(-\omega^2\mathbf{j}^*\right) = -\omega^2\mathbf{r}^* \qquad (282)$$

Putting everything together, we find that

$$\mathbf{a}^* = \mathbf{A}^* + 2\boldsymbol{\omega} \times \mathbf{V}^* - \omega^2\mathbf{r}^* \qquad (283)$$

The roles of each of the terms on the right-hand side will now be examined. Remember that the observer in K^*, who is in actuality rotating relative to absolute space (represented by the system K), is entitled to think of herself as being at rest with the universe rotating around her. This statement is a classical statement of the relativity principle.

If this assumption is made in K^*, then an application of Newton's force-as-rate-of-momentum law allows us to identify each of the three right-hand terms. The force-as-rate-of-momentum law states that

$$\mathbf{f}^* = \frac{\mathrm{d}\mathbf{p}^*}{\mathrm{d}t} = \frac{\mathrm{d}(m\mathbf{v}^*)}{\mathrm{d}t} = m\left(\frac{\mathrm{d}\mathbf{v}^*}{\mathrm{d}t}\right) = m\mathbf{a}^* \qquad (284)$$

If we now multiply the entire expression for $\mathbf{a}^*$ by the mass m, we obtain

$$\mathbf{f}^* = m\mathbf{a}^* = m\mathbf{A}^* + 2m\boldsymbol{\omega} \times \mathbf{V}^* - m\omega^2\mathbf{r}^* \qquad (285)$$

We now see that $\mathbf{a}^*$ is the total acceleration due to external (contact) forces acting on the point under consideration. Since our observer considers herself to be at rest in K^*, she will consider the acceleration $\mathbf{A}^*$ as being that due to all external (contact) forces plus any other field forces that happen to be acting. If no external forces are acting in K^*, she will set $\mathbf{a}^* = \mathbf{0}$ and conclude that the total acceleration $\mathbf{A}^*$ that she observes must be due to the field forces $\mathbf{A}^* = -2\boldsymbol{\omega} \times \mathbf{V}^* + \omega^2\mathbf{r}^*$.

The first term, $-2\boldsymbol{\omega} \times \mathbf{V}^*$, is the velocity-dependent Coriolis acceleration; the second term is the radially outward-pointing centrifugal acceleration.

(N.B.: From our point of view in K, both these terms arise simply enough from the rotation of K^* relative to inertial space. From our observer's point of view, they appear as real, if somewhat mysterious, accelerations that have no visible agents exerting the force that causes them, unless they are to be associated with the rotational motion of the entire universe around the origin of K^*, another argument associated with Ernst Mach.)

This discussion is given here at length because the pseudoaccelerations (as the Coriolis and centrifugal accelerations are often called) have much in common with the gravitational acceleration in general relativity. The fact that the pseudoaccelerations in K^* derive their mathematical form from the nonzero derivatives of the basis vectors is all important. An identical situation is encountered in Einstein's development of the gravitational field equations.

Base Vector Differentials: Toward a General Formulation

The essential idea in the previous section that we must now develop further is this: the derivative of any quantity of higher order than a scalar must take into account the nonzero derivatives of the base vectors as well as those of the individual vector components, since the base vector derivatives carry important information about the system under consideration.

In the previous section, we saw that in a rotating frame of reference, there are accelerations that arise simply because of the rotation, namely, Coriolis and centrifugal accelerations. Such a frame is called a non-inertial frame of reference.

In the more general case, any accelerated frame is non-inertial. The mathematical form of the so-called pseudoaccelerations that arise in non-inertial frames is obtained directly from the nonzero base vector derivatives relative to inertial space. In a frame where these derivatives vanish, there are no pseudoaccelerations. Such a frame is called an inertial frame of reference.

Jumping ahead for just a moment, it should be noted here that Einstein showed that a frame of reference in a gravitational field is equivalent to an accelerated frame of reference in inertial space. The formal expression of this idea is the principle of equivalence. In relativity, the gravitational field, classically an acceleration field,[30] derives mathematically from the general form for base vector derivatives that we are about to develop. The foregoing argument along with this important observation provide the student with an immediate stepping stone to the general theory of relativity.

Note: Before continuing, let us make another change in terminology. In developing a general expression for base vector derivatives, it is more convenient to consider the base vector differentials rather than full derivatives. We will do so starting now and continue until we have a general formula in hand.

[30]Although many people speak of gravity as a force field, formally it is not. The vector field term in Newton's theory of gravitation is not force but acceleration, **g** (m/s^2).

We begin by using the position-velocity-acceleration development that we have just worked through as a springboard and demonstrate in a qualitative way how we come to expect that the base vector differentials must be

1. Linearly dependent on the coordinate differentials
2. Linearly dependent on the base vectors themselves
3. Functions of the coordinate values

The first step is to write the time derivatives of the base vectors as they appeared in the previous section, in differential form:

$$\mathrm{d}\mathbf{i}^* = \omega \mathbf{j}^* \mathrm{d}t \quad \text{and} \quad \mathrm{d}\mathbf{j}^* = -\omega \mathbf{i}^* \mathrm{d}t \qquad (286)$$

Note that these differentials are already linearly dependent on the base vectors. Next, to make these equations appear more complete, we will appropriately add[31] the trivial terms 0**i*** and 0**j*** so that

$$\mathrm{d}\mathbf{i}^* = \left(0\mathbf{i}^* + \omega \mathbf{j}^*\right)\mathrm{d}t \qquad (287a)$$

and

$$\mathrm{d}\mathbf{j}^* = \left(-\omega \mathbf{i}^* + 0\mathbf{j}^*\right)\mathrm{d}t \qquad (287b)$$

Now that zero has been added to each equation, we see that each of the base vector differentials appears as a linear sum over the basis vectors **i*** and **j***.[32] Now there is symmetry between the two equations where there was not a moment ago. Since we are expanding from a restricted (mathematically and physically) example of a rotating system, it is not unreasonable to believe that these trivial terms we have just introduced will not remain trivial in all cases. In fact, it is categorically true in the general case that they will not.

Next, consider the time differential d*t*. It is true that time is an important element in all physics and engineering methods, but not all situations that we can imagine are going to be time dependent. On the other hand, all situations will require coordinate

[31]Always remember that in doing any mathematical development, knowing how to add zero and/or how to multiply by 1 are often times your most important assets.

[32]We are still operating only in the xy-plane, but that is alright. The xy-plane actually is sufficient for representing the whole operating space since the motions we are concerned with are confined to it.

measurements of some type. So, we need to involve the coordinate differentials. If time is to be a coordinate in our overall system (as it is in relativity), then it will fall under the purview of this involvement; if not, we shall not be left wholly without recourse.

Recall that the base vector transformations involved time as a parameter:

$$\mathbf{i}^*(t) = \mathbf{i}\cos(\omega t) + \mathbf{j}\sin(\omega t) \quad (288a)$$

$$\mathbf{j}^*(t) = -\mathbf{i}\sin(\omega t) + \mathbf{j}\cos(\omega t) \quad (288b)$$

As a first step to involving the coordinate differentials, we must use these transformations to show that similar transformations exist for x^* and y^* as functions of x and y. It will turn out again that time will still be a parameter. Let us write out the position vector for any point P in the space mapped by K and K^*. In this special case wherein the origins of K and K^* coincide, the position vector will be the same in both systems. Thus, in this special case, $\mathbf{r} = \mathbf{r}^*$ and in K

$$\mathbf{r} = x\mathbf{i} + y\mathbf{j} \quad (289a)$$

and in K^*

$$\mathbf{r}^* = x^*\mathbf{i}^* + y^*\mathbf{j}^* \quad (289b)$$

Remembering that $\mathbf{r} = \mathbf{r}^*$, let us substitute for $\mathbf{i}^*$ and $\mathbf{j}^*$ in the second of these equations:

$$\begin{aligned}\mathbf{r}^* &= x^*\left[\mathbf{i}\cos(\omega t) + \mathbf{j}\sin(\omega t)\right] \\ &\quad + y^*\left[-\mathbf{i}\sin(\omega t) + \mathbf{j}\cos(\omega t)\right] \\ &= \left[x^*\cos(\omega t) - y^*\sin(\omega t)\right]\mathbf{i} \\ &\quad + \left[x^*\sin(\omega t) + y^*\cos(\omega t)\right]\mathbf{j} = x\mathbf{i} + y\mathbf{j}\end{aligned} \quad (290)$$

By equating the components of $\mathbf{i}$ and $\mathbf{j}$ in the last two expressions, we immediately see that

$$x(x^*, y^*, t) = x^*\cos(\omega t) - y^*\sin(\omega t) \quad (291a)$$

and

$$y(x^*, y^*, t) = x^*\sin(\omega t) + y^*\cos(\omega t) \quad (291b)$$

These are coordinate transformations from K^* to K. Solving for x^* and y^*, we find the inverse transformations from K to K^*:

$$x^*(x, y, t) = x\cos(\omega t) + y\sin(\omega t) \quad (292a)$$

$$y^*(x, y, t) = -x\sin(\omega t) + y\cos(\omega t) \quad (292b)$$

Now, the next step in involving the coordinate differentials is to imagine a point P that is stationary in K (and therefore in inertial space). Since P is stationary, we have the simplification that x = a constant and y = a constant. We may now proceed to differentiate x^* and y^* at P:[33]

$$\mathrm{d}x^* = \left[-x\omega\sin(\omega t) + y\omega\cos(\omega t)\right]\mathrm{d}t \quad (293a)$$

$$\mathrm{d}y^* = \left[-x\omega\cos(\omega t) - y\omega\sin(\omega t)\right]\mathrm{d}t \quad (293b)$$

Note that we may add these two expressions to obtain the new single expression

$$\mathrm{d}x^* + \mathrm{d}y^* = \lambda(t)\,\mathrm{d}t \quad (294)$$

where $\lambda(t) = [-x\omega\sin(\omega t) + y\omega\cos(\omega t) - x\omega\cos(\omega t) - y\omega\sin(\omega t)]$. If we now eliminate[34] the time t in the system of equations

$$x^*(t) = -x\cos(\omega t) + y\sin(\omega t) \quad (295a)$$

$$y^*(t) = -x\sin(\omega t) + y\cos(\omega t) \quad (295b)$$

then $\lambda(t) \rightarrow \lambda(x^*, y^*)$; that is, λ goes from being a function of time to being a function of the coordinate values x^* and y^* exclusively, and

$$\mathrm{d}t = \left(\frac{1}{\lambda}\right)(\mathrm{d}x^* + \mathrm{d}y^*) \quad (296)$$

[33]Since K^* is rotating, the point P will appear, from K^*, to travel in a clockwise circle about the origin. Therefore, if at time $t = t_0$, P is at (x_0^*, y_0^*), then at time $t = t_0 + \mathrm{d}t$, it will have "moved" to $(x_0^* + \mathrm{d}x^*, y_0^* + \mathrm{d}y^*)$. It is the differentials $\mathrm{d}x^*$ and $\mathrm{d}y^*$ in this last expression that we are actually determining in the discussion in the text. Keeping P stationary in K is simply a device chosen to avoid extra work in the differentiation.

[34]Such elimination is theoretically possible but practically is a mess, since the equations involved are transcendental.

The right-hand side is a function exclusively of the coordinate values and the coordinate differentials. By substituting for dt in the base vector differentials **di*** and **dj***, we obtain

$$\mathrm{d}\mathbf{i}^* = \left(\frac{1}{\lambda}\right)\left(0\mathbf{i}^* + \omega\mathbf{j}^*\right)\left(\mathrm{d}x^* + \mathrm{d}y^*\right) \quad (297a)$$

and

$$\mathrm{d}\mathbf{j}^* = \left(\frac{1}{\lambda}\right)\left(-\omega\mathbf{i}^* + 0\mathbf{j}^*\right)\left(\mathrm{d}x^* + \mathrm{d}y^*\right) \quad (297b)$$

With this last equation, we have successfully shown what we set out to show, namely, that the base vector differentials are

1. Linearly dependent on the coordinate differentials
2. Linearly dependent on the base vectors themselves
3. Functions of the coordinate values Q.E.D.

Another Example From Polar Coordinates

Perhaps you are not totally convinced by the argument we have just completed. "There seem to have been some smoke and mirrors," you argue tentatively. Point well taken. Let us look at another example that is both demonstrative and illustrative.

This time, we use a polar coordinate system rather than a Cartesian coordinate system to map the plane. The polar coordinate system differs from the Cartesian in one essential aspect:

> The Cartesian coordinate system consists of straight lines and planes and is therefore a "flat" coordinate system used to map a flat (i.e., Euclidean) space. By comparison, the polar coordinate system is not flat but is a curved coordinate system used to map a flat space. The peculiarities that we are about to note are due to the curvature.[35]

In the polar coordinate system, there are two sets of base vectors. One set $\mathbf{u}_\rho$ is tangent to the radial lines; the other set $\mathbf{u}_\theta$ is tangent to the concentric circles. The two sets are orthogonal at any particular point P in the system. It should be immediately apparent that the directions associated with the base vectors depend on where you are located in the plane relative to the origin of coordinates. Recall that the points in a polar coordinate system are labeled as the ordered pair (ρ, θ) where ρ is the radial distance from the origin and θ is the angle (measured counterclockwise) from a preselected line sometimes called the x-axis (for which $\theta = 0$ by definition).

For points on the x-axis, therefore, $\mathbf{u}_\rho$ points to the right and $\mathbf{u}_\theta$ points straight up. At $\theta = 90°$, $\mathbf{u}_\rho$ points straight up and $\mathbf{u}_\theta$ points to the left. It is apparent that the base vectors and their differentials in this coordinate system are coordinate dependent even if time independent. We may write the base vectors relative to a Cartesian coordinate system with a common origin as

$$\mathbf{u}_\rho = \mathbf{i}\cos(\theta) + \mathbf{j}\sin(\theta) \quad (298a)$$

$$\mathbf{u}_\theta = -\mathbf{i}\sin(\theta) + \mathbf{j}\cos(\theta) \quad (298b)$$

and their differentials as

$$\mathrm{d}\mathbf{u}_\rho = \mathbf{u}_\theta\,\mathrm{d}\theta \quad (299a)$$

$$\mathrm{d}\mathbf{u}_\theta = -\mathbf{u}_\rho\,\mathrm{d}\theta \quad (299b)$$

These expressions certainly involve both base vectors and one of the coordinate differentials. In the polar coordinate system, the base vector differentials are nonzero, not because of acceleration or anything having to do with being inertial or non-inertial but because the coordinate system is curved.

Base Vector Differentials in the General Case

Introductory thoughts.—The time has come to generalize what we have been saying about base vector derivatives. From the rules developed herein, we will be able to derive much of tensor calculus. Consider, first, the contravariant representation of a vector **V**:

---

[35]Some spaces are also curved and are called non-Euclidean spaces or oftentimes Riemannian spaces (after Bernhard Riemann, 1826–1866). In these non-Euclidean spaces, there are only straightest possible curves called geodesics, which possess the same curvature (locally) as the space itself. Geodesics are the natural generalization of the straight line. Coordinate systems constructed of geodesics in a curved space are called geodesic coordinate systems. The Cartesian coordinate system is the geodesic coordinate system of Euclidean space. A given space can only contain curves of curvature greater than or equal to that of the space itself. Thus, a sphere cannot contain a straight line, just as a spherical n-space can never contain a Cartesian coordinate system.

$$\mathbf{V} = v^k \mathbf{e}^{(k)} \tag{300}$$

with summation over all the values of the repeated index k. The contravariant representation has been chosen with a sort of malice of forethought. The development for the contravariant representation will be carried out by employing a unique device involving permutation of covariant tensor indexes. Once we have finished with the contravariant base vector differential, the covariant base vector differential will practically fall into our laps.

Now, we differentiate

$$\mathrm{d}\mathbf{V} = \left(\mathrm{d}v^k\right)\mathbf{e}^{(k)} + v^k\left(\mathrm{d}\mathbf{e}^{(k)}\right) \tag{301}$$

Each term on the right-hand side has a repeated index k, and each term represents a summation over all the values of k, even though the index pairs do not involve the usual covariant-contravariant configuration.

We now proceed to develop a general formulation for the base vector differential $\mathbf{de}^{(k)}$ in view of the three criteria stated below. Our formulation of $\mathbf{de}^{(k)}$ must satisfy these criteria; that is, the base vector differentials must be

1. Linearly dependent on the coordinate differentials
2. Linearly dependent on the base vectors themselves
3. Functions of the coordinate values

We demonstrated these criteria with examples. Now, we raise them to the status of criteria that must be satisfied in general, so let us examine them closely:

1. The coordinate differentials are components of a contravariant vector $\mathrm{d}x^s$. This is a condition of all coordinate differentials. Linear dependence here means that our general formulation must involve a sum of the type $\alpha_s \mathrm{d}x^s$. The term α_s may be a function of the coordinate values.

2. The linear dependence on the base vectors must similarly involve a sum of the type $\beta^m \mathbf{e}^{(m)}$. Criteria 1 and 2 taken together suggest that we are seeking a term of the type $\alpha_s \beta^m \mathrm{d}x^s \mathbf{e}^{(m)} = \lambda_s^m \,\mathrm{d}x^s \mathbf{e}^{(m)}$. The terms β^m and therefore λ_s^m may both be functions of the coordinate values.

3. Finally, we desire an expression of the form $\mathbf{de}^{(k)}$ = (some term) $\lambda_s^m \,\mathrm{d}x^s \mathbf{e}^{(m)}$. Note that the index K is missing on the right side of the equation. We will supply that index by setting the dummy we called “some term” $\rightarrow \varepsilon_k$. Thus $\mathbf{de}^{(k)} = \varepsilon_k \lambda_s^m \,\mathrm{d}x^s \mathbf{e}^{(m)} = \Gamma_{ks}^m \,\mathrm{d}x^s \mathbf{e}^{(m)}$. Summations are understood to be over all repeated index pairs.

We now have the general expression required for the contravariant base vector differential $\mathbf{de}^{(k)}$. Let us write it one more time for completion:

$$\mathrm{d}\mathbf{e}^{(k)} = \Gamma_{ks}^m \,\mathrm{d}x^s \mathbf{e}^{(m)} \tag{302}$$

We are far from finished, for we must now specify the new unknown term Γ_{ks}^m entirely as a function of known terms and then determine whether it is a tensor. Remember the trivial rule that states that the unknown is always defined in terms of the known? We are about to see that this rule is not so trivial after all.

To begin, we inner-multiply both sides of equation (302) by the contravariant base vector $\mathbf{e}^{(w)}$ or more formally, we “left-operate” with $\mathbf{e}^{(w)} \cdot$ (read as “e superscript w dot”):

$$\mathbf{e}^{(w)} \cdot \mathrm{d}\mathbf{e}^{(k)} = \mathbf{e}^{(w)} \cdot \left(\Gamma_{ks}^m \,\mathrm{d}x^s \mathbf{e}^{(m)}\right) \tag{303}$$

Note that there are now two free indexes: w and k.

Next, we will consider each side of this new equation separately. On the left-hand side is $\mathbf{e}^{(w)} \cdot \mathbf{de}^{(k)}$ and on the right-hand side, $\mathbf{e}^{(w)} \cdot (\Gamma_{ks}^m \,\mathrm{d}x^s \mathbf{e}^{(m)})$. The right-hand side is easily reduced:[36]

$$\begin{aligned} \mathbf{e}^{(w)} \cdot \left(\Gamma_{ks}^m \,\mathrm{d}x^s \mathbf{e}^{(m)}\right) &= \Gamma_{ks}^m \,\mathrm{d}x^s \left(\mathbf{e}^{(w)} \cdot \mathbf{e}^{(m)}\right) \\ &= \Gamma_{ks}^m \,\mathrm{d}x^s g_{wm} = g_{wm} \Gamma_{ks}^m \,\mathrm{d}x^s \end{aligned} \tag{304}$$

Note that once the base vectors are eliminated, the summation indexes become covariant-contravariant pairs as they should. Please study these steps until they are clear to you. Every step taken so far derives its validity from what we have previously said and done. When you are satisfied that you understand, go on.

The left-hand side is also easily reduced, since[37]

---

[36]Remember that $g_{wm} = \mathbf{e}^{(w)} \cdot \mathbf{e}^{(m)}$.

[37]Remember that $g_{wk} = \mathbf{e}^{(w)} \cdot \mathbf{e}^{(k)}$ and the rule for differentiating a product.

$$\mathbf{e}^{(w)} \cdot \mathrm{d}\mathbf{e}^{(k)} = \mathrm{d}(g_{wk}) - \mathbf{e}^{(k)} \cdot \mathrm{d}\mathbf{e}^{(w)} = \mathrm{d}(g_{wk}) - g_{km}\Gamma^m_{sw}\,\mathrm{d}x^s \quad (305)$$

Combining the results for the right- and the left-hand sides yields

$$\mathrm{d}(g_{wk}) - g_{km}\Gamma^m_{ws}\,\mathrm{d}x^s = g_{wm}\Gamma^m_{ks}\,\mathrm{d}x^s \quad (306a)$$

or

$$\mathrm{d}(g_{wk}) = g_{km}\Gamma^m_{ws}\,\mathrm{d}x^s + g_{wm}\Gamma^m_{ks}\,\mathrm{d}x^s \quad (306b)$$

Look at this equation and ask yourself, "Having gotten this far, what would I do next?" The most obvious step that should come to mind is to differentiate with respect to x^t:

$$\frac{\partial(g_{wk})}{\partial x^t} = g_{km}\Gamma^m_{ws}\delta^s_t + g_{wm}\Gamma^m_{ks}\delta^s_t = g_{km}\Gamma^m_{wt} + g_{wm}\Gamma^m_{kt} \quad (307)$$

Note that in the second (middle) equality, we have used the relation

$$\frac{\partial x^s}{\partial x^t} = \delta^s_t \quad (308)$$

by virtue of the linear independence of the respective coordinate axes. In a three-dimensional Cartesian coordinate system, we have

$$\begin{aligned} &\frac{\partial x}{\partial x} = 1,\ \frac{\partial x}{\partial y} = 0,\ \frac{\partial x}{\partial z} = 0 \\ &\frac{\partial y}{\partial x} = 0,\ \frac{\partial y}{\partial y} = 1,\ \frac{\partial y}{\partial z} = 0 \\ &\frac{\partial z}{\partial x} = 0,\ \frac{\partial z}{\partial y} = 0,\ \frac{\partial z}{\partial z} = 1 \end{aligned} \quad (309)$$

Similarly, in the polar coordinate system, we have

$$\frac{\partial \rho}{\partial \rho} = 1,\ \frac{\partial \rho}{\partial \theta} = 0;\ \frac{\partial \theta}{\partial \rho} = 0,\ \frac{\partial \theta}{\partial \theta} \quad (310)$$

In the general case, we have

$$\mathrm{d}x^s = \delta^s_t\,\mathrm{d}x^t = \left(\frac{\partial x^s}{\partial x^t}\right)\mathrm{d}x^t \rightarrow \left[\delta^s_t - \left(\frac{\partial x^s}{\partial x^t}\right)\right]\mathrm{d}x^t = 0 \quad (311)$$

But $\mathrm{d}x^t$ is an arbitrary vector (i.e., $\mathrm{d}x^t \neq 0$ generally); therefore, $\delta^s_t = \partial x^s/\partial x^t$. Q.E.D.

> Note that the expression in equation (307) now has three free indexes. The third free index arose when we differentiated. Remember that every time you take a step in a tensor calculation, you must be careful not to repeat an index unless you deliberately intend a summation.

At this point, please pause again and go through what we have just done so that you are clear. We have done nothing new, despite the intimidating appearance of the symbol soup in the last few lines. When you think that you have gotten it, then go on. What is to come next is new and somewhat unusual.

Christoffel's symbols.—To review, in the previous section, Introductory thoughts, we wrote an expression for $\mathbf{de}^{(k)}$:

$$\mathrm{d}\mathbf{e}^{(k)} = \Gamma^m_{ks}\,\mathrm{d}x^s\mathbf{e}^{(m)} \quad (312)$$

We then began to seek a form for Γ^m_{ks}. First, we inner-multiplied by $\mathbf{e}^{(w)}$:

$$\mathbf{e}^{(w)} \cdot \mathrm{d}\mathbf{e}^{(k)} = \mathbf{e}^{(w)} \cdot \left[\Gamma^m_{ks}\,\mathrm{d}x^s\mathbf{e}^{(m)}\right] \quad (313)$$

We then showed that

$$\mathbf{e}^{(w)} \cdot \left[\Gamma^m_{ks}\,\mathrm{d}x^s\mathbf{e}^{(m)}\right] = g_{wm}\Gamma^m_{ks}\,\mathrm{d}x^s \quad (314)$$

and

$$\mathbf{e}^{(w)} \cdot \mathrm{d}\mathbf{e}^{(k)} = \mathrm{d}(g_{wk}) - g_{km}\Gamma^m_{ws}\,\mathrm{d}x^s \quad (315)$$

and we concluded that

$$\frac{\partial(g_{wk})}{\partial x^t} = g_{km}\Gamma^m_{wt} + g_{wm}\Gamma^m_{kt} \quad (316)$$

It is by manipulating this new expression that we now will determine Γ^m_{ks}.

However, before determining Γ^m_{ks}, it is necessary to review briefly the idea of permutations. Consider the numbers 123. Form the following number string: 123123. The first three numbers are our original grouping, 123. Now, remove the initial digit to leave 23123. The first three numbers of this new string, 231, comprise the first even permutation of 123. Now remove the initial digit again to leave 3123. The first three numbers of this string, 312, comprise the second even permutation of 123. (Had we gone the other direction, the resulting permutations would have been the first and second odd permutations.)

Next, in place of 123, write *wkt*, the three free indexes in the last expression (eq. (316)) in the order that they occur from left to right. Now, find the first two even permutations:

Original: *wkt*
First permutations.: *ktw*
Second permutations: *twk*

We will now follow a technique introduced by Elwin Christoffel (1829–1900), the German mathematician who invented covariant differentiation (the process that we are developing here), and use these permutations to generate two more independent equations from our original $\partial(g_{wk})/\partial x^t = g_{km}\Gamma^m_{wt} + g_{wm}\Gamma^m_{kt}$. Remember that a change in free index is a change in what the equation is representing. By flipping indexes in this manner, we generate not a repeat of what we already have, but actual new information. Here are the results for the first and second permutations:

$$\frac{\partial(g_{kt})}{\partial x^w} = g_{tm}\Gamma^m_{kw} + g_{km}\Gamma^m_{tw} \tag{317}$$

and

$$\frac{\partial(g_{tw})}{\partial x^k} = g_{wm}\Gamma^m_{tk} + g_{tm}\Gamma^m_{wk} \tag{318}$$

We will now impose another new requirement on Γ^m_{ks}, namely, that it be symmetrical in the covariant indexes k and s (i.e., we require that $\Gamma^m_{sk} = \Gamma^m_{ks}$. We will have to check to make certain that we have actually satisfied this requirement when we are finished.) We now have three equations:

$$\frac{\partial(g_{wk})}{\partial x^t} = g_{km}\Gamma^m_{wt} + g_{wm}\Gamma^m_{kt} \tag{319}$$

$$\frac{\partial(g_{kt})}{\partial x^w} = g_{tm}\Gamma^m_{kw} + g_{km}\Gamma^m_{tw} \tag{320}$$

and

$$\frac{\partial(g_{tw})}{\partial x^k} = g_{wm}\Gamma^m_{tk} + g_{tm}\Gamma^m_{wk} \tag{321}$$

If we add the first two equations and subtract the third using the new symmetry requirement, we obtain one new equation:

$$\frac{\partial(g_{wk})}{\partial x^t} + \frac{\partial(g_{kt})}{\partial x^w} - \frac{\partial(g_{tw})}{\partial x^k} = 2\left(g_{km}\Gamma^m_{wt}\right) \tag{322}$$

This equation is important because it has a single isolated term involving Γ^m_{wt} and permits us to express this term entirely in terms of known quantities, namely, the fundamental tensor and its derivatives with respect to the coordinates.

We will finally isolate Γ^m_{wt} by left-operating on the equation with $\frac{1}{2}g^{bh}$, then setting $h = k$, and summing over the new repeated index. Please carry out each of these steps yourself on a scratch pad. Here is the result you should obtain:

$$\Gamma^b_{wt} = \frac{1}{2}g^{bk}\left[\frac{\partial(g_{wk})}{\partial x^t} + \frac{\partial(g_{kt})}{\partial x^w} - \frac{\partial(g_{tw})}{\partial x^k}\right] \tag{323}$$

Our task of determining the general form for the contravariant base vector differential $\mathbf{de}^{(k)}$ is now complete. We have specified both the defining equation $\mathbf{de}^{(t)} = \Gamma^b_{wt}\,dx^w\mathbf{e}^{(b)}$ and the term Γ^b_{wt}, which we have expressed entirely in terms of known quantities.

If we formally set $\Gamma_{wkt} = \frac{1}{2}\left[\partial(g_{wk})/\partial x^t + \partial(g_{kt})/\partial x^w - \partial(g_{tw})/\partial x^k\right]$, then we have

$$\Gamma^b_{wt} = g^{bk}\Gamma_{wkt} \tag{324}$$

By convention in tensor analysis, the symbol Γ_{wkt} is called Christoffel's symbol of the first kind, and the symbol Γ^b_{wt} is called Christoffel's symbol of the second kind.

Symmetry of Christoffel's symbol: Remember how we imposed a symmetry requirement on Γ^b_{wt}? Note that the result obtained for Γ^b_{wt} is indeed symmetrical in the covariant indexes w and t just as we required. Start with expression (323):

$$\Gamma^b_{wt} = \frac{1}{2} g^{bk} \left[\frac{\partial(g_{wk})}{\partial x^t} + \frac{\partial(g_{kt})}{\partial x^w} - \frac{\partial(g_{tw})}{\partial x^k} \right] \tag{323}$$

Now interchange the indexes w and t:

$$\Gamma^b_{tw} = \frac{1}{2} g^{bk} \left[\frac{\partial(g_{tk})}{\partial x^w} + \frac{\partial(g_{kw})}{\partial x^t} - \frac{\partial(g_{wt})}{\partial x^k} \right] \tag{325}$$

Since the fundamental tensor is symmetric, that is, since

$$g_{jk} = g_{kj} \text{ for all } j \text{ and } k \tag{326}$$

we also have

$$\Gamma^b_{tw} = \frac{1}{2} g^{bk} \left[\frac{\partial(g_{kt})}{\partial x^w} + \frac{\partial(g_{wk})}{\partial x^t} - \frac{\partial(g_{tw})}{\partial x^k} \right] \tag{327}$$

But this expression is identical to that for Γ^b_{wt}, and we must conclude that $\Gamma^b_{wt} = \Gamma^b_{tw}$. Q.E.D.

The terms Γ^b_{wt} as functions of the coordinate values: We indicated earlier that the terms Γ^b_{wt} may be a function of the coordinate values. Looking again at the expression (eq. (327))

$$\Gamma^b_{tw} = \frac{1}{2} g^{bk} \left[\frac{\partial(g_{kt})}{\partial x^w} + \frac{\partial(g_{wk})}{\partial x^t} - \frac{\partial(g_{tw})}{\partial x^k} \right] \tag{327}$$

it is apparent that Γ^b_{wt} will be a function of the coordinate values provided that the g^{ij} and/or the derivatives of the g_{st} are functions of the coordinate values. For the components of the fundamental tensor and their derivatives to be functions of the coordinate values, it is sufficient to argue that there exists a system K in which the values of the fundamental tensor and its derivatives change as we move about from point to point. However, such a system would involve the base vectors changing from point to point in such a way as to make their inner products vary from point to point. Without going into an actual proof, it should not be too difficult to imagine that this not only can but certainly will be the case in any number of systems—in fact, it is the exception when it is not. So, we may convince ourselves that the terms Γ^b_{wt} may be and usually are functions of the coordinate values.

Differential of a covariant base vector.—Now that we have an expression for the differential of the contravariant base vector, the expression for the differential of a covariant base vector is readily obtained. We start with a simple expression that we already know:

$$\mathbf{e}^{(a)} \cdot \mathbf{e}_{(b)} = \delta^b_a \tag{328}$$

Next, we differentiate:

$$\left[\mathrm{d}\mathbf{e}^{(a)} \right] \cdot \mathbf{e}_{(b)} + \mathbf{e}^{(a)} \cdot \left[\mathrm{d}\mathbf{e}_{(b)} \right] = 0 \tag{329}$$

Then we substitute for $\mathbf{de}^{(a)}$:

$$\Gamma^s_{at}\, \mathrm{d}x^t \mathbf{e}^{(s)} \cdot \mathbf{e}_{(b)} + \mathbf{e}^{(a)} \cdot \left[\mathrm{d}\mathbf{e}_{(b)} \right] = 0 \tag{330}$$

We simplify:

$$\mathbf{e}^{(a)} \cdot \left[\mathrm{d}\mathbf{e}_{(b)} \right] = -\delta^b_s \Gamma^s_{at}\, \mathrm{d}x^t = -\Gamma^b_{at}\, \mathrm{d}x^t \tag{331}$$

We finally observe that if we set

$$\mathrm{d}\mathbf{e}_{(b)} = -\Gamma^b_{mt}\, \mathrm{d}x^t \mathbf{e}_{(m)} \tag{332}$$

then we automatically satisfy the inner product since

$$\begin{aligned} \mathbf{e}^{(a)} \cdot \left[\mathrm{d}\mathbf{e}_{(b)} \right] &= -\Gamma^b_{mt}\, \mathrm{d}x^t \mathbf{e}^{(a)} \cdot \mathbf{e}_{(m)} \\ &= -\delta^m_a \Gamma^b_{mt}\, \mathrm{d}x^t = -\Gamma^b_{at}\, \mathrm{d}x^t \end{aligned} \tag{333}$$

The expression $\mathbf{de}_{(b)} = -\Gamma^b_{mt}\, \mathrm{d}x^t \mathbf{e}_{(m)}$ is the expression sought for the differential of a covariant base vector. Q.E.D.

Tensor Differentiation: Absolute and Covariant Derivatives

Let us repeat our formulas for the differentials of a contravariant and a covariant base vector:

$$\mathrm{d}\mathbf{e}^{(b)} = \Gamma^t_{wb}\, \mathrm{d}x^w \mathbf{e}^{(t)} \tag{334a}$$

$$\mathrm{d}\mathbf{e}_{(b)} = -\Gamma^{b}_{wm}\,\mathrm{d}x^{w}\mathbf{e}_{(m)} \qquad (334b)$$

Next, we write the full expressions for the differential of the vector **V** in both its contravariant and its covariant forms:

$$\mathrm{d}\mathbf{V} = \left(\mathrm{d}v^{k}\right)\mathbf{e}^{(k)} + v^{k}\Gamma^{t}_{wk}\,\mathrm{d}x^{w}\mathbf{e}^{(t)} \qquad (335a)$$

$$\mathrm{d}\mathbf{V} = \left(\mathrm{d}v_{k}\right)\mathbf{e}_{(k)} - v_{k}\Gamma^{k}_{wm}\,\mathrm{d}x^{w}\mathbf{e}_{(m)} \qquad (335b)$$

Since there are no free indexes in either of these two equations, we may do some index swapping and write

$$\mathrm{d}\mathbf{V} = \left(\mathrm{d}v^{k} + v^{t}\Gamma^{k}_{wt}\,\mathrm{d}x^{w}\right)\mathbf{e}^{(k)} \qquad (336a)$$

$$\mathrm{d}\mathbf{V} = \left(\mathrm{d}v_{k} - v_{m}\Gamma^{m}_{wk}\,\mathrm{d}x^{w}\right)\mathbf{e}_{(k)} \qquad (336b)$$

Students should examine these expressions and be certain that they understand how the results were obtained.

Look at the two forms of the vector differential **dV** more closely. Note that as written, the terms enclosed in parentheses are components of a contravariant vector and a covariant vector, respectively. We call these components $\mathrm{d}c^{k}$ and $\mathrm{d}c_{k}$. Then,

$$\mathrm{d}c^{k} = \mathrm{d}v^{k} + v^{t}\Gamma^{k}_{wt}\,\mathrm{d}x^{w} \qquad (337a)$$

$$\mathrm{d}c_{k} = \mathrm{d}v_{k} - v_{m}\Gamma^{m}_{wk}\,\mathrm{d}x^{w} \qquad (337b)$$

These last two expressions are the standard form usually seen in text books. Using these expressions, we may now introduce two types of tensor derivatives, the absolute and the covariant.

Absolute derivative.—Let ds be the differential of a rank 0 tensor and form the derivative of the vector **V**, that is, $\mathrm{d}\mathbf{V}/\mathrm{d}s$. This derivative is the absolute derivative of the vector and has for its contravariant and covariant components, respectively,

$$\frac{\mathrm{d}c^{k}}{\mathrm{d}s} = \left(\frac{\mathrm{d}v^{k}}{\mathrm{d}s}\right) + v^{t}\Gamma^{k}_{wt}\left(\frac{\mathrm{d}x^{w}}{\mathrm{d}s}\right) \qquad (338a)$$

$$\frac{\mathrm{d}c_{k}}{\mathrm{d}s} = \left(\frac{\mathrm{d}v_{k}}{\mathrm{d}s}\right) - v_{m}\Gamma^{m}_{wk}\left(\frac{\mathrm{d}x^{w}}{\mathrm{d}s}\right) \qquad (338b)$$

Acceleration is an absolute derivative. If we set ds = dt, the time differential, then the derivative of the velocity vector with components c^{k} or c_{k} is given above (eqs. (338a) and 338(b)). The term with Γ^{k}_{wt} in each of the expressions above is the term that contributes the components of the pseudoacceleration. (Note that the derivative of the coordinate values in the second term represents a component of the velocity.) In an inertial system, the terms Γ^{k}_{wt} vanish everywhere, that is, $\Gamma^{k}_{wt} = 0$.

Covariant derivative.—Let us now differentiate the vector **V** with respect to one of the coordinate values, say dx^{q}; that is, we wish now to form the partial derivative $\partial\mathbf{V}/\partial x^{q}$. The components of this derivative form the so-called covariant derivative of the vector, which has for its contravariant and covariant components, respectively,

$$\frac{\partial c^{k}}{\partial x^{q}} = \left(\frac{\partial v^{k}}{\partial x^{q}}\right) + v^{t}\Gamma^{k}_{qt} \qquad (339a)$$

$$\frac{\partial c_{k}}{\partial x^{q}} = \left(\frac{\partial v_{k}}{\partial x^{q}}\right) - v_{m}\Gamma^{m}_{qk} \qquad (339b)$$

These components are often abbreviated as

$$v^{k}_{,q} = \left(\frac{\partial v^{k}}{\partial x^{q}}\right) + v^{t}\Gamma^{k}_{qt} \qquad (340a)$$

$$v_{k,q} = \left(\frac{\partial v_{k}}{\partial x^{q}}\right) - v_{m}\Gamma^{m}_{qk} \qquad (340b)$$

The placement of the differentiation index q in the covariant position in both cases is what drives the name "covariant derivative."

We now return to the absolute derivatives and write still further:

$$\frac{\mathrm{d}c^{k}}{\mathrm{d}s} = \left(\frac{\partial v^{k}}{\partial x^{w}}\right)\left(\frac{\mathrm{d}x^{w}}{\mathrm{d}s}\right) + v^{t}\Gamma^{k}_{wt} \times\left(\frac{\mathrm{d}x^{w}}{\mathrm{d}s}\right) = v^{k}_{,w}\left(\frac{\mathrm{d}x^{w}}{\mathrm{d}s}\right) \qquad (341a)$$

$$\frac{\mathrm{d}c_k}{\mathrm{d}s}=\left(\frac{\partial v_k}{\partial x^w}\right)\left(\frac{\mathrm{d}x^w}{\mathrm{d}s}\right)-v_m\Gamma^m_{wk}\times\left(\frac{\mathrm{d}x^w}{\mathrm{d}s}\right)=v_{k,w}\left(\frac{\mathrm{d}x^w}{\mathrm{d}s}\right) \tag{341b}$$

and for the differentials $\mathrm{d}c^k$ and $\mathrm{d}c_k$,

$$\mathrm{d}c^k = v^k_{,w}\,\mathrm{d}x^w \tag{342a}$$

$$\mathrm{d}c_k = v_{k,w}\,\mathrm{d}x^w \tag{342a}$$

We can demonstrate the coordinate independence of $v^k_{,w}$ and $v_{k,w}$ by noting that the vector differential $\mathrm{d}c^k$ is a tensor as is the coordinate differential $\mathrm{d}x^w$. Therefore,

$$\mathrm{d}c^k = \mathrm{d}c^{k*} \tag{343a}$$

$$\mathrm{d}x^w = \mathrm{d}x^{w*} \tag{343a}$$

so that

$$v^k_{,w}\,\mathrm{d}x^w = v^k_{,w}{*}\ \mathrm{d}x^{w*} = v^k_{,w}{*}\ \mathrm{d}x^w \tag{344}$$

and

$$\left(v^k_{,w} - v^k_{,w}{*}\right)\mathrm{d}x^w = 0 \tag{345}$$

Since $\mathrm{d}x^w$ is an arbitrary vector (i.e., $\mathrm{d}x^w \neq 0$ generally), we must conclude that $(v^k_{,w} - v^k_{,w}{*}) = 0$ or that $v^k_{,w} = v^k_{,w}{*}$. Q.E.D.

The argument for $v_{k,q}$ is similar and is left as an exercise for the reader.

Tensor Character of Γ^k_{wt}

Are the Christoffel symbols tensors? The quick answer is no, they are not. The Christoffel symbols are components of a triad, but the triad itself is not the same in all frames of reference; that is, it is coordinate dependent.

Recall that the base vectors are not tensors. They have the same type of coordinate dependence as the position vectors. Thus, in the expression $\mathbf{de}^{(k)} = \Gamma^m_{sk}\,\mathrm{d}x^s\mathbf{e}^{(m)}$, the right-hand side consists of a tensor $\mathrm{d}x^s$, a nontensor $\mathbf{e}^{(m)}$, and the term Γ^m_{sk}. The left-hand side $\mathbf{de}^{(k)}$, on the other hand, is a tensor. This situation should make us suspect[38] the "tensorhood" of Γ^m_{sk}.

Let us now show that Γ^m_{sk} is not a tensor. We will use the fact that the covariant derivative of a covariant vector $v_{k,q}$ is a tensor. Then

$$v_{k,q} = v^*_{k,q} \rightarrow \left(\frac{\partial v_k}{\partial x^q}\right) - v_t\Gamma^t_{kq} = \left(\frac{\partial v^*_k}{\partial x^{q*}}\right) - v^*_t\Gamma^t_{kq}{}^* \tag{346}$$

and, therefore,

$$v_t\Gamma^t_{kq} - v^*_t\Gamma^t_{kq}{}^* = \left(\frac{\partial v_k}{\partial x^q}\right) + \left(\frac{\partial v^*_k}{\partial x^{q*}}\right) \tag{347}$$

Now, even if $v_t = v^*_t$ (i.e., even if the vector with covariant components v_t is a tensor), we still would only have

$$v_t\left(\Gamma^t_{kq} - \Gamma^t_{kq}{}^*\right) = \left(\frac{\partial v_k}{\partial x^q}\right) + \left(\frac{\partial v^*_k}{\partial x^{q*}}\right) \tag{348}$$

and since we cannot guarantee the vanishing of the term $(\partial v_k/\partial x^q) + (\partial v_k{*}/\partial x^q{*})$ everywhere throughout the frame of reference, we cannot directly establish that $\left(\Gamma^t_{kq} - \Gamma^{t*}_{kq}\right) = 0$. Thus, the terms Γ^t_{kq} are not coordinate independent and may not be admitted into the class of objects called tensors.

If we wish to establish our argument even more firmly, we may seek out and find a single actual case where $\left(\Gamma^t_{kq} - \Gamma^{t*}_{kq}\right) \neq 0$. One such case is sufficient to argue that Γ^t_{kq} is not a tensor[39] by counterexample. To do so, let $\partial v_k/\partial x^q \neq 0$ and $\partial v_k/\partial x^q = \partial v^*_k/\partial x^{q*}$. In other words, let $\partial v_k/\partial x^q$ be a nonvanishing tensor.[40] Then

[38]The term $\mathbf{de}^{(k)}$ on the right-hand side is a tensor. The term $\Gamma^m_{sk}\,\mathrm{d}x^s\mathbf{e}^{(m)}$ on the left-hand side comprises a tensor $\mathrm{d}x^s$, a nontensor $\mathbf{e}^{(m)}$, and an unknown Γ^m_{sk}. The unknown is either a tensor or it is not. If it is a tensor, then its combination with $\mathrm{d}x^s$ produces another tensor $\Gamma^m_{sk}\,\mathrm{d}x^s$, whose product with $\mathbf{e}^{(m)}$ results in the nontensor $\Gamma^m_{sk}\,\mathrm{d}x^s\mathbf{e}^{(m)}$. We then have the contradiction that a tensor $\mathbf{de}^{(k)}$ is equal to a nontensor $\Gamma^m_{sk}\,\mathrm{d}x^s\mathbf{e}^{(m)}$. Therefore, by reductio ad absurdum, Γ^m_{sk} cannot be a tensor. This argument is not a proof that Γ^m_{sk} is not a tensor, but it certainly makes us suspect.

[39]The relationship ($\Gamma^t_{kq} - \Gamma^{t*}_{kq}$) = 0 must hold for all cases if Γ^t_{kq} is to be a tensor. Therefore, to demonstrate the existence of even one case to the contrary is sufficient to eliminate Γ^t_{kq} from the tensor family.

[40]Any vector field with a nonvanishing divergence, such as the gravitational field of a point mass or the electric field of an isolated point charge, satisfies this condition. The divergence is the contraction of $\partial v_k/\partial x^q$, that is, the scalar obtained from setting $k = q$ and summing over the repeated index.

$$\left(\frac{\partial v_k}{\partial x^q}\right)-\left(\frac{\partial v_k^*}{\partial x^{q*}}\right)=0 \rightarrow \left(\frac{\partial v_k}{\partial x^q}\right)+\left(\frac{\partial v_k^*}{\partial x^{q*}}\right)=\frac{2\partial v_k^*}{\partial x^{q*}} \quad (349)$$

In this case,

$$v_t\Gamma_{kq}^t = v_t^*\Gamma_{kq}^t{}^* + \left(\frac{2\partial v_k}{\partial x^q}\right) \quad (350)$$

Even if we set $v_t = v_t^*$, this argument again shows that Γ_{kq}^t does not obey the usual transformation law for tensors in the particular case considered. There is an additional term on the right-hand side of the equation. Therefore, since Γ_{kq}^t is not a tensor in this case, it may not be regarded as a tensor in general.

We may also proceed to explore the tensor character of Γ_{sk}^m by writing the complete transformation law for Γ_{sk}^m. The process is somewhat more tedious than what we have just done, but it involves nothing new or out of the ordinary. The result is

$$\Gamma_{qt}^k{}^* = \Gamma_{uw}^s\left(\frac{\partial x^{k*}}{\partial x^s}\right)\left(\frac{\partial x^u}{\partial x^{q*}}\right)\left(\frac{\partial x^w}{\partial x^{t*}}\right) + \left(\frac{\partial x^{k*}}{\partial x^a}\right)\left(\frac{\partial^2 x^a}{\partial x^{q*}\,\partial x^{t*}}\right) \quad (351)$$

Again, the extra right-hand-side term $(\partial x^k{}^*/\partial x^a)(\partial^2 x^a/\partial x^q{}^*\partial x^t{}^*)$ shows that the transformation is not a tensor transformation and, therefore, that Γ_{sk}^m is not a tensor.

To acquire the coordinate transformation for Γ_{uw}^s, let us recognize that the individual terms that are summed to form Γ_{uw}^s are the coordinate derivatives of the components of the covariant fundamental tensor. We know that the fundamental tensor itself transforms according to the rule:

$$g_{st}^* = \left(\frac{\partial x^i}{\partial x^{s*}}\right)\left(\frac{\partial x^j}{\partial x^{t*}}\right)g_{ij} \quad (352)$$

If we form the coordinate derivative of this equation with respect to the coordinate $x^q{}^*$, we will have taken a first step towards obtaining the coordinate transformation of Γ_{uw}^s. Thus,

$$\begin{aligned}\frac{\partial\left(g_{st}^*\right)}{\partial x^{q*}} &= \frac{\partial\left[\left(\frac{\partial x^i}{\partial x^{s*}}\right)\left(\frac{\partial x^j}{\partial x^{t*}}\right)g_{ij}\right]}{\partial x^{q*}} \\ &= \left(\frac{\partial^2 x^i}{\partial x^{q*}\,\partial x^{s*}}\right)\left(\frac{\partial x^j}{\partial x^{t*}}\right)g_{ij} \\ &+ \left(\frac{\partial x^i}{\partial x^{s*}}\right)\left(\frac{\partial^2 x^j}{\partial x^{q*}\,\partial x^{t*}}\right)g_{ij} \\ &+ \left(\frac{\partial x^i}{\partial x^{s*}}\right)\left(\frac{\partial x^j}{\partial x^{t*}}\right)\left[\frac{\partial\left(g_{ij}\right)}{\partial x^{q*}}\right]\end{aligned} \quad (353)$$

We now note that

$$\frac{\partial\left(g_{ij}\right)}{\partial x^{q*}} = \left(\frac{\partial x^k}{\partial x^{q*}}\right)\left[\frac{\partial\left(g_{ij}\right)}{\partial x^k}\right] \quad (354)$$

so that, upon substitution, we get

$$\begin{aligned}\frac{\partial\left(g_{st}^*\right)}{\partial x^{q*}} &= \left(\frac{\partial^2 x^i}{\partial x^{q*}\,\partial x^{s*}}\right)\left(\frac{\partial x^j}{\partial x^{t*}}\right)g_{ij} \\ &+ \left(\frac{\partial x^i}{\partial x^{s*}}\right)\left(\frac{\partial^2 x^j}{\partial x^{q*}\,\partial x^{t*}}\right)g_{ij} \\ &+ \left(\frac{\partial x^i}{\partial x^{s*}}\right)\left(\frac{\partial x^j}{\partial x^{t*}}\right)\left(\frac{\partial x^k}{\partial x^{q*}}\right)\left[\frac{\partial\left(g_{ij}\right)}{\partial x^k}\right]\end{aligned} \quad (355)$$

Now, let us permute the indexes *stq* and *ijk* in this equation just as we permuted them when deriving the original expression for Γ_{uw}^s. We will also take into account certain dummy indexes and the symmetry of g_{ij} in dealing with the right-hand side. We obtain this result:

$$\begin{aligned}\frac{\partial\left(g_{st}^*\right)}{\partial x^{q*}} &= \left(\frac{\partial^2 x^i}{\partial x^{q*}\,\partial x^{s*}}\right)\left(\frac{\partial x^j}{\partial x^{t*}}\right)g_{ij} \\ &+ \left(\frac{\partial x^i}{\partial x^{s*}}\right)\left(\frac{\partial^2 x^j}{\partial x^{q*}\,\partial x^{t*}}\right)g_{ij} \\ &+ \left(\frac{\partial x^i}{\partial x^{s*}}\right)\left(\frac{\partial x^j}{\partial x^{t*}}\right)\left(\frac{\partial x^k}{\partial x^{q*}}\right)\left[\frac{\partial\left(g_{ij}\right)}{\partial x^k}\right]\end{aligned} \quad (356)$$

The nonvanishing scalar divergence guarantees that at least one diagonal term in $\partial v_k/\partial x^q$ will be nonzero.

$$\frac{\partial\left(g_{tq}^{*}\right)}{\partial x^{s}*}=\left(\frac{\partial^{2}x^{i}}{\partial x^{s}*\,\partial x^{t}*}\right)\left(\frac{\partial x^{j}}{\partial x^{q}*}\right)g_{ij}+\left(\frac{\partial x^{i}}{\partial x^{t}*}\right)\left(\frac{\partial^{2}x^{i}}{\partial x^{s}*\,\partial x^{q}*}\right)g_{ij}+\left(\frac{\partial x^{j}}{\partial x^{t}*}\right)\left(\frac{\partial x^{k}}{\partial x^{q}*}\right)\left(\frac{\partial x^{i}}{\partial x^{s}*}\right)\left[\frac{\partial\left(g_{jk}\right)}{\partial x^{i}}\right] \tag{357}$$

$$\frac{\partial\left(g_{qs}^{*}\right)}{\partial x^{t}*}=\left(\frac{\partial^{2}x^{i}}{\partial x^{t}*\,\partial x^{q}*}\right)\left(\frac{\partial x^{j}}{\partial x^{s}*}\right)g_{ij}+\left(\frac{\partial x^{i}}{\partial x^{q}*}\right)\left(\frac{\partial^{2}x^{i}}{\partial x^{t}*\,\partial x^{s}*}\right)g_{ij}+\left(\frac{\partial x^{k}}{\partial x^{q}*}\right)\left(\frac{\partial x^{i}}{\partial x^{s}*}\right)\left(\frac{\partial x^{j}}{\partial x^{t}*}\right)\left[\frac{\partial\left(g_{ki}\right)}{\partial x^{j}}\right] \tag{358}$$

Adding the first two equations, subtracting the third, then substituting Γ_{qst}^{*} and Γ_{ijk} in the result gives

$$\Gamma_{qst}^{*}=\left(\frac{\partial x^{k}}{\partial x^{q}*}\right)\left(\frac{\partial x^{i}}{\partial x^{s}*}\right)\left(\frac{\partial x^{j}}{\partial x^{t}*}\right)\Gamma_{ijk}+\left(\frac{\partial^{2}x^{i}}{\partial x^{q}*\,\partial x^{s}*}\right)\left(\frac{\partial x^{j}}{\partial x^{t}*}\right)g_{ij} \tag{359}$$

And finally, using the relation $\Gamma_{qt}^{k}=g^{ks}\Gamma_{qst}$ in both frames of reference gives

$$\Gamma_{qt}^{k}*=\Gamma_{uw}^{s}\left(\frac{\partial x^{k}*}{\partial x^{s}}\right)\left(\frac{\partial x^{u}}{\partial x^{q}*}\right)\left(\frac{\partial x^{w}}{\partial x^{t}*}\right)+\left(\frac{\partial x^{k}*}{\partial x^{a}}\right)\left(\frac{\partial^{2}x^{a}}{\partial x^{q}*\,\partial x^{t}*}\right) \tag{360}$$

Q.E.D.

Differentials of Higher Rank Tensors

Once having established the basic pattern for vector (i.e., rank 1 tensor) differentials, it is a relatively straightforward process to write the differentials of a general rank n mixed tensor. We will provide an example that points directly to what the general case should look like.

Consider the triad

$$\underline{\mathbf{T}}=\mathbf{ABC} \tag{361}$$

The differential of $\underline{\mathbf{T}}$ is

$$\mathrm{D}\underline{\mathbf{T}}=(\mathrm{d}\mathbf{A})\mathbf{BC}+\mathbf{A}(\mathrm{d}\mathbf{B})\mathbf{C}+\mathbf{AB}(\mathrm{d}\mathbf{C}) \tag{362}$$

where D is used as the differential operator on the left-hand side to indicate that the differential $\mathrm{D}\underline{\mathbf{T}}$ may become either an absolute or a covariant derivative once an appropriate denominator is specified.

Let us assume that the vectors **A** and **B** are given in contravariant representation whereas the vector **C** is given in covariant representation. We also assume that $\underline{\mathbf{T}}$, **A**, **B**, and **C** are all tensors and that the components of $\underline{\mathbf{T}}$ are t_{k}^{ij}, of **A** are a^{u}, of **B** are b^{s}, and of **C** are c_t. Then expressions (361) and (362) become

$$t_{k}^{ij}=a^{i}b^{j}c_{k} \tag{363}$$

and

$$\begin{aligned}\mathrm{D}t_{k}^{ij}&=\left(\mathrm{d}a^{i}+\Gamma_{uw}^{i}a^{u}\,\mathrm{d}x^{w}\right)b^{j}c_{k}\\&\quad+a^{i}\left(\mathrm{d}b^{j}+\Gamma_{sw}^{j}b^{s}\,\mathrm{d}x^{w}\right)c_{k}\\&\quad+a^{i}b^{j}\left(\mathrm{d}c_{k}+\Gamma_{kw}^{t}c_{t}\,\mathrm{d}x^{w}\right)\\&=\left(\mathrm{d}a^{i}\right)b^{j}c_{k}+\Gamma_{uw}^{i}a^{u}b^{j}c_{k}\,\mathrm{d}x^{w}\\&\quad+a^{i}\left(\mathrm{d}b^{j}\right)c_{k}+\Gamma_{sw}^{j}a^{i}b^{s}c_{k}\,\mathrm{d}x^{w}\\&\quad+a^{i}b^{j}\left(\mathrm{d}c_{k}\right)+\Gamma_{kw}^{t}a^{i}b^{j}c_{t}\,\mathrm{d}x^{w}\\&=\left(\mathrm{d}a^{i}\right)b^{j}c_{k}+a^{i}\left(\mathrm{d}b^{j}\right)c_{k}\\&\quad+a^{i}b^{j}\left(\mathrm{d}c_{k}\right)+\Gamma_{uw}^{i}a^{u}b^{j}c_{k}\,\mathrm{d}x^{w}\\&\quad+\Gamma_{sw}^{j}a^{i}b^{s}c_{k}\,\mathrm{d}x^{w}+\Gamma_{kw}^{t}a^{i}b^{j}c_{t}\,\mathrm{d}x^{w}\\&=\mathrm{d}t_{k}^{ij}+\Gamma_{uw}^{i}t_{k}^{uj}\,\mathrm{d}x^{w}+\Gamma_{sw}^{j}t_{k}^{is}\,\mathrm{d}x^{w}\\&\quad+\Gamma_{kw}^{t}t_{t}^{ij}\,\mathrm{d}x^{w}\end{aligned} \tag{364}$$

Again, the use of D as the differential operator in $\mathrm{D}t_{k}^{ij}$ is to indicate that the differential may become either an absolute or a covariant derivative once an appropriate denominator is specified. Careful examination of expression (364) shows that as a general rule in writing out the differential for the third rank mixed tensor t_{k}^{ij}, one proceeds much as for a vector by writing first the total differential $\mathrm{d}t_{k}^{ij}$ and then adding an extra and appropriate Γ term for each index. You may work out as many additional examples as you wish and are encouraged to do so to gain facility with the notation.

Product Rule for Covariant Derivatives

Just as there is a product rule for differentials of functions in basic college calculus, there is also a product rule for covariant and absolute derivatives. The classical product rule is usually written as

$$\mathrm{d}(uv) = u(\mathrm{d}v) + v(\mathrm{d}u) \tag{365}$$

with extension to total and partial derivatives. We will show that the same rule holds for covariant and absolute derivatives. We begin with the rank 2 contravariant tensor c^{km} and form its covariant derivative with respect to the coordinate index s:

$$c^{km}_{,s} = \left(\frac{\partial c^{km}}{\partial x^s}\right) + \Gamma^k_{ws} c^{wm} + \Gamma^m_{qs} c^{kq} \tag{366}$$

Next, we observe that we can always find vectors a^k and b^m such that $c^{km} = a^k b^m$. Therefore,

$$c^{km} = a^k b^m \rightarrow c^{km}_{,s} = \left(a^k b^m\right)_{,s} \tag{367}$$

We now substitute for c^{km} in the covariant derivative (366) and simplify:

$$\begin{aligned}
\left(a^k b^m\right)_{,s} &= \left(\frac{\partial a^k b^m}{\partial x^s}\right) + \Gamma^k_{ws} a^w b^m + \Gamma^m_{qs} a^k b^q \\
&= \left(\frac{\partial a^k}{\partial x^s}\right) b^m + \left(\frac{\partial b^m}{\partial x^s}\right) a^k + \Gamma^k_{ws} a^w b^m + \Gamma^m_{qs} a^k b^q \\
&= \left[\left(\frac{\partial a^k}{\partial x^s}\right) b^m + \Gamma^k_{ws} a^w b^m\right] + \left[\left(\frac{\partial b^m}{\partial x^s}\right) a^k + \Gamma^m_{qs} a^k b^q\right] \\
&= \left[\left(\frac{\partial a^k}{\partial x^s}\right) + \Gamma^k_{ws} a^w\right] b^m + \left[\left(\frac{\partial b^m}{\partial x^s}\right) + \Gamma^m_{qs} b^q\right] a^k \\
\left(a^k b^m\right)_{,s} &= \left(a^k_{,s}\right) b^m + a^k \left(b^m_{,s}\right)
\end{aligned} \tag{368}$$

The last line is the sought-after product rule for covariant derivatives of a rank 2 contravariant tensor. The same operations may be repeated for rank 2 covariant or rank 2 mixed tensors. Hence, the product rule is established for all possible cases. The extension to tensors of higher rank than 2 should be intuitive.

For the case of the absolute derivative, we simply observe that

$$\frac{\mathrm{d}c^{km}}{\mathrm{d}s} = c^{km}_{,w}\left(\frac{\mathrm{d}x^w}{\mathrm{d}s}\right) \tag{369}$$

We set $c^{km} = a^k b^m$ and apply the results that we have just proven for covariant differentiation.

Second Covariant Derivative of a Tensor

Covariant derivatives of order higher than one—that is, second and third covariant derivatives—are often required. Obtaining these derivatives is a straightforward process that is illustrated here again by way of an example.

Let us begin with the first covariant derivative of a contravariant tensor:

$$v^k_{,q} = \left(\frac{\partial v^k}{\partial x^q}\right) + v^t \Gamma^k_{qt} \tag{370}$$

We wish to obtain a second covariant derivative that we write as

$$\left(v^k_{,q}\right)_{,r} = v^k_{,qr} \tag{371}$$

The term on the left-hand side makes it clear that we are dealing with the equivalent of a covariant derivative with respect to the index r of a rank 2 tensor (namely, the covariant derivative with respect to the index r of $v^k_{,q}$) so that we may directly apply the results of the previous section to obtain

$$\left(v^k_{,q}\right)_{,r} = \left(\frac{\partial v^k_{,q}}{\partial x^r}\right) + \Gamma^k_{qm} v^m_{,r} + \Gamma^s_{qr} v^k_{,s} \tag{372}$$

The same logic may be recursively applied to obtain covariant derivatives of any order.

The Riemann-Christoffel Curvature Tensor

Having acquired the second covariant derivative of the tensor v^k, it is important to observe that the order of differentiation is significant. Covariant differentiation is not commutative. Write the symbols $v^k_{,qr}$ and $v^k_{,rq}$.

Note that the order of the covariant indices is reversed between the two terms. Now it may be shown that

$$v^k_{,qr} - v^k_{,rq} = R^k_{rqs} v^s \tag{373}$$

This equation expresses the difference between $v^k_{,qr}$ and $v^k_{,rq}$ as a function of fourth-rank tensor R^k_{rqs} and the vector v^s with summation over the index s. The tensor R^k_{rqs} is called the Riemann-Christoffel curvature tensor. It plays an essential role in the development of general relativity. Using equation (372), it may be shown that

$$R^k_{rqs} = \frac{\partial \Gamma^k_{rs}}{\partial x^q} - \frac{\partial \Gamma^k_{qs}}{\partial x^r} + \Gamma^k_{rm}\Gamma^m_{qs} - \Gamma^k_{qm}\Gamma^m_{rs} \tag{374}$$

Details of this calculation are left to the reader. This tensor vanishes everywhere in a Euclidean n-space (i.e., for all points in any E^n, $R^k_{rqs} = 0$). This tensor does not vanish in the general case of a non-Euclidean n-space. This fact means that the results of vector transport in non-Euclidean spaces is path dependent.

An easy example of such a transport (called parallel transport) is the transport of a tangent vector along a closed path (a spherical triangle) on the surface of a sphere. Recall that a sphere is a non-Euclidean two-space. To form the path, start at a pole of the sphere and draw a geodesic line (great circle) to the equator. This leg of the triangle subtends an angle of 90° at the center of the sphere. Now turn at a right angle, and proceed another 90° along the equator. Turn again at right angles and return along a third great circle to the pole.

If properly drawn, the triangle will consist of three legs of equal length and three right angles. The sum of the interior angles of our spherical triangle is 270°. Remember that a spherical triangle is different from a Euclidean or planar triangle. The interior angles of all planar triangles add to 180°. The interior angles of a spherical triangle add to variable numbers of degrees depending on the triangle, but the sum is always greater that 180°. The difference is called the spherical excess.

In the case of our triangle, the spherical excess is 90°. What is important to remember here is that our spherical triangle is completely contained within our chosen two-dimensional space (i.e., within the surface of the sphere).

Now imagine a vector tangent to the sphere at the pole. Let the vector point along the first leg of the triangle toward the equator. Move the vector, maintaining tangency, along the first leg of the triangle. Maintaining tangency (or equivalently, perpendicularity to a radial line attached to the tail of the vector) assures parallel transport in this case. When the vector reaches the equator, it will have already turned through an angle of 90° from its original position. It arrives perpendicular to the equator, pointing away from the pole from which it started.

Next, move the vector along the equator, maintaining perpendicularity to the equator, until it arrives at the next poleward leg. It will still be tangent to the sphere and will point along the third leg of the triangle. Now move it along this third leg back to the pole. When the vector returns to the pole, it will still point along the third leg, but note that the third leg of the triangle meets the first leg at an angle of 90°. The vector has been rotated through 90° on its journey around the spherical triangle.

In general, this characteristic of a vector to undergo a change when transported along a geodesic line in non-Euclidean space is quantitatively represented by the Riemann-Christoffel curvature tensor.

Derivatives of the Fundamental Tensor

We now recall the equation $g_{ik}g^{kp} = \delta^p_i$. We will rewrite this equation in differential form:

$$\left(\mathrm{d}\, g_{ik}\right) g^{kp} + g_{ik}\left(\mathrm{d}\, g^{kp}\right) = 0 \tag{375}$$

or equivalently,

$$\left(\mathrm{d}\, g_{ik}\right) g^{kp} = -g_{ik}\left(\mathrm{d}\, g^{kp}\right) \tag{376}$$

Differentiating with respect to x^s gives the result

$$\left(\frac{\partial g_{ik}}{\partial x^s}\right) g^{kp} = -g_{ik}\left(\frac{\partial g^{kp}}{\partial x^s}\right) \tag{377}$$

This equation is very useful in building tensor proofs and/or in reducing complicated tensor equations.

Next let us write out the covariant derivative of g_{mk}:

$$g_{mk,s} = \frac{\partial g_{mk}}{\partial x^s} - \Gamma^t_{ms} g_{tk} - \Gamma^r_{ks} g_{mr} \tag{378}$$

For practice, let us derive the expression for $g_{mk;k}$ from the relationship $v_i = g_{ik}v^k$. We begin by writing the covariant derivative of v_i with respect to the index s, and then we reduce the result. In the process, several important facets of basic "tensorship" will be revealed.

We form the covariant derivative with respect to the index s of the covariant rank 1 tensor v_i:

$$v_{i,s} = \left(g_{ik}v^k\right)_{,s} = \left(g_{ik,s}\right)v^k + g_{ik}\left(v^k_{,s}\right) \qquad (379)$$

We expand just the left-hand term $v_{i,s}$:

$$\begin{aligned} v_{i,s} &= \frac{\partial\left(g_{ik}v^k\right)}{\partial x^s} - \Gamma^w_{is}g_{wk}v^k \\ &= v^k\frac{\partial g_{ik}}{\partial x^s} + g_{ik}\frac{\partial v^k}{\partial x^s} - \Gamma^w_{is}g_{wk}v^k \end{aligned} \qquad (380)$$

and next expand the second term on the right-hand side, $(g_{ik,s})v^k + g_{ik}\left(v^k_{,s}\right)$:

$$g_{ik}\left(v^k_{,s}\right) = g_{ik}\left(\frac{\partial v^k}{\partial x^s} + \Gamma^k_{ws}v^w\right) \qquad (381)$$

Let us now combine the two results just obtained:

$$\begin{aligned} \frac{v^k\partial g_{ik}}{\partial x^s} + \frac{g_{ik}\partial v^k}{\partial x^s} - \Gamma^w_{is}g_{wk}v^k &= \left(g_{ik,s}\right)v^k \\ &+ \frac{g_{ik}\partial v^k}{\partial x^s} + g_{ik}\Gamma^k_{ws}v^w \end{aligned} \qquad (382)$$

We then bring all terms to one side of the equal sign and simplify:

$$\begin{aligned} \frac{v^k\partial g_{ik}}{\partial x^s} + \frac{g_{ik}\partial v^k}{\partial x^s} - \Gamma^w_{is}g_{wk}v^k - \left(g_{ik,s}\right)v^k \\ - \frac{g_{ik}\partial v^k}{\partial x^s} - g_{ik}\Gamma^k_{ws}v^w = 0 \end{aligned} \qquad (383a)$$

$$\frac{v^k\partial g_{ik}}{\partial x^s} - \Gamma^w_{is}g_{wk}v^k - \left(g_{ik,s}\right)v^k - g_{ik}\Gamma^k_{ws}v^w = 0 \qquad (383b)$$

$$\left(\frac{\partial g_{ik}}{\partial x^s} - \Gamma^w_{is}g_{wk} - g_{ik,s} - g_{iw}\Gamma^w_{ks}\right)v^k = 0 \qquad (383c)$$

Note the switch in dummy indexes in the last term in the last step. Now, let us argue that since v^k is an arbitrary vector, this last equation is only satisfied when

$$\frac{\partial g_{ik}}{\partial x^s} - \Gamma^w_{is}g_{wk} - g_{ik,s} - g_{iw}\Gamma^w_{ks} = 0 \qquad (384)$$

from which we are able to obtain the sought-after relationship:

$$\frac{\partial g_{ik}}{\partial x^s} - \Gamma^w_{is}g_{wk} - g_{iw}\Gamma^w_{ks} = g_{ik,s} \quad \text{Q.E.D.} \qquad (385)$$

Carefully review the steps in this calculation and be certain that you understand them. This type of exercise provides the best practice for becoming familiar with the exigencies of using tensor notation.

Gradient, Divergence, and Curl of a Vector Field

This section presents the tensor forms of the vector operations that are frequently used in physics and engineering, namely, the gradient, divergence, and curl of a vector field.

First, consider a well-behaved scalar field ϕ over some region of space. Suppose that the scalar is temperature. It is clear that if the field is not perfectly uniform (i.e., ϕ = constant), there will be nonzero heat fluxes: thermal energy will "flow" down the thermal gradients, allowing the warmer regions to cool and the cooler regions to warm.

In conventional notation, the gradient of a scalar field is represented as

$$\text{grad}\ \phi = \nabla\phi \qquad (386)$$

The gradient of a scalar field ϕ defined over some region of space is a vector field defined over the same region of space or at least over that subregion of the space in which the vector function represented by $\nabla\phi$ exists. This new vector field has as its components the first-order coordinate derivatives of ϕ. The gradient, at every point, has the direction along which ϕ increases most rapidly. In tensor notation, the gradient is represented as a covariant derivative of a scalar or rank 0 tensor:

$$\phi_{,r} = \frac{\partial\phi}{\partial x^r} \qquad (387)$$

Since ϕ is a rank 0 tensor, there are no Γ terms added to the partial derivative, and the gradient appears essentially the same in tensor notation as it does in conventional notation. Thus, whatever coordinate system we choose to work with, the coordinate derivatives of the scalar field ϕ are components of the gradient field associated with ϕ.

> Be careful to make appropriate metric adjustments when applying this rule. Remember that dimensional consistency is still of paramount importance in the formulations of physical and engineering equations. The units associated with the gradient field comprise the units associated with the scalar field divided by distance. Thus, if ϕ represents a temperature field in degrees kelvin (°K), grad ϕ represents a temperature gradient field in degrees kelvin per meter (°K/m).

Next, consider the divergence of a vector field **V**. The divergence is represented in conventional notation as

$$\operatorname{div} \mathbf{V} = \nabla \cdot \mathbf{V} \tag{388}$$

The divergence of a vector field is a scalar field. The divergence is a measure of the net outflow from or inflow to a source, preferably a point source. The electric field of a point charge has a nonzero divergence at the site of the charge itself. An imponderable fluid called the electric flux was once thought to flow from the charge through the surrounding space. A negative divergence is sometimes called a convergence.

A nice interpretation of the divergence field derives from Green's theorem that states

> The volume integral of the divergence of a vector field is equal to the area integral of the same vector field over the closed surface that bounds the volume:

$$\int (\nabla \cdot \mathbf{V})\, \mathrm{d}v = \int \mathbf{V} \cdot \mathbf{dS} \tag{389}$$

where dv is a volume element and **dS** is an area element. In other words, if there is a nonzero flow source contained somewhere within a closed volume, the total outflow from that source must cross through the closed surface which surrounds (bounds) the volume.

Recall that in tensor notation, inner products are represented by repeated indexes with summation. Let **V** be a covariant vector with components v_s. To obtain the divergence of this field, let us first form the rank 2 tensor $v_{s,r}$. The values $v_{s,r}$ are components of the dyad $\nabla\mathbf{V}$, which represents the gradient of the vector field. We now set $s = r$ and sum over the repeated index. However, to carry out this operation, we require a covariant and a contravariant index. We know how to find the contravariant components of **V** given the covariant components; we apply the fundamental tensor and contract

$$v^q = g^{qs} v_s \tag{390}$$

We can now write the divergence of **V** directly as

$$\operatorname{div} \mathbf{V} = v^q_{,q} \tag{391}$$

This exercise reiterates an important point: summation indexes must always occur on covariant-contravariant pairs. One important reason for writing the equations relating the covariant and contravariant components of a tensor through the fundamental tensor is illustrated in the example just given.

Finally, we consider the curl of a vector field **V**. The curl of a vector field is another vector field, sometimes called an axial field. In conventional notation and using Cartesian coordinates, the curl of **V** is written

$$\operatorname{curl} \mathbf{V} = \nabla \times \mathbf{V} = \begin{vmatrix} \mathbf{i} & \mathbf{j} & \mathbf{k} \\ \dfrac{\partial}{\partial x} & \dfrac{\partial}{\partial y} & \dfrac{\partial}{\partial z} \\ V_x & V_y & V_z \end{vmatrix} \tag{392}$$

An older name for curl **V** is the rotation of **V**, abbreviated "rot **V**." This name refers back to the time when physicists thought light transmission occurred as oscillations in a mechanical medium called the luminiferous ether. The curl of any physical vector field, such as the magnetic field, was imagined to represent an actual rotation or vortex in the ether. In the representation of a vortex, the rotational axis is the most natural vector direction to choose. That is why the curl at any given point in the field is treated as an axial vector. Similarly in fluid dynamics, if **V** is the velocity vector in a fluid, then $\nabla \times \mathbf{V}$ represents the rotation or vorticity of the flow.

A nice interpretation of the curl field derives from the theorem that states

> The area integral of the curl of a vector field is equal to the line integral of the same vector field over the closed curve that bounds the area.

In other words, if there are nonzero rotations contained within a closed area, the total circulation around the closed perimeter of the area is the (vector) sum of the individual rotations.

In tensor notation, the components of the curl are written as

$$\text{Components of curl}\,\mathbf{V} \rightarrow v_{i,j} - v_{j,i} \qquad (393)$$

where the indexes i and j take on the values 1, 2, 3 sequentially in pairs:

$$(i,j) = (1,2),(2,3),\text{ and }(3,1) \qquad (394)$$

Relativity

Statement of Core Idea

Every mathematical hypersurface has an intrinsic geometry. Spacetime also has an intrinsic geometry that is measurable by physical measuring rods and physical clocks. Light plays a pivotal role in making these measurements in astronomy and astrophysics because light provides the single means of investigating the characteristics and distributions of objects found in distant regions. If the overall geometry of spacetime determined by light beams cannot be made to match the classical geometry of Euclid, then Euclidean geometry cannot be the intrinsic geometry of spacetime, and another geometry must be discovered from which to draw a mathematical description. Tensor analysis allows us to consider very generalized differential geometries and to investigate how they apply to the universe at large. The merger of differential geometry and spacetime was accomplished in the early 20th century by Dr. Albert Einstein.

From Classical Physics to the Theory of Relativity

The theory of relativity was introduced to the world in 1905. It had been developed initially to correct a contradiction that had developed in physics during the 19th century. The contradiction occurred between the classical mechanics of Newton and the electrodynamics of Maxwell. Maxwell's theory very naturally gave the speed of light as a universal constant; according to Newton, no such universal constant could exist.

When a contradiction occurs in any deductive system,[41] it is typically necessary to examine the postulates on which the system is built. Changing or eliminating one or more of them will usually eliminate the contradiction. The special or limited theory of relativity published in 1905 accomplished its purpose by eliminating two fundamental concepts upon which all classical mechanics rested. These concepts were

1. The existence of absolute space
2. The existence of absolute time

Later, another revision would be introduced: in 1917, the general theory would eliminate the insistence that spacetime be thought of strictly in terms of Euclidean geometry. General relativity took the unprecedented step of conceiving spacetime as curved.

Special relativity essentially agrees with classical mechanics for all speeds except those approaching the speed of light. As a moving system approaches this enormous speed, predictable if somewhat surprising, divergences from classical predictions begin to make themselves felt. Also, whereas classical mechanics imposes no speed restrictions on moving systems, relativity provides that nothing but light itself ever move at the speed of light. Everything else may approach arbitrarily close to the speed of light but must always move at least incrementally slower.

Most students do not grasp the enormity of the speed of light c. Numerically, it is easily written as $c = 3\times10^8$ m/s. Physically, it is the equivalent of circumnavigating the Earth at the equator just under eight complete circuits in 1 sec. If an object is moving at some speed $v < c$, then the error between classical physics and relativity is of the order[42] $½(v/c)^2$. For the orbiting space shuttle, which travels at a nominal speed of 7.4 km/s, $½(v/c)^2 = 3\times10^{-16}$. For the Earth's motion about the Sun, 30 km/s, $½(v/c)^2 = 5\times10^{-15}$.

These numbers demonstrate that relativity does not impose significant restrictions at "everyday" speeds, even those speeds we consider "astronomical." But, for a fundamental particle traveling at 3×10^7 m/s or 0.1 times the speed of light, $½(v/c)^2 = 0.005$. This error is 12 orders of magnitude larger than that for the Earth in its orbit. Laboratory measurements of fundamental particles can detect differences of this size and therefore used to support the theory of relativity.

---

[41]As a whole, physics includes classical mechanics and classical electrodynamics and is the deductive system referred to herein.

[42]Actually, $\sqrt{[1 - (v/c)^2]}$. This term is often referred to as the "contraction factor." By approximation, $\sqrt{[1 - (v/c)^2]} \sim 1 - ½(v/c)^2$. The error is taken here as the second term, $½(v/c)^2$.

Astrophysical measurements also lend credence to relativity. Shortly after its initial publication, general relativity predicted a general expansion of the universe. Einstein seriously doubted this result but it was soon confirmed by observation. The expansion is such that galaxies seen from Earth appear to be receding at speeds proportional to their distances. As one looks outward farther and farther, one reaches a distance at which the speed of recession approaches that of light. Beyond this distance, no telescope will ever be able to see. In other words, there is an observational horizon to the universe as we see it.[43]

Today, NASA's Hubble space telescope sees to somewhere around 75 percent of this distance. Hubble telescope observations allow us to answer some of the most perplexing questions about the large-scale structure of the universe and of spacetime itself. Hubble photographs of distant galaxy fields provide tantalizing clues to the large-scale distribution of matter throughout the universe, the overall curvature of the cosmos, and the conditions that prevailed in the early universe. Hubble's descendants, if any, will enable more information to be gathered as astrophysicists gradually piece together the greatest jigsaw puzzle of them all.

In his 1917 paper introducing general relativity, Einstein laid a radical new foundation for the physics of gravitational fields. Whereas Newton conceived of gravity as an action at a distance between individual pieces of matter, Einstein conceived of it as a location and local time-dependent curvature of spacetime. The notion of curved spacetime can be daunting to the student who is not familiar with it. To grasp the concept, it is helpful on one hand to understand non-Euclidean geometry and on the other hand to understand how non-Euclidean geometry is applied to the world at large.

Until the 19th century, the only geometry available to mathematicians and physicists was that of Euclid. Many investigators had long believed that other geometries were possible, but the first of these other geometries did not appear until the 19th century. The point in question was almost always Euclid's parallel line postulate:

> Through any point outside a given line in space, there is one and only one line that can be drawn which is parallel to the given line.

Some mathematicians believed that this postulate could actually be derived as a theorem and therefore should not be called a postulate. Others believed that it was a postulate but that it could be replaced with a different postulate and the result would be a geometry different from that of Euclid.

In fact, in the 19th century, two such postulates emerged, and they produced two very different but internally consistent non-Euclidean geometries:

> 5.1: Through any point outside a given straight line in space, there is no line that can be drawn which is parallel to the given line; all lines drawn through the point will intersect the given line at some finite distance from the point.
>
> 5.2: Through any point outside a given straight line in space, there are an infinite number of other lines that can be drawn parallel to the given line. These other lines exist between two lines which intersect at a finite angle at the point and which themselves are parallel to the given line (intersecting it, one at $+\infty$ and the other at $-\infty$).

The simplest of the new geometries that resulted from these postulates involved the geometry of spherical surfaces on the one hand (5.1) and pseudospherical surfaces ("saddles") on the other (5.2). Both spheres and pseudospheres are two-dimensional surfaces. The concepts developed about their geometries are readily extended to spaces of n-dimensions. Spherical geometries are geometries of positive curvature[44] and collectively are included under the more general title "elliptical geometry." Pseudospherical geometries are geometries of negative curvature and go collectively under the general title "hyperbolic geometry."

To understand how elliptical geometry is applied, one need look no farther than a ship's navigator. He has to apply the concepts of spherical geometry in his calculations because the geometry of the plane does not work over large distances on the surface of the Earth. The shortest distances between various locations

[43] This statement is true for every observer at every location in the universe. Thus, an observer on my horizon will be able to see objects that lie beyond, objects barred from my instruments by the general expansion. I, in turn, am able to see objects barred from his.

[44] The difference between positive and negative curvatures in this case can be understood in the placement of radii of the surface. All the radii of the sphere lie on the concave side of the surface. The radii of the saddle lie on both sides of the surface. Another way of saying this is that the center of the sphere is a single point in space a finite distance from the surface. The two centers of the pseudosphere lie on opposite sides of the surface.

are not straight lines but the curves of great circles. Two ships on parallel paths along two different constant longitudes will eventually approach each other and collide. These characteristics are easily demonstrated with a felt pen on a toy ball. And a quick glance at any mathematics handbook will reveal the trigonometric formulas for spherical triangles and other figures drawn on the surface of a sphere.

Exploring the geometry of a sphere by drawing figures on a ball will reveal the geometry of the spherical surface but will not necessarily demonstrate that that geometry is intrinsic to the surface. The demonstration with the ball is the equivalent of developing spherical geometry by imagining a mathematical two-dimensional sphere embedded in a three-dimensional Euclidean space. However, the geometry of the spherical surface does not require the three-dimensional Euclidean space for its development; it can be worked out entirely from measurements made within the spherical surface. Hence, we say that it is intrinsic to the surface.

As with the sphere, one can also explore the geometry of the pseudosphere by drawing figures on a saddle. Again, the demonstration involves the saddle being in a Euclidean space, but as with the sphere, the geometry of the saddle is also intrinsic. The usual heuristic model for developing the intrinsic geometry of the sphere and the saddle is to imagine measurements made by a two-dimensional being entirely confined to the surface, in other words, "a shadow person" whose entire universe is the two-dimensional surface.[45]

Although we have been speaking of the sphere and the saddle, the development of elliptic and hyperbolic geometry is not confined to two dimensions. Geometries of an arbitrary number of dimensions are possible and have been developed. It is worthwhile to study two-dimensional surfaces at the beginning because examples of them are so readily available. Once the general concepts begin to be grasped, the extension to higher numbers of dimensions is not altogether difficult.

In general relativity, non-Euclidean geometries become the norm for describing the gravitational field. We say that spacetime is curved, and we are now in a position to grasp what this idea means. First, we assert that there must exist a mathematical space that describes the universe. Elements of the space must correspond with elements or properties of the universe. For Newton, this space perforce was Euclidean. For Einstein, it was non-Euclidean.

> We say that spacetime is curved if and only if the mathematical space that best describes it is non-Euclidean.

In other words, the property of curvature or flatness assigned to spacetime derives from a combination of measurements made within spacetime and the specific geometry to which those measurements can best be fitted.

Let us return momentarily to the sphere. We know from the calculus that an incrementally small element of area behaves as though it were flat. In fact, this behavior is true of any curve, surface, hypersurface, and so on that we encounter in the calculus. A similar statement may be made about spacetime. A carefully chosen local region may be considered Euclidean without incurring a large error in calculation or measurement. This is one important property of spacetime in relativity.

The overall curvature of the sphere is constant; in other words, measurements of curvature made on any portion of the sphere will produce results that match measurements made on any other portion. The overall curvature of the saddle is also constant, but the situation is more complicated for spacetime. A simple heuristic statement of Einstein's law of gravity states that local curvature is logically equivalent to local gravity. But we already know from our classical studies that gravity varies from place to place. Thus, it should be no surprise that curvature varies from place to place and time to time in relativity. It is exactly here that tensor analysis enters the picture.

In the 19th century, a generalized differential geometry was developed to include as special cases the hyperbolic and elliptical geometries we have already encountered and to include all other possibilities as well. That differential geometry is exactly represented in the tensor formalisms that we have been exploring. In general relativity, Einstein essentially fused differential geometry with the physics of the gravitational field. In the process, he produced one of the great revolutions in 20th century thought.

It is reasonable to ask whether nature provides motivation for making such a step into the abstract. The answer is that nature, as understood in the present paradigm of physics, certainly does. The following

[45]The analogue in modern astrophysics is ourselves, four-dimensional beings entirely confined to the four-dimensional hypersurface called spacetime. Our entire universe is the four-dimensional hypersurface.

sections will explore some of those motivations using our understanding as derived from classical mechanics and special relativity.

Parallel straight lines.—In considering the geometry of the universe, one question that I must answer is whether I can produce Euclidean parallel lines (two straight lines with some separation) that may be extended indefinitely without changing their separation and without causing their intersection. We have already established that light is the primary means available for exploring the universe, so I will choose to build my lines out of light "pencils," straight, divergence-free beams of light. To do so, I will choose two divergence-free lasers[46] from my stockroom of ideal physics supplies. From my laboratory on Earth, I then fire two laser beams into space, taking every precaution to ensure that the beams are locally parallel (i.e., they make the same angle locally with a third laser beam set up to intersect the other two), and if these beams were gradually to come together and intersect anyway, even at a distance of hundreds or thousands of light years from Earth, then for a cosmic geometry measured with laser beams, the geometry would be non-Euclidean and space would have to be regarded as something other than classically flat. That is, it would have to be thought of as curved.

Why would I ever expect the beams to come together? Newton certainly was not worried about this problem, but he did not know that light paths are influenced by gravity. He thought that light propagated everywhere in straight lines. The influence of gravity on light propagation was not known until the early 20th century, and then it was worked and reworked by Einstein until it assumed its final form in general relativity.

In special relativity, Einstein showed that mass and energy are equivalent and expressed this equivalence in the famous equation

$$E = mc^2 \tag{395}$$

He also merged the conservation laws of mass and energy into one law:

$$E^2 + p^2c^2 = \text{A constant} \tag{396}$$

where E is total energy, m is mass, c is the speed of light, and p is momentum. Elsewhere, it was demonstrated that light was particulate in nature, propagating in discreet "chunks" called quanta. For light of a given frequency (color) ν in inverse seconds, the associated quantum of energy is $h\nu$, where h is Planck's constant, 6.626×10^{-34} J-sec. Using equation (395), we see immediately that a light quantum must possess a mass equivalent

$$m = \frac{h\nu}{c^2} \tag{397}$$

For blue light with a wavelength of 4000 Å, $h\nu$ is approximately 5×10^{-19} J and m is approximately 5×10^{-36} kg. Since the photons in the laser beams have mass, they must exert a gravitational influence on each other, however small. We should therefore expect the photons in each beam to attract the photons in the other beam so that the two beams will gradually approach one another and eventually intersect.

The conditions and measurements that we made in our Earth-bound laboratory gave no evidence of such a large-scale curvature, at least to within the accuracy of our apparatus. Certainly, Newton could not have been expected to produce any experimental evidence that it existed. And in our day and age, even if we had tracked the beams to well beyond the orbit of Pluto, we might not have detected a significant departure from spatial flatness. Even if we had tracked the laser beams out past Alpha Centauri,[47] we would probably have seen nothing to deter us from a sound conviction that Euclid's geometry applied perfectly well to the geometry of space as measured by laser beams. However, if we follow them far enough, eventually we will be able to observe that they really do approach one another and finally intersect. The overall average curvature of the universe can only be determined by making observations over cosmological distances.

We might argue that using laser beams to observe the geometry of the universe was a bad choice. Surely, there must be some means to make observations without invoking curvature. But what else could we use? Light beams are the straightest beams that we can produce. Since even they curve, then the Euclidean

[46] Real laser beams diverge over distance (i.e., their beam diameter increases). A laser fired from the Earth to the Moon will illuminate a spot on the Moon many times larger in diameter than the original beam. For the sake of this argument, such divergence is to be ignored.

[47] A very rough approximation shows that for an initial separation of 1 mm, baring all other perturbing factors, the laser beams would intersect at a nominal distance of 5×10^9 light years from Earth.

straight line is reduced to a mere theoretical abstraction with no counterpart at all in nature. It appears that even a naïve argument is sufficient to bring our classical notions of geometry as it relates to the universe into serious question, at least insofar as understanding observations made with light beams over cosmological distances.

The finite speed of light imposes another constraint on the geometry of the straight line. In college, we took no issue with the idea of extending a line to infinity. To do so would imply either infinite time or an instantaneous extension. We do not have infinite time, and nothing known to physics can exceed the speed of light. So, the idea of infinite extension has no counterpart in physics. Even the gravitational influence cannot propagate from place to place at greater than light speed. A mass disturbance[48] in one part of the universe is felt in another part removed from the disturbance by a distance x only at a time x/c after it originally occurred.

The geometrical point.—As with the physical production of Euclidean parallel lines, we now ask about the physical production of Euclidean geometrical points. Classical physics uses point mass representations of extended objects as the sites to which external forces and torques attach. It also uses point masses and point charges to represent fundamental particles.

A geometrical point has no size at all; its radius is zero. Consider a point mass. The definition of a point mass is a single field point with a mass value attached to it. For example, if the field point is the center of mass of a launch vehicle, then all the forces on the vehicle are assumed to act through the point.

Now consider a sphere of radius r possessing a mass m distributed in some arbitrary way throughout its volume. Take the limit as $r \to 0$ and the result should be a point mass. But what other characteristics should we examine before blithely accepting this idea? Consider mass density, mass per unit volume. As $r \to 0$, density $\to \infty$, regardless of how much or how little mass we start out with. Anything other than zero initial mass produces an infinite density in the limit.

Physical theories are built of numbers and their relationships. Can we admit an infinite quantity into the realm of physics? We can only if infinity is also a number. Mathematicians have investigated infinity for a long time. Although they have a great deal to say about its unusual properties, it seems clear that it cannot be regarded as a number. Thus, it can have no place in physics. The point mass with infinite density, therefore, cannot be admitted into physical theory.

The point mass also has an infinite surface energy density and an infinite surface gravity. There would seem to be many strokes against the point mass as being anything other than a theoretical abstraction or a kind of fiction that can be used in doing calculations based on the dubious premise that it works. Einstein sought a way around this dilemma in his later work by trying to write the equations of general relativity such that finite-sized fundamental particles would emerge as natural solutions to the field equations. He never succeeded.

Fundamental particles are another concept that should give physicists heartburn. For a particle to be fundamental, it must exist in the simplest possible terms in the sense that such irreducible ratios of integers as 2/3 or 4/15 exist in the simplest possible terms. Let us assume that fundamental particles do exist in nature. We then inquire specifically about their size. There are two possibilities:

1. They possess no size, having zero radius, so they are truly point objects. On the basis of the infinities already cited, we have already argued against point objects in nature. A similar argument could have been made for charge or for any other quantity.
2. They possess finite size; however, if they possess finite size, however small, then they can no longer be fundamental because they can be reduced to parts, an interior and a surface. One may then ask about the structure, state, and composition of the surface and, similarly, about the overall constitution of the interior.

Thus, it appears that neither point objects nor fundamental particles have realizations in the physical world. They exist in the realm of theoretical concepts only. As such, it is arguable that they have no formal place in physics if the concepts of physics are to

[48]Physicists have sought to measure gravitational waves propagating from mass dipoles, such as large binary stars. Newtonian physics was silent on the issue of gravitational propagation. Most undergraduate physics students are taught to assume that the gravitational influence is felt everywhere at the same time. Some think that the issue of propagation is best reserved for more advanced cosmological discussions. However, a disturbance on our Sun would not be felt by an observer on the planet Pluto until 5.5 hr after it had occurred—and the distance to Pluto is hardly cosmological.

correspond with measurable aspects of the world at large.[49]

Ability to move figures about without any distortion in their shape and size.—We have already spoken of spherical and hyperbolic geometry. The sphere and the pseudosphere specifically are spaces of constant curvature, as is the plane (a space of zero curvature). In each of these surfaces, figures can be moved about without experiencing any distortion in shape and size. But we also know of surfaces that do not possess this property, surfaces that have variable curvature, such as the surface of an egg. What geometry applies to the surface of an egg? If we were to begin by considering a small enough region (an elemental area) of the egg over which the curvature could be thought of as approximately constant, then spherical or even Euclidean geometry could be used throughout that region to whatever level of accuracy we wished. We could map the entire egg by carefully selecting small adjacent regions and making similar applications of geometry in each. But the overall geometry of the egg, the one obtained when we tried to put all the individual results together into one piece, would be something quite different from what our local observations on their own might have suggested.

With regard to mapping the entire egg, we would find, for example, that there were certain directions on the egg along which geometrical figures could be transported without distortion. Along these directions we would be able to prove concepts such as theorems of congruency and similarity just as we do in the plane, the sphere, and the saddle. However, there would be other directions, orthogonal to this first group, along which transportation of figures could not be accomplished without their requiring significant bending, stretching, or even tearing. Along these directions, theorems of congruency and similarity would be strictly out of the question.

So what about real world figures? Can they be moved about without distortion to their shape and size? A perfectly rigid object can be so moved. In fact, we could define a perfectly rigid object as being one that could be taken from place to place without experiencing any distortions in shape and size. However, perfectly rigid objects do not exist, or if they do, we have no knowledge of them. All real material objects experience nonzero stresses and strains when subjected to material transport. The stresses arise because of time-variable external forces that play across the object. The strains are concomitant geometric distortions. Even objects left stationary will sag with time simply because of their own weight, an example being the wavy glass so highly prized by antique collectors.

These changes in real objects suggest that not only is space curved but, perhaps, so is time. Euclidean geometry has now failed to provide an adequate foundation for thinking about the real world on several counts. The errors in correspondence may be small, but they are not negligible. Einstein's response was to eliminate Euclidean geometry from physical theory and to replace it with non-Euclidean geometry, specifically, a differentially metric geometry wherein local curvature depended on the observer's position and time.

The geometry of general relativity was the brainchild of Bernhard Riemann (1826–1866) and others. The differential geometry that they formulated resulted from their mapping the various individual non-Euclidean geometries onto the theory of partial differential equations. The result, differential geometry, was a grand abstraction that stood in relation to non-Euclidean geometry much as René Descartes' (1506–1650) mapping of planar geometry onto the theory of algebra stood in relation to Euclid. Also, just as earlier investigators in physics spoke of motion in the plane or in a Cartesian space, so 20th century investigators learned to speak of motion in a Riemannian differentially metric spacetime.

The geometry of the theory of relativity cannot be drawn out on paper except for a few special cases. The beauty of differential geometry is that drawing is not necessary because it can represent the most general and most complicated geometric concepts using only pure mathematics. This symbology is incorporated in the indicial notation (along with the associated concepts) that we have been learning in the algebra and calculus sections of this work.

---

[49]If we define an interaction boundary as any n-dimensional surface across which dynamical information (such as momentum or energy) is exchanged and specify that this information may only be exchanged in discreet bundles or quanta of finite size, then we have a natural definition of a particle as the smallest bundle of information that may be exchanged across a given boundary under a given set of conditions. We may have particles of spin, translational energy, momentum, mass, charge, and so on. This type of definition eliminates all questions about what (if anything) actually moves through space from point to point or region to region. We cannot note the progress of a particle through space (as a little hard object, the classical view) without perturbing it in some way, that is, without placing an interaction boundary or a whole series of interaction boundaries in its path. Doing so destroys the very motion that we are trying to observe (Heisenberg's uncertainty principle).

Relativity

The special theory of relativity was introduced by Einstein in 1905. In reformulating the laws of physics, the theory eliminated absolute space and time. Newton had introduced absolute space and time to serve as a reference system in which events took place. Absolute space was rigid and Euclidean. Absolute time ticked away throughout all the ages, independent of events in the universe at large.

Absolute space and time were akin to a theatrical stage on which the actors played out their roles. Remove all matter from the universe and the stage remained behind unaffected. For Newton, empty space had a reality independent of matter. Together, absolute space and time formed an inertial frame of reference. Any frame of reference in unaccelerated relative motion with respect to the absolute frame was also inertial. All accelerated frames were non-inertial and subject to pseudoaccelerations, such as Coriolis and centrifugal.

We see the ideas of Newton aptly played out in the television series Star Trek in which it is possible to bring the ship to absolute rest. The command "All stop" might well be issued on a ship or a submarine on Earth, and in terms of Newtonian philosophy, it makes sense for motion in space as well. But in terms of modern physics, the command has no meaning. Modern physics eliminates all absolute reference systems; thus, it only makes sense to stop relative to some known spatial marker whose motion relative to other markers may or may not be known.

Newton argued that the inertia of a body, its resistance to a change in its state of rest or absolute motion in a straight line, arose when the body was subjected to a nonzero net force that made it accelerate relative to absolute space. The inertia of any given object was for Newton a constant associated with that object. In an accelerated frame, he claimed that so-called inertial forces (pseudoaccelerations times mass) appear and become operative. He tried to demonstrate this notion by using a rotating bucket of water (Hawking, 2002).

Recall that rotation involves centripetal acceleration. The bucket and water were initially placed at rest. The surface of the water was observed to be flat. Then the bucket was set rotating. At first the water initially remained at rest. But as the bucket continued to spin, the water began to acquire a rotation of its own. Finally, the bucket and the water rotated at the same rate. Newton observed that as the water's rotation increased, its surface become more concave due to centrifugal forces operating in the rotating frame of reference. He argued that this response was due to the water's motion relative to absolute space, not relative to the bucket since the water was initially unaffected by the bucket's motion.

Ernst Mach (Mach, 1960) argued against absolute space and time. He correctly noted that there was no adequate means for demonstrating their existence. He believed, however, that acceleration relative to the fixed stars could account for the inertial forces in accelerated frames. The fixed stars set up an "inertial field" throughout all space. Objects responded locally to that field. Einstein noted that such a concept distinguished itself from that of Newton in that the inertia of an object would increase if ponderable masses were piled up in its neighborhood. Such an increase in inertia had no place in Newton's system.

Einstein appreciated Mach's thoroughly modern idea and tried hard to incorporate it in his general theory but never had complete success. Mach's principle (so called by Einstein) stated that distant matter in the universe determined those local conditions under which objects exhibited inertia. Remove all matter from the universe except one test piece, and the inertia of the test piece vanishes. In the case of rotation, with all the rest of the matter gone, there is simply nothing left relative to which to rotate! Remember that Einstein had abandoned Newton's absolute time and space right from the outset.

The consequences of the rotating bucket experiment are very different for Einstein than for Newton. For Einstein and Newton both, the water recedes the same from the axis of rotation as the rate of spin increases. However, if all the matter in the universe were removed except for the bucket, Newton's theory would predict that the water would behave exactly the same as it had with the matter present; Einstein's theory predicts that there would be no change in the surface from its initial flat state.

Unfortunately, there is no way to directly test these notions, but recent experiments with orbiting spacecraft have tested a related phenomenon: gravitational frame dragging. The idea is that a large rotating mass sets up a gravitational field whose overall geometry is affected by the rotation. Newton's theory predicts that the rotation should have no effect on the field geometry. Experiment appears to have decided in favor of Einstein and relativity.

The Special Theory

In the 18th and 19th centuries, a definite ferment was brewing in physics. Many brilliant thinkers sought alternate formulations of Newton's laws to allow classical mechanics to be placed on a foundation other than that chosen by Newton. They believed that the predictions of classical mechanics were correct but that the basic laws themselves needed reformulation. Of these other systems of mechanics, those attributed to Joseph Lagrange (1736–1813) and William Rowen Hamilton (1805–1865) are the best known and most often used. As the advanced student of physics already knows, each man's theory of mechanics involves finding the extremum of an integral involving either energy or momentum. The solutions in each particular case provide the investigator with equations of motion for that case.

Also, in the 19th century, James Clerk Maxwell, a Scottish mathematician and physicist (1831–1879), developed the theory of electromagnetism. This theory made the astonishing prediction that the speed of propagation of electromagnetic waves in free space was a universal constant. That any speed could have this property directly contradicted Newton's kinematics and posed a major problem for the unity of physics. Other issues in physics were also to arise with the advent of Maxwell's theory but they do not directly concern us here. Suffice it to say, physics was suddenly confronted with a startling contradiction that arose despite the apparently complete success of both theories to explain nature in all other aspects.

We have already shown that from the point of view of classical mechanics, the velocity $\mathbf{v}$ of a particle as observed from an inertial reference frame K differs from the velocity $\mathbf{v}^*$ of the same particle as observed from another inertial reference frame K^* in uniform relative motion at velocity $\mathbf{v}_0$ by $\mathbf{v}_0$:

$$\mathbf{v}^* = \mathbf{v} + \mathbf{v}_0 \tag{398}$$

This equation is sometimes referred to as the law of combining velocities or the law of addition of velocities. As a law of physics (even though the term law applies loosely here), it must hold in all possible circumstances. If even a single instance can be found for which it does not hold, then it must be declared false by counterexample, regardless of how well it works in all other cases. If false, then it must also be replaced by another law that holds in all the original cases and holds for the counterexample, too.

The counterexample to the law of combining velocities (and therefore to classical mechanics) arose directly from electromagnetic theory. James Clerk Maxwell gave us the now-famous four equations (laws) relating electric and magnetic fields. These laws are to the science of electromagnetics what Newton's three laws of motion are to classical mechanics. Both sets of laws are so fundamental that they may be regarded as foundational to physics as a whole. In other words, it should be possible to derive all the phenomena of physics from either set taken alone. To do so appeared possible except for the phenomenon of light. Maxwell's theory predicted a universal speed for light propagation that had no place in Newton's theory. Newton's theory applied the law of combining velocities to light as it did to everything else with results that had no place in Maxwell's theory. Here is how Maxwell's prediction came about.

From the four equations of the electromagnetic field, Maxwell derived a single wave equation from which a complete theoretical description of the properties of light and other electromagnetic phenomena was made possible. The veracity of this brilliant effort was first attested to experimentally by Heinrich Hertz (1857–1894), the first experimenter to generate and detect electromagnetic waves in the laboratory and to characterize their properties. From the combined work of Maxwell and Hertz, the age of radio broadcasting had its humble beginnings.

Maxwell's wave equation appears at first glance like any other wave equation, involving second partial derivatives of field parameters with respect to space and time. The issue that concerns us here first arises with the incorporation of certain electromagnetic constants in the equation. These constants are also present in the original four equations and provide fundamental descriptions of the electric and magnetic characteristics of spacetime. From the outset of solving the wave equation, these constants combine to give a speed, which is specifically the speed of electromagnetic wave propagation. The constants are the permittivity ε_0 and the permeability μ_0 of free space. They combine to give a speed of propagation c in free space where

$$c^2 = \frac{1}{\varepsilon_0 \mu_0} \tag{399}$$

Because ε_0 and μ_0 are universal constants, the speed c must be a universal constant, which means that it must have exactly the same value for all observers regardless of their states of relative motion.

In Newton's theory, a light source traveling at speed v relative to an observer ought to produce light waves along the direction of motion whose speed c^* is given by $c^* = c \pm v$, a result to which Maxwell's theory issues a resounding "no!" A fundamental disagreement between two foundational theories of physics meant that somewhere in the vast body of mechanical and electromagnetic thought there must exist a flaw. Something required revision, but what? As the century turned, this question was addressed on a variety of fronts simultaneously and without success.

The necessary revision in physics was ultimately accomplished by Albert Einstein. In 1905 he published in the German physics journal *Annalen der Physik* his paper entitled "On the Electrodynamics of Moving Bodies," and the new theory it advanced became known as the theory of special relativity. Special relativity is built upon only two postulates:

1. All motion is relative (i.e., there is no absolute frame of reference).
2. The speed of light in vacuo is a universal constant for all observers.

The first postulate eliminates absolute space and absolute time. The second postulate places the constancy of the speed of light beyond all question in relativity since the postulates of a given system of thought must be accepted as true a priori.

Since light speed must be the same for all observers, Einstein sought a set of coordinate transformations between observers in uniform relative motion in a Euclidean spacetime for which the constancy of light speed would hold true in a "natural" way. The transformations he derived were later named the Einstein-Lorentz transformations or, simply, the Lorentz transformations after Hendrik Antoon Lorentz (1853–1928), who had earlier derived the same transformations but for entirely the wrong reasons.

One immediate outcome of Einstein's new theory was that space and time could no longer be considered separate entities but must now be thought of as a single fused entity, first christened "spacetime" in the early 20th century by Hermann Minkowski (1864–1909). As for the constancy of the speed of light in spacetime, spacetime must have an intrinsic geometry such that the speed of light being a universal constant emerges quite naturally as a consequence.

In the simple case of two spacetime coordinate systems (Cartesian) in uniform relative motion v along their common x-axes, the Lorentz transformations look like

$$\begin{aligned} x^* &= \frac{x - vt}{\sqrt{1 - \dfrac{v^2}{c^2}}} \\ y^* &= y \\ z^* &= z \\ t^* &= \frac{t - \left(\dfrac{v}{c^2}\right)x}{\sqrt{1 - \dfrac{v^2}{c^2}}} \end{aligned} \tag{400}$$

In essence, the three components of space (x, y, z) and the single component of time t are now to be thought of as components of a four-dimensional rank 1 tensor called (in some texts) a four-vector usually represented (x, y, z, ct).[50] What remains the same for all observers is the four-vector because it is coordinate independent and its components (which are coordinate dependent) are the components of a tensor in Euclidean four-space. With the advent of special relativity, all time and space measurements become subject to "peculiar" variations depending on the relative uniform motions of the observers. The famous time dilatation and length contraction are two such effects.

The magnitude of the spacetime four-vector is a rank 0 tensor s that satisfies the relation

$$s^2 = -x^2 - y^2 - z^2 + c^2t^2 \tag{401}$$

You may verify that $s = s^*$ by using the transformation equations (400).[51] The usual form of the Lorentz transformations uses the differential quantity ds rather than the integral quantity s. We may reformulate the Lorentz transformations using coordinate differentials:

[50]The speed of light is used to multiply the time component for dimensional consistency. Thus, time is measured in meters rather than in seconds.

[51]On the other hand, the usual Pythagorean theorem does not work with the Lorentz transformations; that is, the quantity $x^2 + y^2 + z^2 + c^2t^2$ is not an invariant.

$$dx^* = \frac{dx - v\,dt}{\sqrt{1 - \frac{v^2}{c^2}}}$$

$$dy^* = dy \tag{402}$$

$$dz^* = dz$$

$$dt^* = \frac{dt - \left(\frac{v}{c^2}\right)dx}{\sqrt{1 - \frac{v^2}{c^2}}}$$

Then

$$\left(ds^2\right) = -\left(dx^2\right) - \left(dy^2\right) - \left(dz^2\right) + c^2\left(dt^2\right) \tag{403}$$

and for observers K and K^*, we write

$$ds^* = ds \tag{404}$$

Using the fundamental tensor and recalling that $(ds)^2 = g_{jk}dx^j dx^k$, we may equivalently write

$$g^*_{st}\,dx^{*s}\,dx^{*t} = g_{jk}\,dx^j\,dx^k \tag{405}$$

The expression $(ds)^2 = g_{jk}dx^j dx^k$ is usually presented as the generalized Lorentz transformation.

By examining the expression for $(ds)^2$, we see that in special relativity, the fundamental tensor $\underline{\mathbf{G}}$ must have the form

$$\underline{\mathbf{G}} = \begin{vmatrix} -1 & 0 & 0 & 0 \\ 0 & -1 & 0 & 0 \\ 0 & 0 & -1 & 0 \\ 0 & 0 & 0 & c^2 \end{vmatrix} \tag{406}$$

and that it must be the same for all observers (since each of its nonzero components is a constant).

As with previous arguments that we have already encountered throughout this text, it is reasonable to imagine that this tensor might be generalized in both its diagonal and off-diagonal terms. This generalization is necessary for representing accelerated motion in special relativity and for representing the action of the gravitational field in general relativity. Special relativity, with the fundamental tensor given by equation (406), is correct only for unaccelerated motion. The first generalization would involve replacing three of the diagonal terms with the more general symbols g_{11}, g_{22}, g_{33}, leaving the c^2 term and the zeros as they appear in equation (406). The second generalization would involve replacing the zeros and the c^2 term with terms of the form g_{ij}, where the indices i and j each range over the values 1 through 4. This latter generalization was worked out by Einstein over the years between 1905 and 1917. (The history of his thinking throughout these years makes interesting reading.)

> An equivalent way of saying what we just said above is that in special relativity, the gravitational field is tacitly assumed to vanish (to equal zero everywhere throughout the space of consideration). Equivalently, the spacetime of special relativity is flat; that is, it is a Euclidean manifold.

The vanishing of the gravitational field imposes a very definite and unrealistic physical limitation on the overall theory. It was long accepted from astronomical observations that gravity plays a ubiquitous role throughout the universe. Therefore, a gravity-free spacetime, while teaching us a great deal about local phenomena (where the effects of gravity may be ignored), could never be equal to the task of providing an adequate model of the universe at large.

The next question after the founding of special relativity, therefore, became how to overcome this limitation and to introduce gravity into relativity. Einstein's thinking on this problem makes fascinating reading, but here I will just summarize his conclusions:

> Special relativity deals largely with uniform motion in gravity-free spacetime. The spacetime of special relativity is a four-dimensional Euclidean manifold or E_4. As such, it is flat in the sense that the Euclidean plane is flat: it has a curvature equal to 0 inverse square meters (0 m^{-2}). The postulates of Euclidean geometry hold throughout the spacetime. Parallel lines exist in the usual way; figures may be moved without distortion, and so on. If zero curvature corresponds to zero gravitational field, then what does nonzero curvature correspond to? Einstein discovered, after years of tedious calculation, that the key to understanding the gravitational field was to relax the restriction of using only a flat or Euclidean spacetime and to use non-Euclidean or curved spacetime. The gravitational field is equivalent to

the curvature field everywhere throughout the spacetime. This concept is a cornerstone of general relativity. The curvature at any point in the field is dependent on the mass-energy density at that point; hence, geometry and the material universe become fused into a single entity. No longer do we speak of the geometry of spacetime independently of matter or of matter independently of geometry.

The General Theory

The classical gravitational field is peculiar among the fields of classical physics in that it is an acceleration field. The field term **g** is a radially oriented vector with kinematic units of acceleration (meters per square second). Other fields have dynamic units, such as the electric field **E** (volts per meter, where the volt is equivalent to a joule per coulomb of electric charge) and the magnetic field **H** (amperes per meter, where the ampere is equivalent to the flow of a coulomb of electric charge per second past a given point).

Although the theory of magnetism does not admit the existence of magnetic charges,[52] the theory of electricity does.[53] So it is possible to select an isolated charge (often called a test charge), place it into an electric field, and observe its response to local field conditions. Since, but for exceptional cases, the charge accelerates, we assert that a force must be exerted on the charge by (through) the field. For example, the force **f** on a test charge q in an electric field **E** is a vector given by

$$\mathbf{f} = q\mathbf{E} \tag{407}$$

Since, by Newton's Law, the acceleration **a** of the test charge due to any force acting on it is given by $\mathbf{f} = m\mathbf{a}$, where m is the inertial mass of the test charge, we must have

$$\mathbf{a} = \left(\frac{q}{m}\right)\mathbf{E} \tag{408}$$

In other words, to acquire the acceleration of the test charge at a point, the field term must be multiplied by a scalar term representing the ratio of charge to mass. This ratio is important since it represents the ratio of the quantity (charge) being acted upon by the field to the inertia (resistance to acceleration) associated with the particular quantity.

For the magnetic field, the situation is complicated by the nonexistence of free magnetic charges. However, it is possible to speak of magnetic pole strength p and to use it in a way analogous to the test electric charge.[54] A magnetic test pole p in a magnetic field **H** will experience a force **f** such that

$$\mathbf{f} = p\mathbf{H} \tag{409}$$

This expression yields a formal acceleration for the pole of

$$\mathbf{a} = \left(\frac{p}{m}\right)\mathbf{H} \tag{410}$$

where m is the inertial mass associated with the magnetic pole. Again, to acquire the acceleration of the test pole at a point, the field term must be multiplied by a scalar term representing the ratio of pole strength to mass.

For the gravitational field, we again have free masses, analogous to the free charges encountered in the electric field. Therefore, we may speak of a gravitational test mass μ as the mass acted upon by the gravitational field exactly as the test charge q was acted upon by the electric field or the test pole p was acted upon by the magnetic field. We then have

$$\mathbf{f} = \mu\mathbf{g} \tag{411}$$

Since, by Newton's Law, the acceleration of the test mass due to any force acting on it is $\mathbf{a} = \mathbf{f}/m$, we must have

$$\mathbf{a} = \left(\frac{\mu}{m}\right)\mathbf{g} \tag{412}$$

As before, the field term is multiplied by a scalar term representing the ratio of gravitational mass to inertial mass (the ratio of the mass being acted upon by the gravitational field to the inertia of the test object).

With the argument presented in this fashion, there is no apparent reason for demanding that gravitational mass be equal to inertial mass or $\mu = m$. In fact, experience with the electric and magnetic fields teaches us to expect just the opposite. So, that this

[52]It does not admit to the existence of separate magnetic charges because of Maxwell's equation $\nabla \cdot \mathbf{H} = 0$; that is, there is nowhere a point from which the field diverges.

[53]By contrast, $\nabla \cdot \mathbf{E} = \rho/\varepsilon_0$, where ρ is the local charge density.

[54]Magnetic pole strength is found more in older physics texts. Modern texts treat these problems in such a way as to not invoke this idea.

equality actually exists in nature and has been demonstrated experimentally in a variety of ways, is most amazing. The gravitational field becomes even more peculiar in having not only a kinematical field term but the identity of the gravitational and inertial masses.[55]

The identity of gravitational and inertial masses means that $\mu/m = 1$ and that the acceleration of the test mass is actually identical to the field term multiplied by the dimensionless scalar unity:

$$\mathbf{a} = \mathbf{g} \tag{413}$$

Thus, no other measurement is necessary for determining the local gravitational field than directly observing the acceleration of a test particle. Not only that, all test particles will have the same acceleration regardless of the inertial mass that they carry. An elephant and a feather will both accelerate at the same rate in a gravitational field, even though in an electric field, a charged elephant would accelerate at a ponderously slow rate while an equally charged feather would be whisked out of sight in the blink of an eye.

Another way to state the same argument is to say that the force on a test object at a point in the gravitational field is proportional to its mass.[56] The greater the mass, the greater the force; the acceleration remains the same for all. This is not the case with either the electric field or the magnetic field. For these latter two fields, mass does not enter the picture at all until one seeks to find the acceleration; then it enters as a ratio only as the charge to mass or pole strength to mass.

At this point, you are asked to reread the earlier section entitled "First Steps Toward a Tensor Calculus: An Example From Classical Mechanics." The Coriolis and centrifugal fields that arose in the rotating frame of reference are strangely similar to the gravitational field in terms of what we have just been talking about. The Coriolis field term is an acceleration that has a magnitude $2\omega v$ and kinematic units of acceleration (meters per square second). The same statement holds true for the centrifugal field term $\omega^2 r$.

Also, in a rotating frame of reference, if the force acting on a test object is due to the presence of a Coriolis or a centrifugal field, it is proportional to the inertial mass of the test object. Any test object placed at a point in a Coriolis or centrifugal field will experience the same acceleration regardless of the amount of mass it possesses. The pseudoaccelerations and the gravitational field seem to possess suspiciously similar properties. Gravitation behaves more like a pseudoacceleration than as the type of field obtained from a point charge or magnetic pole.

These statements hold the clue to Einstein's revision of the mechanics and mathematics of gravitation and the gravitational field. Mathematically, the pseudofields arise in accelerated frames of reference because the base vectors in those frames have nonzero derivatives. Gravitation arises in the space surrounding a mass concentration for exactly the same reason. The nonzero derivatives in the rotating frame of reference arose because of the rotation; the nonzero derivatives in the gravitational field arise because of the local curvature of the intrinsic geometry.

Now, how does the foregoing discussion relate to tensors? We simply observe here that the tensor algebra and tensor calculus that we have been developing had no restrictions whatever imposed upon them with regard to the types of spaces to which they would apply. I will here state without proof that they apply to all possible spaces no matter how they are curved and that their equations appear in exactly the same form as we have already seen them developed in the preceding pages. One of the real powers of tensor analysis is that it is extremely general.

Curvature of space around the Sun.—Let us demonstrate that space in the vicinity of the Sun is curved. We will assume a Newtonian context and the result that light has mass. First, imagine the Sun alone in space. Now pass a Euclidean straight line through the poles of the Sun and extend the line outward in either direction to an arbitrary distance. Place three astronauts (α, β, and ε) far from the Sun at the vertices of a triangle such that the line from the Sun passes through the centroid of the triangle. Let the triangle be sufficiently large so that we may pass the Sun through the center without its actually touching the legs of the triangle.

Now, let each astronaut have a mirror and one astronaut also have an ideal[57] laser. The astronaut shines the laser at her neighbor who reflects it to his

[55]Another way to see this argument is to understand that inertia is the resistance of a particle of matter to a change in its state of rest or uniform motion. This resistance has nothing whatsoever to do with gravity. Gravitational mass, on the other hand, is that mass which is acted upon by an external gravitational field (and is also responsible for the particle's own gravitational field). From the classical point of view, that these two should be the same quantity is even more astonishing.

[56]This statement inverts the customary roles played by mass and acceleration: mass is usually the constant of proportionality and force is usually said to be proportional to the acceleration.

[57]Ideal laser has a beam divergence of zero.

neighbor who, in turn, reflects it back to the first astronaut. We have now physically constructed a triangle in space. Each astronaut measures the angle between the local incident and reflected beams. When the three angles are added together, their sum is 180°, which we should expect.

Next, move the center of the Sun onto the centroid of the triangle without disturbing the positions of the astronauts (we can do so because this is a thought experiment only). We know from special relativity that light has mass and that it must therefore be affected by the Sun's gravitational field. In fact, using nothing more than classical calculations,[58] we find that the legs of the triangle now curve inward toward the Sun (see the following sketch). For the astronauts to keep their beams aimed at each other's mirrors, they must slightly adjust their mirrors to reflect each of the triangle legs outward relative to its original position.

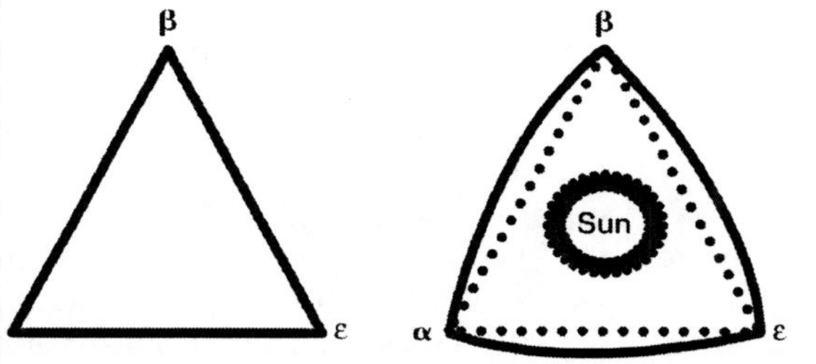

The triangle itself now appears to have outwardly curved rather than straight legs, and the sum of its interior angles is more than 180°. If we shrink the triangle, bringing everybody closer to the Sun, the discrepancy grows larger. If we move everybody outward away from the Sun, the discrepancy becomes smaller. In this naïve argument, the triangle looks like a spherical triangle and space near the Sun appears to be bent into an elliptical geometry, the more so the closer to the Sun.

This thought experiment clearly illustrates that space near the Sun (or by extension near any star or mass concentration) should be expected to be curved, the more so the closer to the Sun or field-generating mass. It also suggests that space far from any field-generating mass should be Euclidean or approximately Euclidean. Special relativity, when linked with Newton's theory of gravity, was already pointing the way to the revision in our concept of space and time, which was finally completed in general relativity.

Now that we know to expect curvature near a massive object, the question becomes one of restating this expectation in rigorous mathematical terms. It was this restatement that cost Einstein so many years of investigation until he arrived at the correct formulation of general relativity.

Curvature of time near a black hole.—Time near a field-generating mass is also curved. The most extreme case of curvature is that near the event horizon of a black hole. A black hole is the remnant of a star that has undergone catastrophic gravitational collapse. The event horizon is the finite (ideally spherically symmetric) region upon whose surface the escape speed equals the speed of light in free space. (Free space is an ideal space in which there are no fields of any kind or for which all the field values equal zero; there is no such space in nature according to most modern thinkers).

The speed of light varies from its free-space value when a gravitational field is present. D. W. Sciama (1926–1969), in The Physical Foundations of General Relativity (Sciama, 1969), visualized the gravitational field as possessing an index of refraction n analogous to the index of refraction possessed by matter. In matter, the index of refraction is a number that permits us to estimate how much the path of a beam of light will bend (refract) at the surface. For free space, the index is set at unity: $n_0 = 1$. For all other matter, $n > 1$. For glass, $n \sim 1.6$ and for diamond, $n \sim 2.5$.

Light also travels more slowly in matter than it does in free space. The speed of light in matter with an index of refraction n is c/n where c is the speed of light in free space, or 3×10^8 m/s. Thus, in glass, $c_g = (3\times10^8 \text{ m/s})/1.6 = 1.9\times10^8$ m/s; in diamond, $c_d = 1.2\times10^8$ m/s. The more refractive the substance, the greater its index of refraction.

The refractivity of space in the gravitational field varies directly with the gravitational field strength: it increases as one approaches the field-generating mass. The bending of light spoken of in the previous section may be thought of as being due to the astronauts' light pencils passing through a region of variable refractive index, increasing as the pencil approached and decreasing as the pencil receded from the Sun. Along with bending, there would also be a variation in the speed of light.[59] This variation may be used to illustrate the curvature of time.

[58] Einstein actually made a similar calculation for light grazing the surface of the Sun. Although correct qualitatively, the result he obtained using this method differed by a factor of 2 from that later obtained from the general theory.

[59] Satellite radar measurements involving the Sun and inner planets have confirmed this variation.

Assume that there are two astronauts stationed in the vicinity of a black hole. One astronaut α is safely at an observation post well outside the hole's gravitational influence (i.e., where the field of the hole does not differ significantly from the fields of other nearby objects in the astronaut's vicinity). The other astronaut β is at a post close to the hole's event horizon.

Each astronaut has a clock and a mechanism for signaling her partner. When the astronauts were together (i.e., before they parted company to go to their respective observation posts), they compared their clocks and found them to be identical in every way; particularly, they found them to run at identical, uniform rates of exactly one tick per second. Each clock was also equipped with a signaling device: at each tick, the clock would emit a pulse of directed laser light that would be sent to the partner astronaut for observation.

Now settled in at their respective stations, the individual astronauts each record that their situations are nominal from their respective points of view. We might be surprised at this, particularly in the case of astronaut β. But then we realize that both astronauts are in orbit around the hole (lest they plummet into the hole) and that being in orbit is equivalent to being in free fall. The astronaut near the hole is therefore not particularly disturbed by the immense gravitational field in her vicinity. Only the fact that the local field varies significantly in magnitude from her head to her toes[60] causes any real discomfort. She feels that she is being mercilessly stretched and realizes that there is nothing she can do about it.[61]

Now each astronaut observes the other. Astronaut α records that β's clock appears very red in color and is running very slowly compared with her own. By her own local measure, many minutes slip by between respective pulses from β's clock. Astronaut α's own clock, of course, continues to run quite normally, emitting one pulse each second as the seconds tick by.

Astronaut α evaluates the situation. She realizes that the light photons are red shifted as they climb out of the immense gravity well below her because they are conserving energy. As gravitational potential energy increases, photon energy decreases.[62] Photon energy is directly measured by frequency. The lower the energy, the lower the frequency. She also remembers that the speed of light is much slower in the gravity well where β is situated than it is at her station. As β's light pulses are emitted, therefore, they start out slowly then speed up as they ascend, and the distance x between successive pulses dramatically increases. Thus, the time interval x/c between arrival of individual pulses also increases.

Astronaut α further reasons that although the clocks were identical when they were side by side, they no longer appear to be identical and in fact no longer have to be thought of as being identical. Astronaut α is not in a classical universe. Refractive effects make direct telescopic observation of β's exact distance from her quite impossible. And she has no other absolute standard of measure, no rigid ruler, to deploy toward the hole to ascertain β's distance. Any material ruler dropped toward the hole would be stretched out of shape as it descended because of the severe local gravity gradients it would encounter. It would be misshapen beyond any usefulness long before ever reaching β's position.

Still, astronaut α is able to compare the light pulses of astronaut β's clock with those of her own as she observes them both in her local reference frame. She concludes that the clock near the event horizon may just as well be thought of as running slow compared with her own. Moreover, having observed β's entire descent into the field, she concludes that the rate of β's clock must have diminished monotonically as β descended into the field toward the hole. When they first parted, she observed no difference in β's clock. It was only as β got farther away that the slowing of her clock became more and more noticeable. Astronaut α is entitled to think of time near the event horizon as being curved. She concludes that Einstein was right.

Meanwhile, astronaut β shifts uncomfortably in the strong local gravity gradient. She finally settles herself into the best position she can and records that α's clock appears vibrantly blue in color and is running very rapidly compared with her own. Hundreds of light pulses from α's clock register on her instruments between respective pulses from her own clock. Astronaut β's clock continues to run quite normally, emitting one pulse each second as the seconds tick by.

---

[60]The gradient of the field becomes extremely steep as the event horizon of a black hole is approached.

[61]Over a distance commensurate with the size of the astronaut, the local gravitational field cannot be "transformed away" (i.e., cannot be made to vanish everywhere at once).

[62]Classically, the operative expression is $h\upsilon - Gm/r = E$, where h is Planck's constant, υ is the light frequency, G is Newton's gravitational constant, m is the mass of the black hole, r is the distance, and E is the total energy. If β's laser operates at frequency υ_0 and she is stationed a distance r_0 from the event horizon, then $E = h\upsilon_0 - Gm/r_0$ and the frequency at any other place along the light path is $\upsilon = \upsilon_0 - [(Gm/r_0 - Gm/r)]/h$. This expression holds relativistically as well as classically.

Astronaut β evaluates the situation. She realizes that the light photons are blue shifted as they descend into the immense gravity well in which she is immersed because they are conserving energy. As their gravitational potential energy decreases, the photon's energy increases. She also remembers that the speed of light is much slower in a gravity well than in free space. As α's light pulses are emitted, they start out at their free-space speed then slow up as they descend, piling up on one another. Astronaut α appears frenetically to rush about as she does her chores.

Astronaut β further reasons that although the clocks were identical when they were side by side, they no longer appear to be identical and in fact, no longer have to be thought of as being identical. Astronaut β engages on a line of reasoning that is essentially the same as that of astronaut α. She decides that she is entitled to think of time in her vicinity as being curved. She smiles. Einstein was right.

Base vector derivatives in curved space.—We have already said that the base vectors in a curved space have nonzero derivatives and that using the Coriolis and centrifugal accelerations as an example, we should expect nonzero base vector derivatives to play an important part in our overall formulation of a revised theory of the gravitational field. To understand how nonzero base vector derivatives arise in curved space, let us consider what happens on the surface of a sphere.

For this discussion, we will make use of the fact that a sphere is a two-dimensional elliptically curved space (surface) that can be viewed from a three-dimensional Euclidean space in which it is embedded.

First, we introduce the idea of parallel transport of a vector. In Euclidean space, a vector may be transported parallel to itself by moving it along a straight line while maintaining a constant angle between the vector and the line. If we wish to accomplish parallel transport along an arbitrary curve, we may subdivide the curve into straight line segments and parallel transport the vector along each of the segments. The finer the subdivision, the closer the approximation to the actual curve. In the limit of infinite subdivision, we have parallel transport along the curve exactly.

In Riemannian space, the geodesic or straightest possible curve replaces the straight line. The geodesic is a "line" that has the same curvature as the local space in which it is contained. In Riemannian space, parallel transport of a vector takes place along a geodesic by carefully maintaining a constant angle between the vector and the geodesic. (We may always assume that a differential region of Riemannian space is quasi-Euclidean and in that region apply the familiar concepts of our school geometry.)

Now we have a means of effecting parallel transport on the sphere. Let us consider the sphere as a whole and imagine a tangent vector $\mathbf{V}$ at a point P on the sphere. Pass a geodesic (a great circle) through P and move the vector a small distance δs (where δ is a small difference) along the geodesic. From the Euclidean space, we observe that for the vector to remain tangent to the sphere, it must change direction in the Euclidean space. From the point of view of a two-dimensional observer in the sphere, the vector has maintained a constant angle with the "line" along which it is being moved.

The change $\delta\mathbf{V}$ in $\mathbf{V}$ resulting from this change in direction as viewed from the Euclidean three-space must be a tensor and must be the same in all coordinate systems, including the two-dimensional coordinate system embedded in the sphere. Thus, the ratio $\delta\mathbf{V}/\delta s$ has a nonzero value in the Euclidean space and in the sphere. This value, in the limit of vanishing δs, is the nonzero vector derivative, and it arises solely because of the curvature of the sphere's surface. Since $\mathbf{V}$ is any vector we like (provided that it is tangent to the sphere), we will let $\mathbf{V}$ be a base vector. Our argument is complete.

In reality, if the vector experiment just described were to be done by a two-dimensional observer whose entire world was the spherical surface and who had no recourse to the three-dimensional Euclidean space, it would proceed differently from what was described above. The test vector $\mathbf{V}$ would actually be carried around a closed loop (arbitrarily chosen) starting from P and ending at P. When it returned, $\mathbf{V}$ would be observed to have changed direction. If $\mathbf{V}$ had rotated through an angle $\delta\theta$ during its parallel transport around the closed loop and if δs were the area enclosed by the loop, then the derivative in question would be the real derivative $\delta\theta/\delta s$ rather than the path derivative originally described. The ratio $\delta\theta/\delta s$ would have units of inverse square meters (m^{-2}), the proper units for measuring curvature.

That a vector actually changes direction when parallel transported around a closed loop on a sphere is easily seen if a macroscopic path is chosen. Let the path start at an arbitrarily chosen point P that we will call a pole of the sphere. Let the first section of the loop be a great circle extending from the pole to the equator (as a line of constant longitude would on

Earth). It will subtend 90° at the center of the sphere. Let the next section subtend another 90° at the center, but this time advance along the equator. The two sections will thus meet at an angle of 90° as observed by the two-dimensional observer in the sphere. Let the final section be another line of constant longitude returning to *P*.

Next, choose a vector tangent to the sphere and directed along the first great circle (e.g., with its head pointing in the direction it would have to advance toward the equator). When it reaches the equator, it will stand at right angles to the equator. Now, parallel transport the vector along the equator. When it reaches the third great circle, it will still be perpendicular to the equator. Now parallel transport it along the third great circle back toward *P*. When it reaches *P* again, it will have been rotated 90° relative to its initial position.

The area δs enclosed by the path is one-eighth the entire area of the sphere. Therefore,

$$\delta s = \left(\frac{1}{8}\right) 4\pi r^2 = \left(\frac{1}{2}\right) \pi r^2 \tag{414}$$

where r is the radius of the sphere measured in the three-dimensional Euclidean space. The angle through which the vector is turned during its traverse around the loop is $\delta\theta = \pi/2$. The ratio of these two quantities is

$$\frac{\delta\theta}{\delta s} = \frac{1}{r^2} \tag{415}$$

which is the measure of the sphere's curvature as we first learned in calculus and analytical geometry.

The reader can conduct this experiment with a ball and a toothpick to grasp the idea of parallel transport, which is of paramount importance in more advanced texts where the concept of curvature is more rigorously developed than it will be here.

Geodesics in curved space.—We have used the term "geodesic" several times throughout this text and given examples of what we mean by using a great circle on a sphere. Let us now examine the concept of the geodesic more closely and, without delving into the detailed mathematics, learn enough about its general properties to become comfortable with it. To review what we have already said, the geodesic in a given Riemannian space is equivalent in every way to the straight line in Euclidean space:

1. It is the straightest curve possible between two points of the space in question.
2. It is an extremal distance between two points (either maximal or minimal; the straight line of Euclidean space happens to be minimal).
3. At every point in the space, it possesses the same curvature as the space itself (the line possesses the same curvature as the plane, zero).
4. Geometric figures, such as triangles, rectangles, and so on, are always constructed of geodesics; thus, on the sphere for which the geodesic is the great circle, we speak of spherical triangles and spherical geometry.

The general equation expressing the geodesic is a second-order differential equation obtained by applying the calculus of variations to the invariant differential element

$$(\mathrm{d}s)^2 = g_{jk}\,\mathrm{d}x^j\,\mathrm{d}x^k \tag{416}$$

In the calculus of variations, one seeks a path along which a particular integral is external. That path is usually given as a function of the coordinates, the coordinate derivatives, and some other parameter, usually time. Historically, the original problem to be solved with variational techniques was the bachistochrone problem, which sought the particular path between any two points in a gravitational field along which a free particle would move in minimum time[63].

If between two points *P* and *P**, we have an infinite number of nonintersecting possible (homologous) paths along which to integrate the differential d*s*, at least one of those paths will yield a maximal or minimal solution for the integral.[64] It is the task of the calculus of variations to determine the general equation for finding that path. Typically, the integral of concern is represented in its general form as

$$\int f\left[y, \left(\frac{\mathrm{d}y}{\mathrm{d}t}\right), t\right] \mathrm{d}t \tag{417}$$

The calculus of variations uses concepts very similar to those used in the maximum-minimum problems encountered in basic calculus. Recall that given a function $y(x)$, a minimum or a maximum of the function could be found by forming the derivative of

[63]Newton solved the problem in a single night. The account is fascinating, and I recommend that you find it and read it.

[64]Either all the paths will yield the same value, in which case all are extremal, or all paths will not yield the same result, in which case there must be at least one path for which an extremal value is obtained.

$y(x)$ with respect to x and setting the result equal to zero:

$$\frac{dy}{dx} = 0 \tag{418}$$

The process of forming the derivative at a point P on the curve $y = y(x)$ involved taking a point to the right of P and another point to the left of P, connecting the two points with a straight line, determining the slope of that line, then finding the limit of the sequence of slopes formed as the two points converged on P.

The calculus of variations works in much the same way. For any given path P, we choose two adjacent paths (one to the right and one to the left, metaphorically) and determine the integral along each of those paths. The integrals are compared by forming their difference. The path P for which the difference approaches zero in the limit of convergence of the adjacent paths is the extremal path sought. In the notation of the calculus of variations, we write

$$\delta \int f\left[y, \left(\frac{dy}{dt}\right), t\right] dt = 0 \tag{419}$$

where δ means the difference between the values of the integral taken along slightly different (and adjacent) paths connected only at their end points. To find the general equation of the geodesic, we begin with the differential arc length ds, which we have already represented in general form via equation (416), repeated here:

$$(ds)^2 = g_{jk}\, dx^j\, dx^k \tag{416}$$

Recall that ds is the physical length associated with the differential position vector **dr** whose components are the coordinate differentials dx^w. By applying the calculus of variations to this expression, we are seeking the minimal (or maximal) distance between two points in the space under consideration. The straight line is a special case of this more general situation.

The integral of interest[65] is $\int ds$ where

$$\int ds = \int \sqrt{\left(g_{jk}\, dx^j\, dx^k\right)} = \int \sqrt{\left[g_{jk}\left(\frac{dx^j}{ds}\right)\left(\frac{dx^k}{ds}\right)\right]}\, ds \tag{420}$$

And the variation of interest is

$$\delta \int \sqrt{\left[g_{jk}\left(\frac{dx^j}{ds}\right)\left(\frac{dx^k}{ds}\right)\right]}\, ds = 0 \tag{421}$$

When the variation is carried out, we obtain the second-order differential equation

$$\left(\frac{d^2 x^t}{ds^2}\right) + \Gamma^t_{jk}\left(\frac{dx^j}{ds}\right)\left(\frac{dx^k}{ds}\right) = 0 \tag{422}$$

whose solutions $x^w = x^w(s)$ are the required geodesics.[66] Since the solution of this equation in the plane is the straight line, we may argue (nonrigorously) that the equation represents an equation of motion for particles upon which no forces are acting. (This statement can actually be proven by rigorous methods.) We may then write a more general equation of the form

$$\left(\frac{d^2 x^t}{ds^2}\right) + \Gamma^t_{jk}\left(\frac{dx^j}{ds}\right)\left(\frac{dx^k}{ds}\right) = a^t \tag{423}$$

where a^t are the contravariant components of the particle's acceleration (classically, s represents absolute time). We now have the equations of motion for any particle on which some force is acting (including the force $\mathbf{f} = \mathbf{0}$ for which $a^t = 0$ for all values of the index t). Einstein used this equation, with $a^t = 0$ as his equation of motion for all particles in the gravitational field. Note that the more general quantity ds replaces the quantity dt in Einstein's formulation.

In general relativity, it is strictly the curvature of space that comprises the gravitational field. Unlike classical mechanics, there is no gravitational force in general relativity. Particles in the gravitational field undergo force-free (acceleration-free) motion ($a^t = 0$) along their local four-dimensional spacetime geodesic. The spatial part of this motion is typically seen as a curved path. For "small" gravitational fields, such as

[65]Careful examination of the integrand in the second integral above shows the identity $g_{jk}(dx^j/ds)(dx^k/ds) = 1$.

[66]Note that in Euclidean space, all the values of Γ vanish; that is, $\Gamma^t_{jk} = 0$. The resulting differential equation is simply $d^2x^t/ds^2 = 0$, the differential equation of the straight lines $x^t = \alpha^t s + \beta^t$, where α^t and β^t are constants.

our Sun's, this path is approximately a Keplerian conic section.[67]

The spacetime of general relativity is differentially curved: the curvature varies smoothly from place to place. In a differentially curved geometry, figures cannot be moved from place to place without bending, stretching, and sometimes even tearing. This property of the geometry is mirrored in the spacetime of general relativity by the nonexistence of rigid matter. All matter in general relativity undergoes variations in stress and strain as it moves from region to region. The deformations (strains) reflect the fact that no absolute measurement of space or time is possible. All measurements are local; all are related through the generalized Lorentz transformation repeated here:

$$(\mathrm{d}s)^2 = g_{jk}\,\mathrm{d}x^j\,\mathrm{d}x^k \tag{416}$$

Locally, spacetime always appears flat to the observer. More distant observations (in space and time) reveal the curvature. The "differential" region in general relativity over which the observer may assume quasi-flatness must be carefully chosen. Within that region, the observer is entitled to apply special relativity to his or her observations.

Let us now try to gain some further insight into Einstein's concept of the gravitational field. We will begin with the foregoing equation of motion:

$$\left(\frac{\mathrm{d}^2 x^t}{\mathrm{d}s^2}\right) + \Gamma^t_{jk}\left(\frac{\mathrm{d}x^j}{\mathrm{d}s}\right)\left(\frac{\mathrm{d}x^k}{\mathrm{d}s}\right) = 0 \tag{422}$$

and rewrite it as

$$\frac{\mathrm{d}^2 x^t}{\mathrm{d}s^2} = -\Gamma^t_{jk}\left(\frac{\mathrm{d}x^j}{\mathrm{d}s}\right)\left(\frac{\mathrm{d}x^k}{\mathrm{d}s}\right) \tag{424}$$

We will consider only the spatial components of the motion for the moment. These components correspond to the index t having values equal to 1, 2, and 3. (The value $t = 4$ is reserved for the time component.) It should be apparent that the terms $\mathrm{d}^2x^t/\mathrm{d}s^2$ are equivalent to the components of classical acceleration. In classical theory, we have

$$a^t = g^t \tag{425}$$

where $t = 1, 2, 3$. The terms $\Gamma^t_{jk}\,(\mathrm{d}x^j/\mathrm{d}s)(\mathrm{d}x^k/\mathrm{d}s)$ must therefore be the relativistic equivalent of the classical g^t; that is, they must represent either the gravitational field components or something closely related to them. The terms $\mathrm{d}x^j/\mathrm{d}s$ and $\mathrm{d}x^k/\mathrm{d}s$ on the right-hand side are apparently velocities (reminiscent of the Coriolis term that also involved velocity); therefore, the actual field terms must be Γ^t_{jk}. The Christoffel symbols in the equation of motion carry information about the gravitational field and are in fact its components.

In general relativity, these symbols are evaluated in a Riemannian spacetime with variable curvature. Recall that the Christoffel symbols are related to the coordinate derivatives of the fundamental tensor:

$$\Gamma^b_{tw} = \frac{1}{2}g^{bk}\left[\frac{\partial(g_{kt})}{\partial x^w} + \frac{\partial(g_{wk})}{\partial x^t} - \frac{\partial(g_{tw})}{\partial x^k}\right] \tag{426}$$

The 10 independent components[68] of the fundamental tensor therefore become 10 gravitational potentials in general relativity. Why? Consider the classical equation relating gravitational acceleration **g** (i.e., the gravitational field term) and the gravitational scalar potential ϕ:

$$\mathbf{g} = -\kappa\nabla\phi = -\kappa\left[\left(\frac{\partial\phi}{\partial x}\right)\mathbf{i} + \left(\frac{\partial\phi}{\partial y}\right)\mathbf{j} + \left(\frac{\partial\phi}{\partial z}\right)\mathbf{k}\right] \tag{427}$$

where $\kappa = 4\pi G$ is a universal constant involving Newton's gravitational constant G. The field term derives from the first coordinate derivatives of the potential term with a constant of proportionality. In general relativity, the field terms Γ^t_{jk} derive from the first coordinate derivatives of the 10 gravitational potentials g_{uv}. Only the differential operator is much more complicated, involving both space and time.[69]

[67]The approximation is most noticeable in the case of Mercury's orbit. Kepler's law predicts a closed ellipse. Einstein's law predicts an open ellipse, one that does not return upon itself. As a result, Einstein's theory predicts that the perihelion of Mercury rotates around the Sun at a rate of about 64 sec of arc per century. This advance of perihelion has been observed and in fact was first discovered and reported in the late 19th century by the French astronomer Leverrier (1811–1877). At that time, an intramercurial planet named Vulcan was postulated to account for the "perturbation" in Mercury's orbit. Needless to say, Vulcan was never seen.

[68]There are 10 independent components in this case because the g_{jk} are symmetric and the space is four dimensional.

[69]The rough classical equivalent of a spacetime operator is the d'Alembertian operator $\Box^2 = \nabla^2 - (1/c^2)\partial^2/\partial t^2$ where ∇^2 is the Laplacian operator, $\nabla^2 = \nabla \cdot \nabla$.

How do we acquire the 10 potentials? In general relativity, there is a field equation that involves curvature and is roughly akin to the classical

$$g = \frac{Gm}{r^2} \tag{428}$$

with which we calculate the classical field term from the magnitude of the field-generating mass and its radius. To glimpse the more general equation, we must recall how curvature is expressed as a tensor.

Recall that curvature is a rank 4 tensor R^i_{jkm} that satisfies

$$v^i_{,jk} - v^i_{,kj} = R^i_{jkm} v^m \tag{429}$$

The tensor R^i_{jkm} is called the Riemann curvature tensor. It relates the difference between the second covariant derivative of a rank 1 tensor v^i taken with respect to the indices first j then k and the second covariant derivative of the same vector taken with respect to the indices first k then j to the actual components of the vector itself. Equation (429) tells us that in a non-Euclidean space, the order of differentiation in a second covariant derivative makes a difference to the result. Recall that in Euclidean space, the order of differentiation made no difference; that is, that

$$\frac{\partial^2 f(x,y)}{\partial x \partial y} = \frac{\partial^2 f(x,y)}{\partial y \partial x} \tag{430}$$

This simple and convenient rule is not true in the general case. In Euclidean four-space, $R^i_{jkm} = 0$; that is, all 256 components of R^i_{jkm} vanish everywhere throughout the space. This vanishing is the equivalent of saying that Euclidean space is everywhere flat.

The general form of the curvature tensor may be obtained by writing out the expressions for the two second covariant derivatives, forming their difference, and simplifying the result. To do so requires nothing more than you have already learned from this text. The procedure becomes untidy because of the number of symbols to keep track of, but a little care in bookkeeping will pay off for the student who is willing to try. Here is the result you should obtain:

$$R^i_{jkm} = \Gamma^s_{jm}\Gamma^i_{sk} - \frac{\partial \Gamma^i_{jk}}{\partial x^m} - \Gamma^s_{jk}\Gamma^i_{sm} + \frac{\partial \Gamma^i_{jm}}{\partial x^k} \tag{431}$$

Once we have the curvature tensor, we may contract it to form a rank 2 tensor:

$$R^k_{jkm} = R_{jm} \tag{432}$$

Einstein did so because the 256 independent equations that the full tensor R^i_{jkm} provided overly constrained the theory. He next separated the contracted curvature tensor into two terms:

$$R_{jm} = G_{jm} + H_{jm} \tag{433}$$

One of these terms involved the derivatives of the fundamental tensor components that were considered necessary for a proper generalization of Newton's own theory of gravity. He set up the following expression:

$$H_{jm} - \alpha g_{jm} H = -T_{jm} \tag{434}$$

where $H = g^{jm} H_{jm}$ and α is a constant to be determined. The right-hand side term T_{jm} is the stress-energy tensor (referred to as an "empirical" term in the 1917 paper). It is symmetrical and has 10 independent components. He next required the vanishing of the divergence of T_{jm} to ensure the conservation of stress energy everywhere in the universe. This condition constrained the constant α to assume the value ½. The result was the field equation

$$H_{jm} - \frac{1}{2} g_{jm} H = -T_{jm} \tag{435}$$

One of the first solutions of this equation for the case of locally vanishing stress energy was attributed to Karl Schwarzschild (1873–1916), a German astronomer, mathematician, and physicist, who set $T_{jm} = 0$ to approximate the spacetime conditions outside a large field-generating mass, such as our Sun or a particular planet. Following his lead, we obtain

$$H_{jm} - \frac{1}{2} g_{jm} H = 0 \tag{436}$$

Rewriting this expression in mixed form yields

$$H^s_m - \frac{1}{2} \delta^s_m H = 0 \tag{437}$$

Setting $s = m$ and summing, we find that

$$H = 0 \tag{438}$$

so that the gravitational field equation reduces to

$$H_m^s = 0 \tag{439}$$

that is, the second rank tensor H_m^s vanishes everywhere in the space under consideration. This Schwarzschild equation has yielded the following three famous effects in which predictions from general relativity differ from those of Newtonian theory. The observation of these effects by astronomers has lent considerable support to the veracity of the general theory:

1. Rotation of a planet's perihelion with time
2. Deflection of starlight passing near a massive object
3. Red shift of light moving away from a massive object

Of the three, the first was observed in the orbital motion of the planet Mercury and accounts for the anomaly in the planet's orbit (Leverrier, 1811–1877); the second was first observed during the famous 1919 eclipse expedition of Sir Arthur Stanley Eddington (English astronomer, 1882–1944); the third has not been definitively observed, although from observations of massive stars, there is spectral line-shift evidence that tends to agree with relativity.

Later, Schwarzschild's equation also led to the first prediction of radical gravitational collapse of massive stars and to the theoretical existence of black holes.

Glenn Research Center
National Aeronautics and Space Administration
Cleveland, Ohio, January 18, 2005

References

Bell, E.T.: The Development of Mathematics. Second ed., McGraw Hill, New York, NY, 1945.

Hawking, Stephen: On the Shoulders of Giants: The Great Works of Physics and Astronomy. Running Press, Philadelphia, PA, 2002.

Mach, Ernst: The Science of Mechanics: A Critical and Historical Account of Its Development. Open Court, LaSalle, IL, 1960.

Sciama, D.W.: The Physical Foundations of General Relativity. Doubleday, Garden City, NY, 1969.

Suggested Reading

Born, Max: Einstein's Theory of Relativity. Dover Publications, New York, NY, 1962.

Lorentz, H.A., et al.: The Principle of Relativity: A Collection of Original Memoirs on the Special and General Theory of Relativity. Dover Publications, New York, NY, 1959.

Spiegel, Murray R.: Schaum's Outline of Theory and Problems of Theoretical Mechanics With an Introduction to Lagrange's Equations and Hamiltonian Theory. Schaum Publishing, New York, NY, 1967.

Spiegel, Murray R.: Schaum's Outline of Theory and Problems of Vector Analysis and an Introduction to Tensor Analysis. McGraw-Hill, New York, NY, 1959.

REPORT DOCUMENTATION PAGE

Form Approved
OMB No. 0704-0188

Public reporting burden for this collection of information is estimated to average 1 hour per response, including the time for reviewing instructions, searching existing data sources, gathering and maintaining the data needed, and completing and reviewing the collection of information. Send comments regarding this burden estimate or any other aspect of this collection of information, including suggestions for reducing this burden, to Washington Headquarters Services, Directorate for Information Operations and Reports, 1215 Jefferson Davis Highway, Suite 1204, Arlington, VA 22202-4302, and to the Office of Management and Budget, Paperwork Reduction Project (0704-0188), Washington, DC 20503.

1. AGENCY USE ONLY (*Leave blank*)	2. REPORT DATE	3. REPORT TYPE AND DATES COVERED
	April 2005	Technical Paper

4. TITLE AND SUBTITLE

Foundations of Tensor Analysis for Students of Physics and Engineering With an Introduction to the Theory of Relativity

5. FUNDING NUMBERS

WBS–22–332–41–00–01

6. AUTHOR(S)

Joseph C. Kolecki

7. PERFORMING ORGANIZATION NAME(S) AND ADDRESS(ES)

National Aeronautics and Space Administration
John H. Glenn Research Center at Lewis Field
Cleveland, Ohio 44135–3191

8. PERFORMING ORGANIZATION REPORT NUMBER

E–14609

9. SPONSORING/MONITORING AGENCY NAME(S) AND ADDRESS(ES)

National Aeronautics and Space Administration
Washington, DC 20546–0001

10. SPONSORING/MONITORING AGENCY REPORT NUMBER

NASA TP—2005-213115

11. SUPPLEMENTARY NOTES

Responsible person, Joseph C. Kolecki, organization code RPV, 216–433–2296.

12a. DISTRIBUTION/AVAILABILITY STATEMENT

Unclassified - Unlimited
Subject Categories: 31, 59, 70, 88, and 90

Available electronically at http://gltrs.grc.nasa.gov

This publication is available from the NASA Center for AeroSpace Information, 301–621–0390.

12b. DISTRIBUTION CODE

13. ABSTRACT *(Maximum 200 words)*

Tensor analysis is one of the more abstruse, even if one of the more useful, higher math subjects enjoined by students of physics and engineering. It is abstruse because of the intellectual gap that exists between where most physics and engineering mathematics leave off and where tensor analysis traditionally begins. It is useful because of its great generality, computational power, and compact, easy to use, notation. This paper bridges the intellectual gap. It is divided into three parts: algebra, calculus, and relativity. Algebra: In tensor analysis, coordinate independent quantities are sought for applications in physics and engineering. Coordinate independence means that the quantities have such coordinate transformations as to leave them invariant relative to a particular observer's coordinate system. Calculus: Non-zero base vector derivatives contribute terms to dynamical equations that correspond to pseudoaccelerations in accelerated coordinate systems and to curvature or gravity in relativity. These derivatives have a specific general form in tensor analysis. Relativity: Spacetime has an intrinsic geometry. Light is the tool for investigating that geometry. Since the observed geometry of spacetime cannot be made to match the classical geometry of Euclid, Einstein applied another more general geometry—differential geometry. The merger of differential geometry and cosmology was accomplished in the theory of relativity. In relativity, gravity is equivalent to curvature.

14. SUBJECT TERMS

Scalar; Vector; Tensor; Algebra; Calculus; Physics; Engineering; Relativity; Foundations

15. NUMBER OF PAGES

91

16. PRICE CODE

17. SECURITY CLASSIFICATION OF REPORT	18. SECURITY CLASSIFICATION OF THIS PAGE	19. SECURITY CLASSIFICATION OF ABSTRACT	20. LIMITATION OF ABSTRACT
Unclassified	Unclassified	Unclassified	

CPSIA information can be obtained at www.ICGtesting.com
Printed in the USA
LVOW09s0921220515

439405LV00028B/296/P

9 781289 256425